CULTURAL SURVIVAL REPORT 20

POLITICS AND THE ETHIOPIAN FAMINE 1984-1985

Jason W. Clay and Bonnie K. Holcomb

Cultural Survival, Inc.
11 Divinity Avenue
Cambridge, MA 02138
617-495-2562

Cultural Survival, Inc., 11 Divinity Ave., Cambridge, Mass. 02138

© 1986 by Cultural Survival, Inc. All rights reserved
Originally published in 1985 as Occasional Paper No. 20
Revised edition published 1986
Printed in the United States of America
by Transcript Printing Company, Peterborough, N.H. 03458

 Distributed by Transaction Books
New Brunswick (U.S.A.) and Oxford (U.K.)

Cultural Survival Report No. 20
The Cultural Survival Report series is a continuation of the Occasional
Paper series.

ISBN 0-939521-34-2 (cloth)
     0-939521-25-3 (pbk.)

For too long the ruling classes have attributed to "Nature" ... the inequalities for which the organization of society is responsible."

Sebastiano Timpanaro (cited in M. Watts,
*Silent Violence: Food, Famine and Peasantry
in Northern Nigeria*, 1983).

CONTENTS

MAPS

Preface

When first issued, this book was intended primarily for relief agency personnel whose organizations had programs for famine assistance in Ethiopia. Consequently, the report was particularly concerned with the kinds of information necessary to discern the impact of humanitarian assistance on agricultural production in the context of the Ethiopian famine. When the report was first made available, however, we found that many other readers were interested in first-hand accounts of the Ethiopian famine from peoples directly affected by it. We have kept the general reading public in mind when preparing the second edition. The book remains a report of research findings, but changes have been made in style and exposition. Some adjustments were introduced to improve the readability, others for clarification and emphasis. Those familiar with the original version should know that no data have been added to or deleted from this edition.

The most significant alteration has been to make more explicit the distinction between what we originally termed the "short-term" and the "long-term" causes of famine. This distinction was utilized in our research design and maintained through the conclusions and analysis. However, referring to both kinds of information with the general term "causes of famine" made it unnecessarily tedious to sustain the distinction throughout the text. Therefore, in this edition we refer to the short-term or immediate factors that bring people to the point of starvation as the *causes of hunger*. By contrast, we refer to the factors that affected the systems of production and availability of food in what are now famine-stricken areas as *causes of famine*. This change in terminology, made throughout the current edition, does not indicate a different analysis. Rather, it more accurately underscores the analytical approach that characterized the original research, examination of the findings, and the process by which the conclusions were reached.

In this edition we have expanded the introduction (Chapter I). The remainder of the book — the chapters containing our findings, conclusions and recommendations — stands as it was, except that errors found in the original have been corrected and some sections have been rearranged. We have decided not to update this work a year after publication, though events and processes addressed here have proceeded apace and substantially confirmed our analysis. Instead, we have chosen to present new research data and to develop further the analytical approach in a companion volume. That book, forthcoming from Cultural Survival, also includes contributions from Peter Niggli and Sandra Steingraber, and bears the title *The Spoils of Famine: Ethiopian Famine Policy and Peasant Agriculture*.

Jason W. Clay and Bonnie K. Holcomb
November 17, 1986

Acknowledgments

The goal of the research on which this book is based was to bring forth information about the Ethiopian famine from a source too often neglected, the people most directly affected by it — the victims of the food shortages. In the course of undertaking the research, however, many others also provided information and otherwise assisted us. We wish to acknowledge both groups here.

Given the lack of free access to famine-stricken areas and to people residing inside Ethiopia, we conclude that refugee camps across the borders in Sudan or Somalia may be the only place that people affected by food shortages experienced in Ethiopia can speak freely to an outside observer about their predicament and its causes. Those we spoke with immediately understand the significance of the questions we were asking and patiently responded in detail. Most of all, therefore, we want to thank the refugees we interviewed in Sudan.

Next we wish to draw attention to the indispensable contribution of Peter Niggli. Only days before we arrived to begin this work, Peter had reached Sudan, prepared to investigate the resettlement program of the Ethiopian government by interviewing escapees from the resettlement sites. Through discussions with Peter in Khartoum we agreed to collaborate. Only distance — Peter lives in Zurich, Switzerland — prevented him from co-authoring this report.

Work conducted in such a politically charged situation requires translators independent of political affiliation. We thank Atakilt Ambaye, Haile Tsehaya and Solomon Haile Eba for their impartial translations.

The research was not without disappointments. We had planned to collaborate with Mary Dines while in Sudan, but in the end she was unable to join us. Her involvement and assistance was, however, invaluable.

A great number of individuals and organizations assisted us before, during and after our research trip to Sudan. In addition to the 277 interviews with affected people whose testimony is the subject of this work, we conducted scheduled interviews with 71 people from 42 different organizations involved with various aspects of the famine crisis. In these discussions also people were generous with their time and candidly shared details of events that they had witnessed and their views regarding the causes of the famine and the most appropriate solutions. Although these discussions were of great value to us and our research, they were most enlightening when considered in conjunction with the testimony from refugees. It is our hope that those who gave us their time and expertise will recognize that we have addressed in this report, in one form or another, most of the points or questions that they raised. Most importantly we have focused specifically on those data from famine-affected people which the assistance personnel regarded as essential for developing appropriate solutions to the present food shortage crisis.

We have chosen to single out for special mention only those groups that gave us essential logistical support in Sudan — assisting with our travel permits, administrative details or lodging in the refugee areas. We would like to thank the Sudanese Commission on Refugees for permission to undertake this independent research. In addition, we would like to extend our appreciation to the United Nations High Commission for Refugees for its assistance in Wad Kauli and Fau II, the Relief Society of Tigray for its assistance in Damazine and the Oromo Relief Association for its assistance in Demazine and Yabuus. These groups provided assistance when requested (such as making personnel available to accompany us or to provide supplementary translators of Arabic and Amharic when necessary). Most importantly, however, all these groups left us to ourselves in all our contact with the refugees including selecting, surveying and interviewing the refugess. For this freedom of movement, above all, we thank them.

Glossary

agilgili	picnic baskets
ambas	resettlement villages
awaraja	districts
balabat	local administrative official during Haile Selassie's regime
birr (E$)	Ethiopian currency equivalent to approximately US $.50 at time of study.
chooma	fertile land
dado	traditional Oromo mutual aid association
dega	high cold regions found mostly in the northern half of the Ethiopian plateau
Dergue	committee; term used to designate the ruling military body
farenjis	foreigners
gada	socio-political system by which Oromos governed themselves prior to their incorporation into the Ethiopian Empire in the early twentieth century
galla	a pejorative term for Oromo people
gashas	square measurement equivalent to 40 hectares; land was measured in gashas from 1974 until 1976 when the Dergue approved of Oromo farmers' principles of agricultural production and expanded their land base
gesso	hoe
gollo	hot, dry lowland areas of Ethiopia
gombisa	locally made granary; can vary in size from 50 to 100 quintals (5,000 to 50,000 kg)
hectare	2.47 acres
hidda	vine
kebeles	the lowest organizational level of urban and rural administration
kiltu	local fruit tree
kulaks	a pejorative term for rich peasants in Ethiopia
mahiber	formerly a voluntary organization of the Ethiopian Orthodox church; now it refers to any voluntary association

neftanya	gun-carrying settler
oda	local shade tree of the sycamore family; the symbol of the Oromo Liberation Front
saffia	liquid measurement equivalent to a gerry can
shiftas	euphemism for guerrillas, usually national liberation front fighters; bandits
SL	Sudanese Pound equivalent to approximately US $.35 at time of study
tchokorsa	vine
Walla wye inde Wollo	they do not have a clear stand like the Wollo
woreda	subdistrict
woyna dega	lower highland areas of Ethiopia which range from temperate to subtropical
ye galla meret	Galla land or Oromo land
ye genye agar	colonial lands
zari tokitcha	one seed

Acronyms

AEPA	All-Ethiopian Peasant Association
AFP	Agence France Presse
AMC	Agricultural Marketing Corporation
COR	Sudan Commission of Refugees
CRS	Catholic Relief Services
EDU	Ethiopian Democratic Union
EEC	European Economic Commission
EPLF	Eritrean Peoples' Liberation Front
ERA	Eritrean Relief Association
ERC	Eritrean Relief Committee
OAU	Organization of African Unity
OLF	Oromo Liberation Front
ORA	Oromo Relief Association
PMAC	Provisional Military Administrative Council; the Dergue
PVO	Private Voluntary Organization
REST	Relief Society of Tigray
REYA	Revolutionary Ethiopian Youth Association
RRC	Ethiopia's Relief and Rehabilitation Commission
TPLF	Tigrayan People's Liberation Front
UNHCR	United Nations High Commissioner for Refugees
WFP	World Food Program
WPE	Workers' Party of Ethiopia

Chapter I

INTRODUCTION

The Ethiopian famine of 1984-1985 was discovered by the Western media in October of 1984, eliciting an unprecedented public interest and response. During the following February and March, we conducted research on the causes of the famine by interviewing 277 farmers who had fled to Sudan from three major famine-stricken regions of Ethiopia. This book presents and examines what we learned about the development of the famine from its victims, draws out the implications of these findings for different actors and explains in detail how the work was carried out so that the research can be replicated.

We introduce the work by looking at the events that prompted the research, drawing attention to the obstacles and issues that Western agencies faced in attempting to provide relief assistance in a situation about which there was little reliable information.

Four weeks after the enormous celebrations in September 1984 for the tenth anniversary of the rule of the "military committee" (or *Dergue*) in Ethiopia, a film crew was finally granted official permission to photograph victims of starvation in the Ethiopian administrative region of Wollo, located north of Addis Ababa, the capital city. The team went to a feeding center where famine victims had been collected on one of the country's main roads. Reporters from the United States who had been in the country to cover the anniversary festivities had been denied access to the same region when they had requested permission one month earlier (*Washington Post*, September 18, 1984, and *The New York Times*, September 18, 1984). Millions of people in the West learned on October 22 and 23, 1984, that great numbers of people were starving to death inside the Ethiopian empire when that film footage of the famine victims encountered in Wollo was distributed through the British Broadcasting Corporation.

Many groups in the West, faced with the news of the Ethiopian famine, reached the same conclusion: respond immediately and on a large scale. For persons who were familiar with Ethiopia and its problems, several aspects of the public response to the famine aroused great concern about the incompleteness of the public record regarding its causes. The research reported here was stimulated by similar concerns. One troubling aspect was the fact that there was virtually no background information in the West about the situation in the famine-affected rural areas. A second was that there was no unrestricted access to the rural areas producing famine victims. A corrolary to this was the tight control placed on the movements and observations of visitors and relief agency personnel and on the distribution of relief assistance. A third aspect was the untested, unreliable nature of the explanations for famine that were offered in the media. A fourth was the inability of agencies to acquire and their failure to demand the independent information necessary to measure the impact of their aid. Without such information, they faced the danger of making the situation worse by unwittingly exacerbating the causes of the famine. The Cultural Survival research team was formed specifically to address these issues as we watched them unfold in November and December 1984. These issues constituted a part of the story only partially revealed in the early media coverage.

As anthropologists and persons who were familiar with the region and its problems, we closely followed the events, and became increasingly concerned about the disparity between what we knew about the situation in rural areas of Ethiopia and what was being presented as fact in the midst of the unprecedented transfer of foreign assistance to that country.

The general public in the West, who had had little intimate knowledge of Ethiopia, became alarmed by the thousands of deaths witnessed nightly on the television screen, and responded with the largest outpouring of humanitarian contributions in memory. In just over a year, more than $1.2 billion was raised or allocated for relief assistance in Ethiopia by governments and nongovernmental agencies in the West. US-based agencies alone had pledges of some $200 million.

On the political level, Western officials encouraged the public exposure of Ethiopia's internal problems. It should not be overlooked that politicians in the West had been dismayed only recently when the Dergue announced at the anniversary festivities in September the formation of the Workers Party of Ethiopia. This gave notice that Ethiopia was securely within the Soviet bloc. Official Western famine policy from the outset seemed based on challenging the security of this attachment by responding generously to a problem which the West presumed it was in a far better position to solve than was the USSR. There was, as a result, no opposition to the transfer of large amounts of private and even public aid.

Western groups who delivered aid in Ethiopia did so in an information vacuum. Ethiopia's pro-Soviet stance meant that there were no Western observers in rural areas and consequently that there was virtually no independent base of information available to Western agencies about the extent or the causes of famine. As the West came to the threshold of delivering famine relief, reliable independent avenues for seeking information about production in Ethiopia remained closed.*

Agencies took the position that under ideal conditions information about the nature of the famine among peasants might be useful in planning their programs and later in determining the impact of their assistance. But when presented with the prospect of administering famine relief in Ethiopia using only government-supplied data, Western agencies made the decision to initiate or expand programs in Ethiopia on the government's terms. They em-

---

*By October 1984 Ethiopia and the United States were exchanging *chargés d'affaires* rather than full ambassadors. Government-to-government developmental assistance from the US to Ethiopia was prevented by legislative act, the most well known being the Hickenlooper Amendment. The US Agency for International Development maintained only a token presence to oversee a certain amount of emergency assistance legally allowed under the provision. The handful of US personnel that remained kept a strictly low profile on the tacit understanding with the government that this was the only way to ensure the renewal of their visas. Most US missionaries withdrew in the face of severe restrictions on their movements and on their work. Academic research by Westerners and Western-trained scholars had been virtually halted. The little research that was conducted did not address famine-related issues.

phasized that they were certain thousands of people were dying in front of them and that their mandate was to save lives.

Specifically, and significantly, Western relief assistance went only to restricted areas. The media spotlight was not allowed to turn elsewhere. The Ethiopian government did not take over the distribution of food from the agencies. Rather, it directed when deliveries could begin and where they would take place; that is, it shaped and controlled the structure of the food delivery system. Arriving foreign agency personnel and their locally employed counterparts functioned solely within a preordained food delivery structure. The government selected and administered the locations to serve as feeding centers, establishing a network of sites along the main roads from Addis Ababa. Agency personnel who distributed food there were not privy to government announcements in the countryside about the location or availability of the food or the conditions of its distribution. They were not allowed to travel or to set up programs in the areas beyond the feeding centers to which they were assigned. They assisted and photographed only people who arrived at the feeding center. Government representatives determined who would be called and who qualified for admission to the feeding centers. The occasional exception to this was that foreign medical personnel were called on to screen exceptional cases for treatment.

Relief agencies complied with all these restrictions without complaining or drawing attention to the constraints. In fact, most aid professionals setting up programs in Ethiopia were willing to do whatever was necessary in order to ameliorate as soon as possible a disastrous situation in a place that had been practically closed to Westerners for a decade. Their respective governments encouraged them in this stance. There was an air of grateful surprise that the government of Ethiopia, which had the reputation as a hard-line Marxist-Leninist client of the Soviet Union known for constantly denouncing the West, was admitting Western assistance at all.

For the most part the media, public figures and government officials supported the agencies in their decisions. Incontrovertible proof of the suffering was offered daily in the media — the victims of starvation who arrived and were photographed at the feeding centers were absolutely destitute. With these horrifying images saturating North American and European media, few Westerners raised questions about why the people were starving or how they had come to such a state. No one challenged the advisability of shipping in as much food as possible as fast as possible to reach as many of these people as could be reached. The public was demanding that all aid go directly to buying and delivering food. Agencies even competed indirectly for public donations by assuring that very small percentages of donated funds would go toward administrative costs.

Asking questions — doing research — of any kind at such a time was considered luxurious overhead by the agencies and the people sending them money. It also would have required rocking the boat to insist on proper conditions for research — such as being allowed to travel in the country to assess the nature and the extent of the overall situation and then making suggestions about where and how food and other supplies would be delivered. Agency and government representatives alike kept quiet on these issues and went to work distributing food.

By 1985, some elements that the earlier accounts of famine downplayed or omitted began to emerge as sidelights to the main story, which was the delivery of food. The enormous food delivery effort soon brought attention to certain political and military "complications" that hindered efforts to reach all of those in need. Before long, humanitarian agencies, journalists and government personnel began to report on the wars between the government troops and liberation fronts operating in areas where large numbers of famine-affected people were located. In this way the public learned of the wars between Ethiopian state forces and several liberation fronts. These wars were primarily reported in sidebars intended to explain delays in food delivery. Opponents in these conflicts issued proposals and counter-proposals for food truces to allow safe passage of food to affected people who lived in disputed territory, but donors of food tended to downplay the complications in order to stress that many people were in fact getting food. Significantly, the issues of how the wars had contributed to food shortages and famine and how food assistance was used as a weapon were not clearly spelled out.

Shortages of transport vehicles, which impeded food delivery, brought the first mention of the government's use of trucks and buses to move massive numbers of people from northern Tigray and Wollo regions south to Wollega and Illubabor.

Explanations Offered in the Media to Account for the Famine

Television, newspaper and radio outlets circulated essentially the same explanations for how the famine came to be. Daily headlines and feature stories on the Ethiopian famine gave the overriding impression that a record-breaking failure of rains had brought on the misfortune; nature had conspired against the peasants, and their poor farming practices and general underdevelopment had made them incapable of responding. War was presented as a factor that merely compounded an already disastrous situation. (We discuss each of these explanations in Chapter III.)

Journalists' accounts were written in the heat of the rush to deliver assistance and most often either cited Ethiopian government officials' explanations of the causes of the famine or turned to United Nations representatives and other officials who likewise consulted official Ethiopian government data for their responses. Occasionally these reporters drew on scholars or regional experts for commentary or referred to the claims of the liberation fronts for contrast. (See Appendix F for a compilation of examples of the major print media coverage of the explanations for famine.)

The explanations offered by scholars and regional specialists pointed to global processes and long-term trends, but none of them had concrete, first-hand observations on agricultural production in any part of Ethiopia which would have enabled them to give an authoritative picture of how the situation had come about.

Liberation fronts operating among populations affected by the famine did issue statements from time to time about the extent and the causes of the famine. These groups often laid the entire blame for the catastrophe on the government, with which they were engaged in armed conflict. The statements used language that sounded inflammatory and extreme to many Western agency personnel and offered little systematic evidence to substantiate claims. These statements were rarely pursued or followed up by the press and were dismissed by many who read them as politically inspired and therefore suspect. Few found the polemical language convincing.

Information from affected people themselves appeared only as a quotation or two intended to provide human interest, an embellishment to a story whose main point lay elsewhere. The experience of someone standing in a food line or waiting in a clinic was adduced to confirm the rain shortage, lack of harvest and subsequent sale of animals. People were not asked what had brought them to the point of starvation. It was not possible to understand what had happened in the lives of peasant producers to bring about such disaster. In short, the victims remained bellies; they did not have brains.

Background to the Research

This research was proposed in late 1984, at the time when Ethiopian feeding centers were swelling with people seeking food, and Western public interest in the Ethiopian famine reached its height. At this time two major developments were reported. A huge number of refugees seeking food began pouring out of the Ethiopian administrative region of Tigray into Sudan, and it was also disclosed that the Ethiopian government had implemented a gigantic program to resettle famine victims from the drought-stricken northern regions to areas south and west of their homelands said to be uninhabited. In January 1985, refugees from the resettlement areas began to arrive in a different part of Sudan, farther south from where those from Tigray entered. Both of these developments offered windows onto the famine-afflicted areas and the appropriateness of measures taken to relieve it.

The overriding objective of our investigation was to fill in some of the gaps by collecting information from the victims and to shed light on the nature of the famine in order to assess the appropriateness of measures being proposed to resolve the crisis. Newly arriving refugees in Sudan meant that researchers had access to many people with first-hand knowledge of the conditions that led to the famine in areas inaccessible to outside observers. (The research design is discussed in Chapter III.)

An important assumption underlying the work was that a problem cannot be solved unless it is understood, and that a full picture requires talking to the people affected by the problem. This latter assumption is basic to anthropology: the experience and testimony of participants should be given a central position in the reconstruction and analysis of events. With this perspective, we believed it necessary to focus on productive processes and what affected them as the famine developed, as well as the human rights or persecution of affected peoples.

One of our objectives was to make precise, well-documented information derived from the experience of the affected people available to the agencies operating in Ethiopia. Thus, part of our work was to talk to these organizations. It had become clear to us during the end of 1984 that neither the governmental nor the private donors were prepared or inclined to collect data systematically themselves, yet they needed concrete information to use as a basis for decision making and program planning. A wide variety of popularly based groups, from the local to the international level, would continue to make critical judgments about the famine crisis based on almost no independent information, unless some measures were taken to collect the information required. Consequently, during 1984 and early 1985, we approached relief agencies in the United States which were involved with famine relief programs in Ethiopia to propose such research.†

Agency responses varied, often according to the nature of their programs. Some agencies had had a continuing presence in Ethiopia; some had not but were receiving funds from constituents alarmed by the famine and were evaluating appropriate actions. Most of them shared with us the belief that the type of information we were proposing to collect was essential to their program planning, implementation, monitoring and evaluation. Discussions with the personnel of these agencies enabled us to determine what types of information about the famine in Ethiopia they had at their disposal and what information they were lacking. Our research design was adjusted in order to elucidate those data that relief agencies deemed important to their programs or concerns. We then shared drafts of our questionnaires with these agencies, requesting that they comment on the appropriateness to their concerns.

We also invited agencies to participate in or to contribute to the proposed research, or both, so that it could be undertaken in a timely manner. Several agencies expressed a keen interest in our findings; some were prepared to cooperate with us by conducting systematic surveys in the feeding centers. In line with the proposed cooperation, one of the agencies requested that we eliminate one of the more sensitive aspects of the questionnaires, specifically the question in our survey regarding nationality. We complied. Ultimately, however, none of the agencies, including the one that made that request, cooperated in the research or supported the project financially. A typical response was, "We depend upon this type of information to plan our programs, yet we cannot collect it or even be seen to support its collection without jeopardizing our relief efforts in Ethiopia." Some were direct and others indirect about not wanting the names of their organizations associated with anything that contained a criticism of the Ethiopian government. This was our introduction to the subtle yet highly effective silence that surrounded the transfer of unprecedented amounts of relief supplies into Ethiopia. (We address this situation in our recommendations section, Chapter XI.)

Funding for the Research

A consequence of the agencies' reluctance to provide support for the research meant that it was funded independently from any group involved directly in Ethiopian famine assistance. This turned out to be a blessing in

†Copies of the letters sent to the agencies, the research project proposal, its budget, and all related documents were printed as appendices to our original report (Cultural Survival Occasional Paper 20) and are available from Cultural Survival, 11 Divinity Avenue, Cambridge, MA 02138.

disguise, although had funds been available from the outset, we could have published the first edition of the report in a more timely fashion. One-half of those funds actually needed to carry out the research work were raised through a one-time advertisement placed in *The Boston Globe* and then mailed separately to Cultural Survival's 8,000 members. The 141 individual contributions to the project amounted to $13,000.90. Cultural Survival provided approximately $8,000 for the research, cartography and publishing expenses. No other funding was received for the project. We draw attention to the total cost of such research in order to point out how it compares with the $1.2 billion in humanitarian assistance spent in Ethiopia in a year's time amid uncertainty about the effectiveness of relief efforts in the long and short run. Such a discrepancy should indicate to agencies involved that appropriate research is neither exorbitantly expensive nor overly time-consuming. An essential ingredient for such research, however, is the will to undertake it in the first place.

Organization of the Book

We realize that the kind of approach entailed in research like this requires a profound shift of focus and of procedure. We present this book with the assumption that systematic, small-scale, duplicable research of this type is an appropriate beginning for a process that can be refined and expanded by others who see the value of this approach and the type of information it generates. In keeping with this belief, the book is organized as follows: the findings, which present the concrete experience of the affected people, comprise the bulk of the work and lie at its center in Chapters IV, V, VI, VII, VIII and IX. This chapter has introduced the research work in the context of the events that generated it. Chapter II is a summary of historical and structural issues that we think need to be understood in order to assess the findings. It is a perspective constructed and confirmed through the course of our work. It is placed at the outset in order to shed light on the data that come in the following chapters. Chapter III sets out the development of the research design and how it was implemented; this is done in enough detail that it can be replicated either within Ethiopia or in other countries. Conclusions are summarized in Chapter X. The recommendations in Chapter XI outline the implications of our findings for those whose activities affect the Ethiopian famine and have consequences for its eventual resolution.

Chapter II

THE CREATION OF THE ETHIOPIAN EMPIRE: BACKGROUND TO THE CURRENT CRISIS

Schematic Introduction to the Region and Its Peoples

With over 1.2 million sq km, Ethiopia is roughly the size of South Africa and one of Africa's largest states. Assessing population in Ethiopia has always been more an art than a science. Its inhabitants number from 32 million to 45 million, depending upon who is making the assessment and for what purpose.

Most general introductions to Ethiopia indicate that its surface consists of three major topographical regions — the lowlands and two types of highland areas. What is normally omitted from such descriptions is that the ecological regions widely acknowledged as distinct (qolla, woyna dega, and dega in Amharic) are also largely inhabited by distinct groups of peoples. Semitic highland agriculturalists — the Abyssinians (including Amharas and Tigrayans) — occupy the high, cold regions found mostly in the northern half of the Ethiopian plateau. Mostly Cushites — the largest Cushitic groups are the agricultural and agro-pastoral Oromo and Sidama — inhabit the lower highland areas of the empire which range from temperate to sub-tropical. Other pastoral Cushitic groups, such as the Somalis in the east, and also Nilotic peoples in the west, inhabit the hot, dry, lowland areas within Ethiopian boundaries as well. The association of peoples with specific ecological niches is an enduring feature of regional dynamics that is often overlooked or even misconstrued.

Highlands and lowlands each account for about half of Ethiopia's surface area. Nearly 75 percent of the population, however, resides in the highlands. The environment varies from desert, thornbush and savannah grasslands in the lowlands to tropical forests and cleared areas in the highlands. Nomadic and transhumant pastoralists predominate in the lowlands. In the highlands, both hoe cultivation and mixed farming economies based on ox-drawn plows characterize subsistence and even cash crop production. Prior to the nationalization of land in 1975, land tenure systems varied greatly: generally, tenancy dominated the south and communal, village tenure dominated the north. Our research indicates that while in theory such differences may have been eliminated, in fact differential access to land and control of production continue to distinguish farmers in different parts of the country.

In addition to the peoples that constitute Eritrea, several major distinct peoples (listed alphabetically) — Afar, Amhara, Gurage, Oromo, Sidama, Somali and Tigrayan — make up most of the country's population. A number of other smaller Semitic, Cushitic and Nilotic groups are found throughout the empire.

Christianity, Islam, numerous traditional religions and Judaism are practiced. Adherents of the different religions have a long history of conflict and conquest. During the last millennia, the boundaries controlled by adherents to different religions have moved back and forth numerous times, playing a secondary role to interactions among nations indigenous to the area.

The Politics of Empire

The politics of Ethiopia are the politics of an empire. While Ethiopia was formally declared to be a "republic" in 1975, and officially dropped the designation "Empire of Ethiopia," many factors indicate that "empire" remains a more accurate description. The country's current boundaries (see Map 1), social and political dynamics, and diverse national, cultural and religious identities have characterized Ethiopia since the establishment of the empire at the turn of the twentieth century.

A brief historical background is presented here at the outset in order to provide a context in which to interpret the findings of our research into the causes of famine. It is equally valuable when assessing the impact of existing and proposed humanitarian assistance to the region. Many of the causes of famine are rooted in the relations between historically constituted nations, something which became clear through the course of the research. In that sense what follows embodies a portion of our conclusions.

Map 1

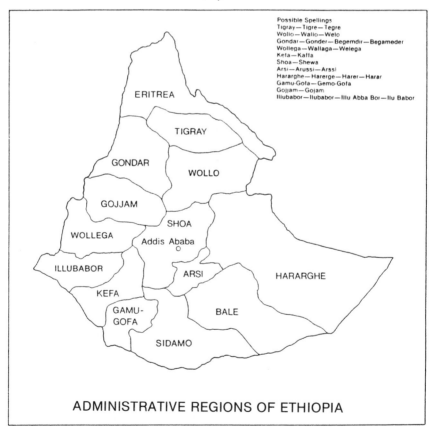

Possible Spellings
Tigray—Tigre—Tegre
Wollo—Wallo—Welo
Gondar—Gonder—Begemdir—Begameder
Wollega—Wallaga—Welega
Kefa—Kaffa
Shoa—Shewa
Arsi—Arussi—Arssi
Hararghe—Harerge—Harer—Harar
Gamu-Gofa—Gemo-Gofa
Gojjam—Gojam
Illubabor—Ilubabor—Illu Abba Bor—Ilu Babor

ERITREA

TIGRAY

GONDAR

WOLLO

GOJJAM

SHOA

WOLLEGA

Addis Ababa

ILLUBABOR

ARSI

HARARGHE

KEFA

GAMU-GOFA

BALE

SIDAMO

ADMINISTRATIVE REGIONS OF ETHIOPIA

The Creation of the Empire

The Ethiopian empire, as it is constituted today, was first envisioned in the nineteenth century by a Shoan Abyssinian prince aspiring to control all of Abyssinia and neighboring regions. This prince, Menelik, eventually claimed the title King of Kings in 1889 by first ruling over one kingdom, that of Shoa, in the Semitic highlands, and then conquering some unrelated neighboring Oromos. He finally succeeded Emperor Yohannes, a Tigrayan, and became absolute ruler over all the kingdoms of Abyssinia. The fact that this occurred during a period of European colonial expansion in the Horn of Africa in the late nineteenth century is no coincidence. Earlier kings and emperors of Abyssinia had attempted to control wider areas but prior to the European entry their attempts had failed. Menelik intensified military expeditions (see Map 2), mostly into areas controlled by Oromo and Sidama, to expand the empire after he became king of kings in Abyssinia. Competing European colonial powers, each jockeying for indirect control over the northeastern Africa region, made available to him modern weapons that made these military conquests possible. Each European country's fear of territorial expansion by the others worked to Menelik's advantage, and he was able to acquire enough arms to create an army enviable to every Western power attempting to gain a foothold in the area. After conquering what makes up at least 70 percent of the land mass of the present-day empire—areas primarily lying to the south of Abyssinia—Menelik signed boundary treaties with the European colonial powers. The Tripartite Treaty of 1908, signed by Britain, France and Italy, officially recognized these boundaries.

Menelik's military expeditions, mounted primarily between 1883 and 1904 from Abyssinia, more than doubled the area he ruled and assembled the core of the Ethiopian empire (see Maps 4 and 5). Later additions to Menelik's empire included Eritrea, which was originally carved out as an Italian colony, an eastern region along the coast which was mostly Afar-inhabited, and a portion of Somaliland.

The legacy of Menelik's military conquests, which took place less than a century ago, and the structure of the state built to incorporate the conquered peoples are a major underlying cause of many of Ethiopia's problems today. The boundaries created as a result of Abyssinian military victories were no less arbitrary than those created by competing European colonial powers in the rest of Africa; in the west, Anuak, Nuer, Berta and Komo were split between Ethiopia and present-day Sudan; in the south, Oromo were split between Ethiopia and present-day Kenya; in the east and southeast, Somali were split between Ethiopia, Kenya and present-day Somalia and Djibouti; and in the northeast, Afars were split between Ethiopia and present day Djibouti. A number of other smaller groups were divided in the north, west and south.

Prior to Menelik's conquests, peoples indigenous to different areas were connected primarily through trade contacts. In the late nineteenth century they were independent groups with separate cultures, identities and different histories. Menelik's goal to bring together the territory stretching "from Khartoum to Lake Nyanza"—an area that had never been ruled by a single power—was little more than a bold bid to control a region pursued by European powers scrambling for Africa's last bits of uncolonized land.

Map 2

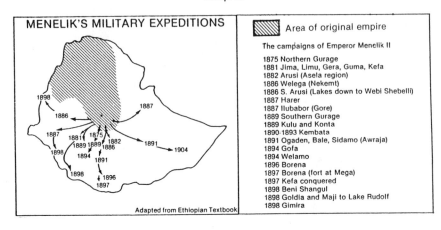

MENELIK'S MILITARY EXPEDITIONS

▨ Area of original empire

The campaigns of Emperor Menelik II

1875 Northern Gurage
1881 Jima, Limu, Gera, Guma, Kefa
1882 Arusi (Asela region)
1886 Welega (Nekemt)
1886 S. Arusi (Lakes down to Webi Shebelli)
1887 Harer
1887 Ilubabor (Gore)
1889 Southern Gurage
1889 Kulu and Konta
1890-1893 Kembata
1891 Ogaden, Bale, Sidamo (Awraja)
1894 Gofa
1894 Welamo
1896 Borena
1897 Borena (fort at Mega)
1897 Kefa conquered
1898 Beni Shangul
1898 Goldia and Maji to Lake Rudolf
1898 Gimira

Adapted from Ethiopian Textbook

Map 3

ETHIOPIAN RESETTLEMENT SITES

Adapted from Eshetu and Teshome 1984

Only a cursory examination of the placement of resettlement sites reveals their striking relationship with Menelik's military expeditions which began more than a century ago. Where bullets have failed to fully incorporate recently conquered peoples, humanitarian assistance from the West used to support the resettlement program, which is being used to dispossess people of fertile land and to establish a surveillance and "security" presence in the area, will certainly succeed. While Ethiopia could only resettle between 200,000 and 250,000 people in the previous decade, from November 1984 to the present between 700,000 and 800,000 people have been forcibly moved. The drastic increase in the numbers of people moved has resulted, in large part, from the massive influence of Western trucks and foodstuffs.

12   Politics and the Ethiopian Famine 1984-1985

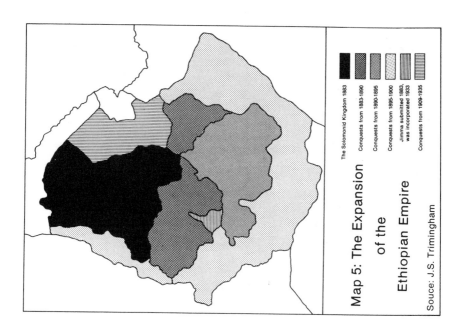

Map 5: The Expansion

of the

Ethiopian Empire

The Solomonid Kingdom 1883

Conquests from 1883-1890

Conquests from 1890-1895

Conquests from 1895-1900

Jimma submitted 1883,
was incorporated 1933

Conquests from 1909-1935

Souce: J.S. Trimingham

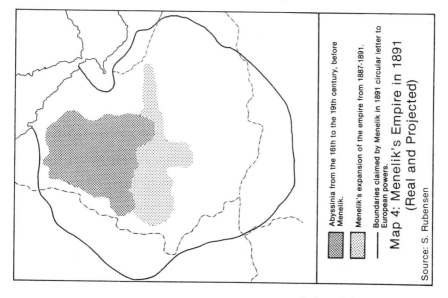

Abyssinia from the 16th to the 19th century, before Menelik.

Menelik's expansion of the empire from 1887-1891.

Boundaries claimed by Menelik in 1891 circular letter to European powers.

Map 4: Menelik's Empire in 1891
(Real and Projected)

Source: S. Rubensen

Incorporation of Conquered Regions

The conquered peoples neither saw nor accepted any historical justification for the conquests, especially considering their long histories of conflict with the Abyssinians to the north over trade, land and religion. Various conquered groups to the east and south of Abyssinia now believe the expansion of the northern kingdom resulted from the Shoan Amhara's desire to control production of the region's exports with strategic European support. With few exceptions, cash crops and trade goods originated in Oromo and neighboring Cushitic areas but were exported through Abyssinia to Europe and elsewhere. The once-conquered peoples point out that the same relations continue today.

The conquest intensified the contradiction between southern Cushitic peoples and the Abyssinians who lived north and west of them. The conquests were brutal and involved much killing, property destruction, looting and abduction of slaves. Destruction of the agricultural base was so extensive in some Oromo and Sidama regions that severe famines followed military campaigns.

Menelik's Agrarian Policies

The atrocities of the conquest, though not forgotten, were quickly overshadowed by the large-scale land grab that immediately followed, by the colonization of many areas by Amhara settlers and by the establishment of military and administrative posts throughout the region. These posts eventually evolved into armed garrisons, then urban centers.

Menelik changed land tenure throughout the conquered areas. He declared all conquered people his subjects and all land the property of the crown. These decrees, upheld by the military, laid the foundation for the relations of production within the empire and set the stage for the conflict between nations that continues today. Soldiers from Abyssinia who helped win the military campaigns — most had been victims of the Great Famine of the 1890s — were rewarded for their role in state building with grants of land in the conquered regions as well as the right to use subjugated indigenous peoples as slaves to fulfill labor requirements in absence of labor-saving technology. Local elites from the conquered populations who collaborated with the conquering power during the formation of the new political system were also given land-use rights in return for their service to the Abyssinian, now Ethiopian, emperor. They could not, however, pass these rights on to their children.

Land tenure in the south was transformed — quickly in some areas, more gradually in others — from a system in which land was centrally allocated by indigenous authorities or regional representatives to one in which most residents became sharecroppers or serfs who were expected to give most of their crops to resident and visiting landlords in addition to other payments and obligations in service or in kind. These northern landlords also served as tax collectors, judges and functionaries in the state administration of the empire-cum-state.

Throughout the conquered areas in the south the standard of living plummeted. Most new tenants had Abyssinian landlords, many of whom were infamous for their harsh treatment of local people from whom they were to wrest their livelihood. Some were such poor farm managers that large numbers of tenants had to be sold as slaves in order to pay their debts or to acquire currency.

At first, pastoralists and others who practiced a mixed agro-pastoral economy were less directly affected by the changes in land tenure due to the lack of local administrative capacity in their areas. They lived on the periphery of the new empire, so central control of them and their resources was delayed. Although a livestock tax was imposed by fiat, it could be enforced only sporadically. However, as the southern half of the new empire's population increased and as colonists from other parts of the empire were transplanted into the conquered lands, and granted land as well as authority derived from the state, the land base of the stockkeepers was also steadily eroded. Similar to most farmers in the conquered regions, livestock herders had also lost their land rights by proclamation and were in the same structural position vis-a-vis the central state. The major difference was that it took more time, in some cases decades, before the herders realized that they had no land rights. This realization occurred as the state built up the capacity to implement imperial law.

The conquests incorporated unwilling subjects into the empire, exploited them economically and increased the diversity of the country's population; all these factors contributed to the currently widely acknowledged conflict and crisis within the empire.

Attempts at Assimilation of Conquered Areas

As a result of the expansion of the empire, the following peoples were added to the existing Christian, Amhara-Tigrayan kingdom, which supported itself by practicing ox-drawn plow agriculture and trading extensively with the Middle East: the Sidama of the southwest highlands who practiced a traditional religion and hoe cultivation; Oromo of both Islamic and traditional beliefs from the central, south central, eastern and western parts of the present empire, who prior to conquest practiced a combination of herding, agriculture and commercial trading; and the Moslem Somali to the south and east of Abyssinia.

Cultural diversity did not inspire cultural pluralism, tolerance or flexibility among the dominant Amharas who were numerically a small group in the new empire. The Abyssinians considered their own culture and religion superior to those of the conquered peoples who lived south and east of them and developed a corresponding ideology of superiority. They strove to Amharicize the conquered peoples through various programs: Amharic was taught in the schools and public use of other languages was restricted. Higher education was conditional upon passing exams in Amharic. State support for Coptic Christianity was instituted while Islam was denigrated. The Ethiopian legal code, grounded in ancient Abyssinian texts, replaced indigenous legal systems in the conquered regions. The settlers' economic and political organizations replaced those of pre-existing polities which were officially denounced as "pagan" and "primitive." In short, the Amhara-created and -dominated empire dismantled the pre-conquest economic, political and social systems of the conquered peoples throughout the Cushitic and Nilotic western, southern and eastern regions.

Although certain individuals chose to accept assimilation, Amhara policies polarized the majority of conquered peoples. It made them aware of their differences and particular ethnic identities. During the early part of the twentieth century, for example, attempts to spread Christianity as part of the expansion of the empire inspired numerous conversions to Islam among the conquered peoples as a form of resistance and assertion of separate identity.

Despite this awareness among the conquered peoples during this period, they were unable to organize to evict the Amhara from their lands. This failure to expel the invaders was the result of several factors. In the first place, the conquest was spread over a period of two decades. Some of the peoples were incorporated into the empire before others were even conquered. Consequently, there was not an immediate awareness of collective experience of domination and repression. In addition, many local elites were persuaded to collaborate with the conquerors. Although this deflected violent conquest, it helped consolidate the conquerors' power. Another factor was that the Amhara quickly gained control of local trading routes. They transferred large stockpiles of European weapons to the conquered areas and established military garrisons to guard trading posts, thus preventing the free flow of information. Separated by wide terrain, and with their own overarching, integrating mechanisms dismantled, many from the most populated areas were only connected with one another and the outside world by these routes. Finally, and perhaps most importantly, the European superpowers helped the new empire enforce order and administer "newly acquired" regions. In their attempts to curry favor with the empire, the Europeans sold weapons to the Ethiopians and provided military and technical advisors. Once established, this policy continued under Haile Selassie. In 1942, after expelling Italy and reinstating Haile Selassie on the throne, the British even shaped the new state's bureaucracy. As Margery Perham observed of the relations between Ethiopia and Great Britain: "After the liberation of the country the Emperor [Haile Selassie] found himself in a wholly new position. The country had been reconquered in the main by the armies of the British Commonwealth and Empire, and for a period the whole structure of the country was dependent on the cooperation and financial support of Britain" (1969:93).

Reform in the Idiom of "Modernization" Under Haile Selassie

Most of the empire was incorporated by forceful means. Administrative and economic policies were enforced despite resistance. As a direct result of the empire's strict economic measures against the peasantry, their poverty increased throughout the twentieth century. From the 1940s onward, imperial land takeovers intensified. More Abyssinian settlers were brought into the conquered regions, overtly referred to in Amharic as ye qenye agar (colonial lands) and ye galla meret (Galla land or Oromo land).

After World War II, when commercial agriculture was introduced in the empire's recently conquered areas, many indigenous peoples finally realized that they had indeed lost the legal right to their lands some 50 years before. Tenants were evicted in areas designated for tractor farming and agribusiness; "green revolution" technology introduced through integrated development schemes made labor nearly superfluous since the technology was expected to produce more crops than the tenants could produce. These schemes were funded with bilateral or multilateral assistance from the West.

Evicted tenants were often forced merely to "move" and ended up squatting in areas only marginally suited for rain-fed cultivation, where they led a poorer and more precarious existence. Those agriculturalists who kept livestock as well as cultivated crops were often forced to abandon their arable land and depend exclusively on livestock herding, i.e., they were forced into pastoralism from a mixed mode of livelihood.

In the empire's eastern areas, hundreds of thousands of agriculturalists were prohibited from working lands they had traditionally used for agriculture and stock rearing so that capitalist-style agriculture using irrigation technology could be introduced. By providing army and police protection as well as agricultural credit, the government ensured the implementation, if not success, of this high-technology agricultural settlement in the name of modernization. If conquered inhabitants were involved at all with these innovations, it was normally as laborers. Most of the wealth generated went to landlords or traders who were not native to the local area and were, in fact, settlers.

Resistance of Once-Conquered National Groups

As the conquered peoples became aware of their position — both of the importance of their produce to the economic stability of the Amhara-dominated state and of their political marginalization — they increased their resistance to the central state. There were precedents for this resistance. In 1936, when the Italians invaded Ethiopia from the north, Oromo leaders in the west of the empire appealed for British assistance to maintain an Oromo federation until they achieved self-government. Under Italian occupation of Ethiopia, the Oromo and others were encouraged to evict Amhara settlers from some areas. At the same time, the Italians and British ruled the Somali in their own, separate administrative units that increased the group's identity as a political unit. Most importantly, perhaps, Italian occupation demonstrated to many subordinated peoples that Amhara dominance and colonization could be overthrown.

In the late 1940s and early 1950s, even after Haile Selassie was returned to the throne by the British (along with the imported constitution), attacks against Amhara dominance and against Abyssinian settlers in the conquered regions continued and increased with the reimposition of imperial tax-gathering. Unrest also increased during this time in response to specific policies; for example, livestock herders rebelled when the government attempted to prevent the untaxed export of animals by restricting pastoralists' mobility.

In 1948, the British failed to act on western Oromo leaders' requests to negotiate the Oromo's independence and it seemed the Oromo's fate was sealed. In 1952, Eritrean decolonization was scheduled according to a United Nations' timetable, but Ethiopia, with the aid of the US in the UN, annexed the region in 1962 as a "province" of Ethiopia, and Eritrea alone was denied the independence that was granted other former colonies in its position.

Following the independence and union of British and Italian Somalilands in 1960, the Somali who remained under Ethiopian control made a strong push for independence. Radio broadcasts from independent Somalia heightened their discontent.

Such developments encouraged the protracted revolt of Somalis and Oromos by the early 1960s. At the heart of this opposition was the exploitation of the peasantry — the continued takeover of land by colonists. The central government responded to resistance with a brutal but unsuccessful military campaign. Through accommodation of individual leaders, resistance was minimized, but not before even more hatred was generated between Oromos and Somalis on the one hand and Abyssinian settlers and officials — who interpreted events to the rest of the population through control of the media.

Even economic and social associations among the conquered peoples were tolerated only to a point. In 1966, for example, educated Oromos in Addis Ababa established a self-help association, the Macha-Tulama, that spread to the rural areas. Expression of wide-spread dissatisfaction with the Amhara-dominated government and with the Oromos' position within the empire followed. Although the organization was banned in 1968, it indicated to Abyssinian officials and Oromos alike that there was considerable opposition throughout the country even among those Oromos who had been considered Amharicized.

While there had been sporadic outbreaks in the previously conquered areas prior to the overthrow of Haile Selassie in 1974, the Ethiopian empire's military superiority by and large subdued most people indigenous to the region. A tenuous truce existed between conquered and conqueror groups, but over time, population growth and competition for resources in the conquered regions deepened the rift. Thus, by 1974, peoples in many conquered areas had begun to settle grievances over the political and economic conditions they had suffered the preceding 70 to 80 years. This was when the military stepped in to replace Haile Selassie's regime.

The Northern Highlands: Resistance of Subjugated National Groups

The Amhara-dominated imperial government also faced challenges from the Abyssinian northern highlanders, especially Tigrayans, even though many of those in the area had historical, ethnic and religious ties with the Amhara. Neither emperor — Menelik nor Haile Selassie — had received support from the area's Tigrayan inhabitants. Historically, local and regional leaders had established their own principalities and vied with each other to dominate the entire Abyssinian area. Difficult terrain and isolation intensified power struggles. While regional political groupings could become relatively strong, it was logistically difficult for one person to rule all the northern highlands for sustained periods.

Even today in the northern highlands, first loyalties go to the regions and administrative units that correspond roughly with past kingdoms. Amhara domination was attained through European assistance, conquests of peoples south of them and overt repressive economic measures taken specifically by Menelik's and Haile Selassie's governments to subdue particular groups of fellow Abyssinians and thus prevent their effective rivalry. These measures combined formed their regional loyalties and the basis of other northern highland groups' dissatisfaction with central government.

Tigray, specifically, developed strong grievances against Amhara-dominated governments because from the time of Emperor Menelik they were gradually excluded from power. Even prior to Menelik, Tigrayans had claimed that the position "Kings of Kings" of the Abyssinian kingdoms had legitimately belonged to them since the time of Axum. Thus, for a century, Tigrayans saw even their rightful place in the empire usurped by Amhara. For example, under Haile Selassie, Tigrayans resented Amhara officials assigned to their area. They felt the Amhara oppressed and starved them economically in order to monopolize and retain power.

Each reform Haile Selassie implemented, designed to increase the centralization of government power in the hands of Amharas, was opposed by other northerners. These measures included the dismissal of local armies and the assignment of central government troops to the area. Amharas who replaced local tax collectors were also resented in Tigray and in other Abyssinian regions. Revolts in Gondar in 1930 just prior to Selassie's inauguration were a clear attempt to prevent his rule over the area. Other revolts followed in Tigray and Gojjam.

Another period of unrest in various Abyssinian regions followed the restoration of the emperor in 1941. Haile Selassie's attempts to reimpose central government in Gondar and Tigray met resistance that almost toppled the government. Yet even so, revolts from within Abyssinia — based on different grievances from those of conquered peoples — could be handled differently from those that arose in regions of alien, conquered peoples where no internal controls operated.

In 1944 attempts to introduce revised land taxes following the expulsion of the Italians met with militant opposition in Gondar and Tigray. Later that year the emperor rescinded the measure in those provinces. Gojjam was the scene of two other major revolts against the imperial government in 1951 and 1968, as well as numerous other actions that occurred when government policies were seen as imperial interference in local matters.

Resistance of an Annexed Former European Colony

In 1962, Haile Selassie's government unilaterally announced the dissolution of the United Nations mandate over the peoples of the former Italian colony of Eritrea. With diplomatic assistance from the US, the Ethiopians summarily annexed Eritrea as an "Ethiopian province." This occurred at the time when all former European colonies in Africa were attaining their independence. Eritreans, arguing that they had formed the basis of an independent state, resisted vehemently. A full-scale war began, which continues today.

Attempts at Unification

Faced with threats from both annexed and subordinated nations to the north and the nations of the conquered regions to the south of the Abyssinian heartland, the government sought to create unity by attempting to augment and tighten central authority. Administrative boundaries were established and then changed in order to break the power of regional leaders and erode the homogeneity of national groups. To prevent administrators from building regional power bases, they were transferred frequently. Provincial government was brought under central authority, and political parties and political campaigning were banned in order to give regional politics a low profile. Revolts were dealt with harshly; this quelled them temporarily, but tended to intensify ethnic identity and exacerbate conflict along these lines. Finally, to placate the provinces, the emperor juggled tax amnesties, removed harsh governors and distributed titles to revolt leaders who laid down their arms. The recurrence of unrest in several areas over a number of decades, however, indicates that such measures were, at best, only temporarily successful and did not resolve the cause of the problems.

The Case of Wollo

Due to the facts that a large number of the affected population included in this study were people from Wollo; that food supplies — while in sufficient supply in the country as a whole — did not appear to have reached Wollo residents in sufficient quantity in 1984 or 1985; and that according to government estimates some 65 to 70 percent of all those being resettled are from Wollo — nearly 9 percent of the region's population, it is important to discuss the historical relationship of the residents of this administrative region to the empire.

The Ethiopian administrative region of Wollo is a transitional area in every sense of the term. It is a critical ecological buffer zone between the arid lowlands of the nomadic Afar people and the highlands of the Amhara Abyssinians. The middle region, a long finger of fertile plains, has long been inhabited by agro-pastoral Oromos. Their transhumant lifestyle enabled them to exploit efficiently a topographical niche where cattle thrived and rains for agriculture were not certain, but where in good years large surpluses could be produced. These surpluses provided grain supplies during the dry years to supplement animal products. The transitional nature of the ecology occupied by Oromos in Wollo is characteristic terrain for their agro-pastoral productive systems throughout present-day Ethiopia.

Wollo is the name of one of the major branches of the Oromo nation, and the Oromo people of that branch were a functional part of the Oromo *gada* generation grade system until the nineteenth century. At that time a long-standing struggle began over the alliance and identity of Oromo people in the area which now occupies the central part of the empire.

By the sixteenth century, Oromos firmly ensconced in the Wollo area had nearly entirely converted to Islam, a religious affiliation that created an additional barrier between themselves and neighboring Amhara and Afar peoples (in addition, that is, to the national economic/cultural barriers).

The Oromos of Wollo, particularly Yejju, were known for their courageous, well-equipped, trained cavalry. These attributes acquired significance in the late eighteenth century when a skirmish broke out between neighboring Abyssinian kingdoms. During a major conflict between Amhara and Tigray principalities for supremacy within the Abyssinian kingdom — best described as a feudal monarchy — the contending Amhara prince appealed to Cushitic Oromo neighbors to assist him in battle against the Tigrayans to the north. Many Oromos did not partake in this internal jockeying for power, not being Abyssinian or even of Semitic stock, but the Wollo branch of the Oromo polity had been in competition for land with Tigrayans to the north of them, so they complied and sent 20,000 well-armed cavalry to assist the Amhara against their enemy. Their support was decisive, the Amhara king became emperor, and he sent an invitation and a plea for the fighting force to stay on in Gondar to defend the emperor and to act as a deterrent to future threats from Tigray. Many of the Oromo cavalry and their families stayed on in the Gondar region, especially after the

Amhara emperor married the widow of a high-ranking Oromo. The son born of this union was sent to Wollo to be raised as an Oromo and eventually returned to rule in Gondar. The period of nearly a century (1760-1855) that followed in Abyssinia is known as the "Era of the Princes." During this time several emperors of mixed Wollo Oromo and Amhara blood ruled in Gondar, and Oromo became the language of the royal court.

In 1855, Theodoros came to power with the expressed holy mission of clearing the alien *Galla* (Oromo) out of Abyssinia. His Amhara nationalist zeal drove him to attempt to unite Abyssinia under the banner of Christianity and expel the former Oromo security forces who had moved into powerful positions. Theodoros attempted to maim and punish as many Oromos as possible to prevent their return to dominate the Abyssinian kingdoms. Most of the Moslem Oromos returned to Yejju from where they had originally come. Some who had converted to Christianity stayed on in Gondar and became assimilated with the Amhara population. A few descendants who followed Islam remained in the Debra Tabor region. Theodoros' campaign eventually foundered, and by the time Napier's celebrated expedition made its way to Abyssinia to save British hostages held by Theodoros, the emperor was surrounded by hostile Oromos who gave every assistance to the British.

In his push to expand the area of Abyssinian rule beyond its historical limits, Menelik first conquered the Wollo Oromo and created a single administrative region that he called Wollo. In this province, Oromos were sandwiched between Amhara on one side and Afar on the other. This administrative unit still exists with the name Wollo. It remains common for the name of the region and the people to be confused.

A number of observers have commented on the importance of the Wollo Oromo to instability of Amhara rule. Margery Perham writes of the Wollo Oromo, "who on the eastern escarpment of the northern plateau ... have been in long and close contact with the Amharas [but who] have resisted absorption and have therefore been the source of grave weakness to the Amharas" (1969:303).

Lipsky also notes in a survey of the peoples of the empire, "The *Galla* [Oromo] to the north of Shoa [in Wollo] particularly the Wollo, Yejju and Raya Gallas [called Azebu by the Tigrayans], have never been thoroughly assimilated and remain a political liability" (1962:46). Accounts of Haile Selassie's journey from Addis Ababa in 1936 indicate that the Wollo Oromo spat at him as he passed through their areas and he refused to travel there again (Shepherd 1975:9).

The identity that the people from Wollo will eventually assume in the current national conflict, i.e., "Ethiopian," "Oromo" or other, is an open question in the empire — and a matter of some importance as an indicator of the strength of the social formations demanding their loyalty and allegiance. The battle over those from Wollo is one of the battles being waged in the resettlement process. Taking Wollo Oromo from their homeland and making them dependent upon the present regime, a ruling military committee/junta, is a gambit for control of those from Wollo based on the assumption that they will see it is in their own interest to support the state in return for possible amenities in the resettlement site. But resettling them in the midst of a people with whom they have cultural and social ties and where an Oromo liberation movement is active is a risky move for the government. It could be based on any one or some combination of the three following scenarios: the Ethiopian government does not feel there is any threat of a united Oromo resistance because many of the Wollo Oromo no longer speak the Oromo language, the government is concerned that those from Wollo will respond to the appeals of the TPLF (Tigrayan People's Liberation Front) and join the TPLF and this fear outweighs its fears of a united Oromo resistance, or the government does not believe that many from Wollo will survive the resettlement.

A weakness in our own research design was introduced when we agreed not to inquire directly about nationality in our survey (a point which we conceded to the concerns of aid agencies who were to cooperate in the research). As a result we do not know how people from Wollo would identify themselves at this juncture. They see themselves as victims of the regime. The primary avenue open to them to improve their condition is to become militiamen, which turns them against the local Oromo population; yet they have deserted the settlements in droves in efforts to return home. Further researchers would do well to explore this issue.

People from Wollo have a reputation for their tendency to watch and wait for the proper time to act and then for going with the stronger force. *Walla wye inde Wollo*, for example, which means "they do not have a clear stand like the Wollo," is a common saying in Addis Ababa. Future political alliances in the area may well turn on the events in the struggle for the loyalty of the people of Wollo.

Reform in the Idiom of "Socialism" Under the Dergue

Even in such multinational and multicultural areas as Wollo, Ethiopia's imperial governments were unsuccessful in creating a unified and integrated "state" despite specially designed centralizing and modernizing policies. On the eve of the 1974 revolution, Ethiopia was a loose gathering of distinct peoples whose diverse cultural identities had actually become more intense as a result of imperial government policies.

In 1974, widespread resistance throughout the empire finally toppled the government of Haile Selassie. In the course of taking power, the military factions who organized the "Committee" that became known as the "Dergue" recognized that the imperial government had grown weaker and was exacerbating ethnic-based opposition throughout the empire.

The military government's own range of reforms, couched in the idiom of "Ethiopian Socialism," were desperate attempts to hold the empire together. The Dergue fashioned responses to quell the widely divergent expressions of unrest referred to above. A proclamation announcing the nationalization of all land in Ethiopia, made in 1975, appeared to be the most sweeping of several reforms. Each group in the empire had been concerned about the issue of land, the primary means of production in a peasant economy. Many had put forward the demand "Land to the Tiller" and expected that after the revolution they would be granted the land that in most cases had belonged to their peoples prior to the creation of the present empire. Their demands led them to expect a liberation of the land, and its placement under their control. Instead the leaders announced the nationalization of the land.

The country-wide confusion between liberation of land and nationalization of land lasted for nearly two years while the Dergue consolidated state power. Then, as the Dergue's Provisional Military Administrative Council (PMAC) moved to implement its programs in a top-down fashion based on state ownership of all rural land, it met resistance from the same quarters as its predecessors—from conquered, subdued and annexed nations. Our findings correspond with this interpretation of events. Current refugees date their opposition to the state to widespread reversals in elections, tax policy, agricultural programs and recruitment for militia/military which began in 1977-1978 (see especially pp. 127-128).

The fundamental issue for most peoples in Ethiopia is what kind of state holds the land. Individual families were to be given up to 10 hectares for use. All the land, however, remained the state's property. In the northern highlands and southern conquered areas peasants were required to join peasant associations in order to use land. But the implementation of government policies regarding land appears different in the north among suppressed nationalities than in the south among formerly conquered peoples.

The military government was able to reorganize local, rural, agrarian production in large part because it initially recognized the existence, even officially condoned the expansion, of local systems of self-government that had sprung up. Many of these had even been instrumental in the demise of Haile Selassie's government in the rural areas, particularly in many Oromo areas. The government's program of peasant associations co-opted these movements by incorporating them by proclamation into central government ministries and then placing them on a timetable toward collectivization. The government has announced its intention that by 1990 peasant associations will have converted voluntarily into producers' cooperatives that would undertake production collectively. To date, however, they have not. Even though there appear to be considerable incentives and pressures to form cooperatives, not even one percent of producers have moved along this projected timetable. The resettlement program is one way to speed up this process (see Map 4); "villagization" is another.

Recently the government has announced that over the next nine years 33 million people will be moved into nucleated villages "where the government can more easily provide services to them." The only services to date in the new villages are centrally located, flag-draped buildings that are used for party headquarters. The nucleation of rural populations has been explained by the government as a necessary step in their education/indoctrination. Through political education programs, it is assumed, peasants will voluntarily choose to convert their peasant associations to producers' cooperatives.

Reemergence of Resistance from the National Groups

The demise of Haile Selassie's regime resulted from the explosion of the above-mentioned variety of economic, regional, religious and ethnic forces which the imperial government failed to acknowledge, much less keep under control. After the the Selassie regime fell and the nature of the Dergue became clear, various national groups pressed the military government for specific changes. While the Dergue's political and military attention was focused on changes taking place in the capital in 1976-1977, national groups planned that they would be able to establish strong positions in their home areas to be able to influence the new government.

Eritreans and Somali were quick to attack the Dergue's army and achieved unprecedented military control over contested areas. But when the new regime successfully appealed to the USSR for military assistance, and when a sizeable Cuban fighting force was dispatched to Ethiopia, the Eritreans and Somalis were forced to retreat.

By 1977, Eritrean liberation movements controlled not only all of the Eritrean countryside, much of which they had already controlled for a decade, but also all of the urban centers in the region with four exceptions — two interior cities and two ports. Three of these towns were surrounded for several months. Oil supplies headed for Addis Ababa were often disrupted. The Eritrean situation was critical for the Dergue military regime. The contested area included the country's most important ports and industrial areas as well as extensive commercial agriculture areas established during the Italian occupation.

The Western Somali Liberation Front (WSLF) also launched a major military campaign in 1978-1979 among Somali living in the Ogaden region of the eastern Ethiopian province of Harar. They gained control of the region, which they designated Western Somalia. During the fighting, the railroad from Addis Ababa to Djibouti, Ethiopia's only railroad connection to a port, was cut, and the major industrial town in the east, Dire Dawa, surrounded. Grain shipments from the eastern highlands, which the capital city and the military depended on for crucial food supplies, were threatened.

The success of these campaigns coincided with similar uprisings in neighboring areas. In Tigray, the TPLF emerged out of the continued dissatisfaction of the Tigrayan population with Amhara domination and the gradual realization that the Dergue was continuing, even furthering, the Amharas' dominance of the central state and direct repression of Tigrayans. It became clear that the autonomy promised at the time of the revolution for Tigray and others was a low priority for the Dergue at best.

Support for the TPLF grew as more Tigrayans realized that once again they were being systematically excluded from the new military government. When the Dergue began forcibly to conscript young men to fight against Eritreans and Somali, peasant support for the TPLF increased dramatically. Since the dominant Amhara comprised only 15 percent of the country's population, the Dergue had to recruit young men from among the conquered peoples to form sub-Saharan Africa's largest army. Amhara representation in the army is less than their representation in the empire as a whole. Support and enlistments for the TPLF grew as the government raised local taxes, demanded contributions, reorganized peasant associations and orchestrated redistribution of land. Tigrayans were also forced to work without pay on state farms in the north and resettle as colonists on state farms in many of the previously conquered areas in the south.

In Oromo-inhabited regions — the east, south, southwest and western areas of the empire — the Oromo Liberation Front (OLF) gradually acted upon the momentum created by Oromo resistance movements operating from 1963-1970. In Bale, for example, Oromo never gave up their arms. From 1978-1979, the OLF was particularly active in Ethiopia's eastern areas.

24   Politics and the Ethiopian Famine 1984-1985

Since then, it appears to have expanded its base by organizing Oromos throughout areas to which Oromo were indigenous (the OLF refers to these Oromo homelands as "Oromia"). In 1981, the OLF became militarily active in the western part of the country—specifically in Wollega and Illubabor administrative regions, a fact that takes on significance in light of the Dergue's ongoing resettlement programs in precisely those areas (see Chapter VI).

Comprising, according to some estimates, 60 percent of the population—some 18 million to 20 million people—Oromo are potentially the most serious threat to Ethiopia's central government. As a direct result of the Dergue's policies, OLF support has increased. The land nationalization program, which took land from both tenants and individual owners and placed it in the hands of an Amhara-dominated state, appeared to Oromos as a revival of Menelik's old agrarian policy—"all lands belong to the crown-cum-state." The Dergue's program, which forced producers to join peasant associations and, in some cases, producers' cooperatives, increased peasant support for the OLF dramatically.

The military government also faces other challenges that stem from the introduction of socialist economic strategies and the reluctance of producers and traders to adjust to new incentives. Food shortages are the major problem. The military government is particularly worried that a lack of food in the cities will lead to unrest in urban areas or in the military. Supporting both of these sectors is essential to the survival of the government.

Food shortages can be traced to agrarian and agricultural policy, beginning with the land reform program. Initially, land reform, tax and marketing policies led many peasants to retain larger portions of their produce for themselves or to sell it through private traders—where they could get a better price—rather than through the government marketing system. After 1977, when the government's ability to enforce sale of produce to the state-run AMC (Agricultural Marketing Corporation) increased, however, many farmers simply did not plant extensive areas in crops for fear of expropriation.

Guaranteeing enough food for urban areas remains a problem. Low, fixed government prices are disincentives for producers to plant or, as in 1984, even to harvest crops that must be marketed through the government agencies or AMC. Joseph Collins (personal communication) and numerous other observers driving east and south from Addis Ababa during the critical 1984-1985 famine witnessed unharvested fields even near the main roads. As the government has tightened its control of private traders' activities, the option of selling to the private sector has been curtailed as quotas are increased.

From the beginning, the Dergue was aware—as a result both of the drought, which ended in 1973, and of the decline in food production following 1977—of the rural populations' potential to undermine its power. In attempting to guarantee a food supply for urban residents and the military, it redoubled efforts to pursue the establishment of state farms, producers' cooperatives and even peasant associations, all or large portions of whose collectively produced crops go to the government, in many areas without compensation. Agricultural credit, equipment, technical advice and services are concentrated on the production controlled by the government in state farms or producers' cooperatives. The orchestration of the events which created the famine as well as the programs that were intended to alleviate it constitute a direct extension of the central power of the state over individual producers.

The Role of Resettlement in the Creation and Maintenance of the Ethiopian Empire

The famine and the resettlement of people from northern regions to southern ones is best understood in light of the above described historical relations among the peoples of the empire. The movement of people from "north to south" has been a constant feature of Ethiopian society since the present-day empire was created. While those who write about the phenomenon draw attention to the continuity in the process from era to era since the time of Menelik, they refer to it in widely differing ways. Some say the movement of peoples has been "spontaneous," others a part of "political conquest." Some call the movement a "natural flow" of people responging to population pressure on the northern lands (Hoben 1973; Marcus 1975), while others say the government has designs to implement policy through population control. McClellan (1976), Wood (1983) and Eshetu Chole and Teshome Mulat (1984) have drawn special attention to the processes of settlement as they have taken place under succeeding regimes in Ethiopia. Each has pointed out the enormous logistical, economic, cultural and political constraints involved in the attempt to orchestrate the introduction and settlement of culturally different people into homelands of other groups.

Through resettlement, people who have been problematic to the ruling regime in their own homes are made dependent on the central state by being placed into regions where residents are predictaby hostile to the newcomers. This policy has become a major part of a formula for dividing and conquering distinct peoples in the empire. By making people dependent upon the central state the government can dominate those who might otherwise organize effectively to push for more local power in the form of either autonomy or independence. It should be noted that most of Menelik's conquering armies who helped build the empire were comprised of famine victims, restless and desperate for resources, who later became loyal settlers in the early 1900s. As *neftanya* (gun-carrying settlers) in conquered lands, they derived benefits directly from the indigenous farmers/laborers. These *neftanya*, primarily of Amhara nationality, occupied the garrison posts that eventually evolved into urban centers. Other Abyssinians and local Oromos also participated, and as a result received benefits from the government. The state structure that emerged was an apparatus designed to link and organize these clusters of settlers — or, more appropriately, colonies — systematically. Successive Ethiopian states have channeled a vast proportion of their resources into maintaining and strengthening the ability of Ethiopia's strategically located settlers to uphold the law and to administer the outpost regions. The extent to which the current resettlement program fits this pattern is striking.

The colonization of "southern lands" was first made possible by designating them "government" lands and distributing them to "patriots," soldiers, landless and unemployed persons, and others in return for "meritorious" service. The supreme rights of the regime in power (whether

Map 6

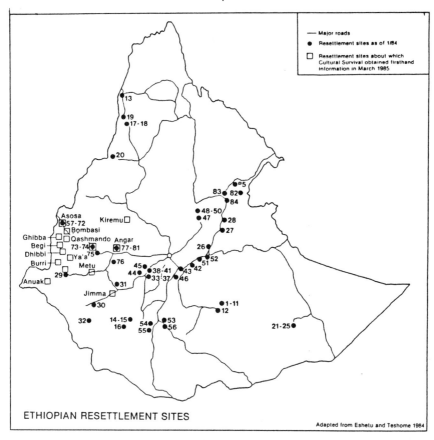

ETHIOPIAN RESETTLEMENT SITES

Adapted from Eshetu and Teshome 1984

Though woefully incomplete, this map provides an indication of the pattern of resettlement as of mid-1984. Some of the sites overlap with those for famine victims from Tigray and Wollo. This map does not indicate areas that have already been affected by the rapidly expanding villagization program (scheduled to move 33 million people over the next nine years) for which the Ethiopian government also appealed for international funding throughout 1985 (see accompanying map for greater detail of resettlement sites in southwest Ethiopia).

referred to as "monarch," "crown" or "state") have been used to reallocate "government" land as it saw/sees fit.

The resettlement program of the Dergue government in Ethiopia, regardless of socialist explanations offered for the transfer of populations within the boundaries of the state, fits precisely the colonizing settlement patterns of a century of preceding rulers. The key, common features are:

1. All land belongs to the government.

2. Lands of indigenous peoples are reallocated to settlers as a reward for compliance and services rendered to the state.

3. Settlers receive greater benefits than do local populations (e.g., transport and communication facilities, health, education, marketing and administrative services).

4. Armaments are dispensed to settler populations in return for cooperation; though arms are initially granted to settlers under the rubric of "self-protection from hostile, local populations," they are later employed in the enforcement of constantly revised laws.

5. Settlers are mandated to build a "New Ethiopia" against local opposition.

6. Officials encourage conjugal unions and marriages between settlers and local peoples.

7. Settlers are encouraged to appropriate and consume local surpluses.

A retrospective assessment of settlement under Haile Selassie led Eshetu and Teshome to conclude, "the exercise of the monarch of his land administrative powers did not always result in beneficial settlement patterns. Often political and short-term considerations were given more weight than long-term gains" (1984:6). The data provided by these authors show that when land was provided to grantees, agricultural production declined. Our research findings indicate that such problems have been magnified under the Dergue and are reaching an irreversible crisis point with the 1984-1985 resettlement and villagization programs.

The Dergue's Resettlement Apparatus

The proclamation of the "Public Ownership of Rural Lands" and the elimination of private property has empowered the Dergue government to move populations around on the land even more dramatically than its predecessors. Peasant associations have been useful vehicles for implementation of settlements on both ends. For example, settlers have been successfully recruited through peasant associations that are administered centrally through the All-Ethiopia Peasant Association (now, significantly, simply Ethiopian Peasant Association).

Structures explicitly devoted to settlement have been central to the Dergue's administration of the empire from the formation of this government. In 1978, the Settlement Authority operated as an autonomous unit within the Ministry of Agriculture and Settlement. In 1979, the Relief and Rehabilitation Commission was made to encompass the Awash Valley Authority, the Settlement Authority and the old RRC. It was to function independently and was answerable only to the chairman of the Council of Ministers. With considerable and wide-ranging powers, it was this body that designed the 1983-1985 settlements. Site selection was conducted by WPE personnel during 1983 and 1984. Unemployed persons and drought victims were targeted for participation. Drawing on peasants almost exclusively from Tigray and Wollo, where peasant populations have proved to be political liabilities to the Dergue (see above), the program for 1984 was orchestrated despite the agricultural production failures and the high death rates associated with the earlier settlement sites of the previous decade. All internal government reports as well as those such as Eshetu and Teshome's (1984) had revealed that in Ethiopia "settlements show consistently the lowest levels of land and labor productivity" in comparison with all other forms of agricultural organization.

Even though traditional methods of producing all crops in all regions showed higher levels of production, settlements — which largely displaced traditional communities — were proposed as the Dergue's principle solution to "solving the food production crisis" of 1983-1984. Results of government and university studies comparing settlements occupied by drought victims with settlements mainly comprised of jobless laborers show the drought victims to be only 20 percent as productive as the laborers. The current resettlement program was planned and implemented despite overwhelming negative evidence concerning the economic viability of the program. Furthermore, no alternative programs to rehabilitate the northern famine areas received serious consideration or investment.

Background to the 1984-1985 "Resettlement Program for Famine Victims"

In November 1984, the Ethiopian government presented its ongoing resettlement program as its officially endorsed solution to the 1984 famine crisis. Following the Dergue's establishment of the Workers' Party of Ethiopia in September 1984, the decision had been taken to reverse previous policy and open famine-striken northern regions of Ethiopia to the Western media in October 1984. The resulting television broadcasts that revealed conditions of starving people in Wollo shocked the world and prompted a generous monetary response from private and public sectors in the West. In a series of public announcements transmitted over Radio Addis Ababa, government spokesmen declared Ethiopia's intent to move 1.5 million people from the country's "famine-affected areas" in the north of the country to "uninhabited virgin areas" in three administrative regions in the southwest by the end of 1985. This program was officially put forth as the government's strategy for ensuring the survival of famine victims and for alleviating the conditions that led to the famine. As such, the program was introduced as an active candidate for international funds.

The declaration of intent by the Ethiopian government to resettle 1.5 million people unleashed a torrent of controversy. The Tigray People's Liberation Front and the Oromo Liberation Front immediately released a joint statement denouncing the program as politically motivated. Their statement also accused the government of coercing Tigray and Oromo peoples to participate in this program in order to break their resistance to central government policies and to increase control over both groups by attempting to settle one group on top of the other (Joint Statement by the TPLF and OLF, 29 November 1984). The reluctance of the West to become involved in the program without evaluating it first did not cause the Ethiopians even to hesitate. The prearranged Soviet transport support arrived on schedule and the program proceeded apace. By early 1985 Mengistu Haile Mariam boasted that,

Map 7

RESETTLEMENT SITES ABOUT WHICH CULTURAL SURVIVAL
OBTAINED FIRSTHAND INFORMATION

In the first chapter [phase] during this year the plan to resettle 50,000 peasant families or 250,000 people in the western and southwestern regions of our country and integrate them among the scattered organized peasant associations has, through the prestigious cooperation and efforts of the people of the region, been implemented between 17 November 1984 and 19 December 1984.

The number of these 250,000 peasant families or 1.5 million people who are to be resettled in two chapters [phases] is very small compared to the number of peasants who must still be resettled (Radio Addis Ababa, 13 February 1985).

The United States' response to the resettlement program was changed from skepticism to condemnation when Soviet aid, in the form of transport vehicles, was billed by the Ethiopians as "humanitarian assistance from the USSR." The Soviet transport equipment, delivered to the Ethiopian government subsequent to the establishment of the Workers' Party of Ethiopia (WPE) in September 1984, was devoted immediately and entirely to the rapid movement of hundreds of thousands of settlers from Tigray and Wollo to the southwest provinces. It took some time before the contours of this program became clear to Western observers. On 19 November 1985, *The New York Times* reported,

The four transport helicopters at Kembolcha are part of 24 sent by Moscow with 300 trucks and a dozen Antonov-12 transport planes to carry food and relief supplies to the 6.4 million people said by the Ethiopian government to be suffering from prolonged drought and famine.

Later, *The New York Times* reported,

The helicopters are to be based at the northern towns of Aksum, Mekelle, Kembolcha and Gondar and used for short shuttle flights, Ethiopian officials said.

On 3 January 1985, *The Washington Post* observed,

The Ethiopian government has proclaimed resettlement as its most important priority and with the help of 12 Soviet built Antonov cargo aircraft and more than 300 Soviet built trucks, about 20,000 peasants are moving south each week.

By March between 300,000 and 400,000 residents of northern administrative regions had been relocated into resettlement sites. It was clear that "logistical" problems confronted in the distribution of donated food from the West would not impede the resettlement program. Although food often could not be cleared from the docks, adequate fuel and vehicles were made available for resettlement through May, precisely the time when stories began to surface that the donated food was rotting on the docks for lack of transport. In April and May, an additional 100,000 people had been resettled.

Pressure began to mount in US official circles and in Congress to condemn resettlement. By June there was a move afoot to impose a US trade embargo on Ethiopia. These moves coincided with the onset of the rainy season and the impassability of the roads into the southwestern regions. Resettlement slowed considerably. Official Ethiopian statements were issued at that time stating that the resettlement program was being shelved, or at least reconsidered. These announcements elicited a hopeful and satisfied response from Western observers who wanted to believe that

Map 8

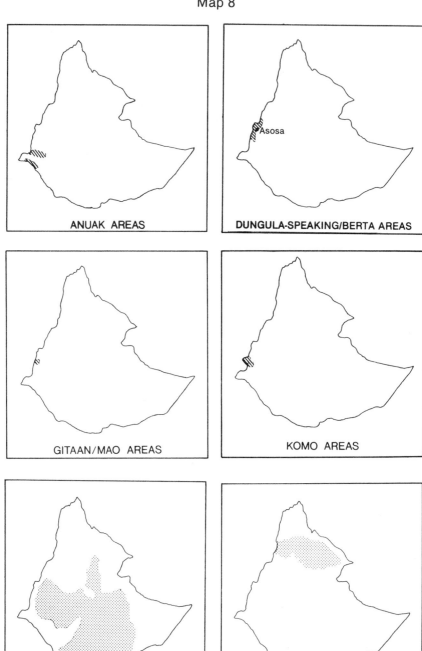

ANUAK AREAS

DUNGULA-SPEAKING/BERTA AREAS

Asosa

GITAAN/MAO AREAS

KOMO AREAS

OROMO AREAS

TIGRAY AREAS

PEOPLES AFFECTED BY RESETTLEMENT PROGRAMS

Ethiopia might actually reverse several long-standing policies. These responses did not take into account, however, that the resettlement program is an extension of the ongoing settlement strategy and centralization policies described above.

Mengistu referred to resettlement in his speech to the WPE Congress on the occasion of the tenth anniversary of the Dergue's coming to power in Ethiopia as an indispensable policy within the agricultural development program: "One of the main focuses of our prospective plan is the expansion of settlement programs so as to hasten agricultural progress and improve peasants' living standards" (Radio Addis Ababa, 6 September 1984). Mengistu went on to say that "there is no other reliable solution [besides resettlement] to today's problem of unemployment in our towns."

Peter Niggli (1985b:16-17) has observed that resettlement is perceived by the Ethiopian officials as

> ... only the beginning of a long-range remedy against famine in the government's planning, the necessity of which will become clear to the masses only after its implementation. In Rama in Tigray a party cadre explained to the just captured peasants that the relation of the government to its people in respect to the resettlement plans was the same as the relation of the parents to a sick child. The child would reject a bitter medicine, just as the peasants refused to be resettled. But the government, just as the parents, did not have an alternative but to force its people, whom it had to protect, to accept this cure because the government knew best. This paternal self-assertion not only corresponds to the communistic varnish of the Ethiopian government machinery with its claim to "historical truth" but also to the immense distance between the Ethiopian educational elites and the "backward," "primitive" peasantry which was still producing with "archaic methods."

Resettlement was revived, in short, as a political party move, justified in terms of what was necessary for the suffering people of Ethiopia "for their own good" and implemented despite their noncompliance. The voluntary nature of resettlement has never been an issue in Ethiopia. Resettlement has had to be packaged for external consumption, however. The initial announcement of the resettlement program as a cure for famine was accompanied by assurances that relocation would be voluntary and that families would be moved intact. Relief and Rehabilitation Commission (RRC) officials, in interviews with the press, reported that settlers were being sent to fertile, unoccupied regions and that each family would be given 10 hectares of land to farm as they chose. Since observers from the West initially were not allowed to visit resettlement sites, their reports on resettlement were based entirely on the projections of Ethiopian officials. Administratively, settlements were to be incorporated into the All-Ethiopian Peasant Association (AEPA) structure and eventually organized into producers' cooperatives.

> Thus far, the government has restricted outside access to the newly settled areas, allowing brief guided tours by outside delegations ... that it apparently believes are predisposed to support the program.
>
> The government claims it is moving only those peasants who volunteer, that it is keeping families together, and that it is giving each family about five acres of land. Reports from diplomats in Addis Ababa who have seen the resettlement areas support these claims.

Farmers in the new areas will be allowed to grow what they want on their parcels of land and will be able to keep all of their profits, according to Tamrat Kebede, a chief planner. But, Kebede said, they will not own the land and, in time, all the resettlement farms will join in "producers' cooperatives" with shared production and shared profits. . . .

Kebede would not say how quickly the resettlement farms would be collectivized. "We will leave it to its own historical process," he said. . . .

It [the Ethiopian government] desperately needs outside help to make the resettlement work, but its plans to collectivize the new farms, turning them into proven money-losers, seem likely to keep out western money and technical help (*The Washington Post*, 3 January 1985).

The government announced that it would provide the settlers with houses, farm equipment, oxen, food and even clothing until a crop was harvested. Yet, by February 1985 the RRC had not officially budgeted any funds for the move, though 200,000 to 300,000 people had already been resettled.

A month after the Ethiopian government made its initial announcement about the resettlement program, it adjusted its public statements. In the *Addis Zemen*, the official national newspaper, it claimed that local residents (ironically those from areas originally slated as "uninhabited regions") were "voluntarily" providing their "fellow Ethiopian comrades" the basic materials necessary to survive in the resettlement sites (the full text appears in Appendix G). The government announced that "in the spirit of Ethiopian unity," these people were building houses for the newcomers and giving them farm tools and oxen. The government also announced that these indigenous inhabitants had even planted extra fields that the newcomers would harvest and keep for themselves until they could plant and harvest their own crops.

In addition, in February 1985 the government announced that it would call upon all citizens to give one month's salary to help support the resettlement program (Radio Addis Ababa, 2 November 1985). Until February, however, funding for it appeared to come from three sources: 1) the USSR and its allies provided most of the transport vehicles (trucks, trailers, buses, helicopters and airplanes), some of the transport operators, and the fuel; 2) local residents in the areas targeted for resettlement provided houses, furniture, utensils, farm equipment, oxen and food until they had nothing left to give; 3) when their food supplies were depleted, food from the EEC and from other Western donors via the World Food Program started to flow through the resettlement pipeline. Refugees interviewed had carried their possessions in bags that were marked in English as being wheat from Canada, "Food Aid sent from the European Economic Community to the people of Ethiopia," and from the Federal Republic of Germany via the Red Cross. Since the summer of 1985, Canada has funded resettlement directly through the Irish aid agency Concern. Italy has also approved funding for the program.

The government has been unable to eliminate the national liberation movements; in fact, the guerrilla operations have gained increasing public support both in the north and the south. Their success draws into question the Dergue's capability, even with billions of dollars worth of imported Soviet weapons, of imposing its will on rural areas whose primary identity is still linked to home and community and whose allegiance remains with the only forms of production that they consider valuable — ones that ensure self-sufficiency. The nature of the international response to the 1984-1985 famine, however, introduced new factors into this scenario. Humanitarian assistance may, if present policies and programs continue to be followed, succeed in coercing peasant producers where bullets have failed.

Thus, famine policy, including resettlement and villagization, must be seen in light of the history of interactions among the peoples of the Ethiopian empire.

Background Readings

A more detailed summary of some of the information in this chapter can be found in Adrian P. Wood, "Rural Development and National Integration in Ethiopia," in *African Affairs* 82(329) October 1983:509-539. For further information see Abir (1968), Baxter (1978), Bereket (1980), Blackhurst, Bondestrom (1974), Cohen (1975), de Salviac (1901), Getahun (1974), Gilkes (1975), Knutson (1969), Lipsky (1962), Marcus (1975), Markakis (1974), Pankhurst (1966, 1967), Perham (1969), Salale (1979), Shepherd (1975), Stahl (1974, 1977), Trevaskis (1960), and Trimingham (1952).

Chapter III

THE RESEARCH DESIGN

Introduction

This research project was conceived and originally designed to collect information from peoples directly affected by the famine in Ethiopia about the causes of the present famine and to discern the impact of assistance programs designed to alleviate it. Directly affected peoples were to include those in Ethiopia on their lands and in feeding centers, those displaced from their land, and those who had entered Sudan as refugees. In Ethiopia, peoples who had remained in their homes as well as those who had been displaced by famine were to be interviewed. But persons traveling to Ethiopia who were willing and able to cooperate in our research, although not formally connected with it, could not obtain visas. When we conducted this investigation travel in Ethiopia was limited for most outside observers. As a result, no research has been conducted inside Ethiopian boundaries to date which, independently from the government, has assessed systematically the extent or causes of famine in all the affected areas of the country.

Fully aware of the debate over the nature of refugee testimony, both its strengths and weaknesses, we proceeded to interview people who fled from Ethiopia to Sudan regarding the causes and solutions to the crisis of food shortages in the Ethiopian empire. These groups were Eritreans and Tigrayans who arrived in Sudan in 1984-85, people who had been resettled from the north to the southwest and then escaped from the resettlement sites to Sudan and finally indigenous peoples in the southwest who were displaced by resettlement in their homelands. It is our position that though information derived from refugees provides only a part of a complex picture, it is an indispensable part. Unfortunately, due to a limitation of funds and personnel, we were unable to conduct our surveys among Eritreans in Sudan during the 1985 trip.

Because we were unable to carry out research in Ethiopia or with Eritreans in Sudan there are a number of unavoidable gaps in our report. In this regard we are quite willing to discuss with interested social scientists or humanitarian agency personnel the extension of this research methodology to approach other famine-affected peoples of the area, either those who fled or those who remain inside the borders of Ethiopia.

In a country such as Ethiopia where access to regions and to peoples outside the closely guarded urban areas and feeding centers is severely restricted, the recorded observations, descriptions and assessments of peasant farmers regarding long-term as well as immediate causes of food shortages that affected them directly is rare and unusually instructive, especially in reconstructing a scenario of practices and the impact of policy at the local level. It was our assumption that data from food producers who had experienced famine could shed light on little-understood processes in a chronically famine-ridden country regardless of where the interviews were conducted. Their accounts could provide important glimpses of the type of information that is essential for more detailed analyses, without which appropriate assistance programs become "hit or miss" propositions. The data presented in Chapters IV-IX confirm our belief in the value of the testimony of former food producers from Ethiopia as to the causes of famine. Aside from devoting a sizable section of our report to a discussion of the conditions reported by those people we interviewed, we also propose a number of guidelines for humanitarian assistance to the Horn of Africa and suggest a number of avenues for further research along these lines (see Conclusions and Recommendations).

The Nature of Refugee Testimony

Cultural Survival has been interviewing refugees from Ethiopia for more than five years. Our data have revealed that political persecution and coercive, dictated economic changes are closely related to the creation of refugee populations from Ethiopia. In 1985 new refugees were also famine victims. Since no one had systematically questioned any famine victims about the causes of their plight and the relationship of Ethiopian government policies to their present conditions, the presence of farmers from Ethiopia in Sudan provided the occasion for correcting this omission. In fact, the voices of the victims have been consistently ignored as reliable sources. Based on previous research both in the Horn of Africa and in countries throughout the world, we concluded that such information is essential for the design of appropriate and responsible assistance programs. It is no secret that in some of the world's greatest disasters, the voices of refugees have been ignored to the peril of many.

The reliability of refugees' testimony is always a controversial topic. It is our position that while their testimony may be no more reliable, perhaps, than that of other actors in the present famine disaster, it is no less reliable than that of other spokesmen, e.g., government officials, particularly when those displaced are from different ethnic groups than the officials who are designing government policies and programs that, according to our findings, appear to be a major cause of the famine.

Any account of events and processes in Ethiopia that fails to include the experience of refugees and other famine-affected peoples is incomplete and consequently inaccurate.

Research in a Political Minefield

This research was designed to compare the assumptions embedded in information on the famine from as many sources as possible: refugees or displaced peoples, government officials, journalists and humanitarian agency officials. Systematic research on the scope and causes of the Ethiopian famine is effectively prohibited inside Ethiopia at the present time (see Maps 9 and 10). Even short trips by journalists or agency personnel are limited in scope, with the government demanding approval of all site visits and with a government employee/translator accompanying the traveler at all times. Perhaps more importantly, the safety of interviewees cannot be guaranteed once the investigator leaves the area. This undoubtedly affects the "truths" that are to be uncovered. While these problems might be overcome on an occasional visit, information collected in Ethiopia is at best impressionistic

Map 9

UNICEF 5/1984

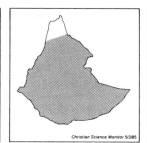

Christian Science Monitor 5/3/85

Indian Ocean Newsletter 22/11/84

The Christian Science Monitor 6/5/85

The Christian Science Monitor 28/11/84

The Christian Science Monitor 26/12/84

The New York Times 18/9/84

AREAS OF ALLEGED FAMINE REPORTED BY THE PRESS DEMONSTRATE CONFUSION CONCERNING AREAS AFFECTED BY FAMINE

Map 10

Indian Ocean Newsletter 22/11/84

The Guardian 7/11/85

The Christian Science Monitor 26/12/84

ALLEGED AREAS OF ETHIOPIAN RESETTLEMENT REPORTED BY THE PRESS DEMONSTRATE CONFUSION OVER TARGET AREAS FOR THE PROGRAM

Map 11

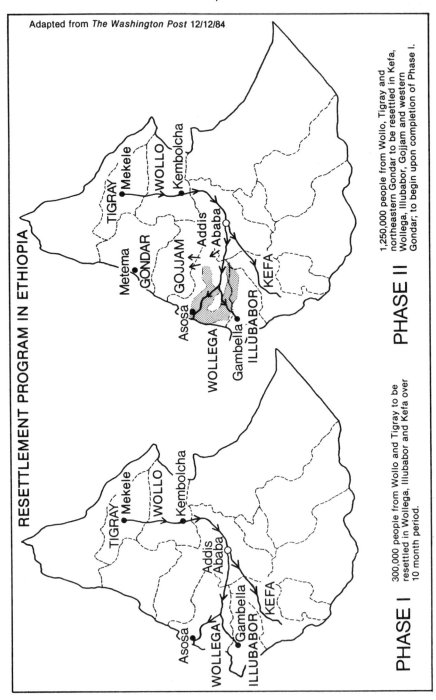

RESETTLEMENT PROGRAM IN ETHIOPIA

Adapted from *The Washington Post* 12/12/84

PHASE I

300,000 people from Wollo and Tigray to be resettled in Wollega, Illubabor and Kefa over 10 month period.

PHASE II

1,250,000 people from Wollo, Tigray and northeastern Gondar to be resettled in Kefa, Wollega, Illubabor, Gojjam and western Gondar; to begin upon completion of Phase I.

Map 12

Area where Cultural Survival documented displacement of local people by resettlement

Route into Sudan of resettlement escapees and those displaced by resettlement

Resettlement routes

Administrative regions

Figures are minimal estimates of those resettled by late summer 1985

60,000 +

15,000 +

105,900 +

135,000 +

90,000 +

THE ETHIOPIAN RESETTLEMENT PROGRAM

Adapted from *The Times* 3/11/85

In the absence of precise information regarding resettlement, *The Washington Post* (Map 11) and *The Times* (Map 12) attempted to create more precise maps. Cultural Survival has indicated areas (see shading) where local people would have been displaced by the settlers. *The Washington Post* and *The Times* overlooked this aspect of the program.

and unsuitable for program design, implementation or evaluation. Furthermore, reports based on research or journalism carried out under the above conditions rarely indicate who the author talked with, who else was present at the interview, who translated, or how representative the findings are for the area in question, let alone other areas affected by the problems under investigation. Only recently have some journalists and would-be visitors begun to make public the denial of visas to them.

Our research design was based on a review of available information found in the literature (both scholarly and popular) and obtained from interviews with firsthand observers, travelers, journalists, agency personnel, etc. From these sources of information on the causes of the famine, the dimensions of the crisis and the existing and proposed programs for alleviating the famine, we identified key areas about which little is known and key assertions that, although not yet proven, nevertheless were guiding policies and programs in the area. Some of the quotations are included below; most are contained in Appendix F.

Topics Examined by the Research

As reflected in the introductory and follow-up letters sent to agencies and the newspaper advertisement used to raise funds for the research (see Appendix I), our primary objective was to investigate the causes of food shortages that led to famine and the appropriateness of the proposed solutions.

At the time that the extreme nature of food shortages in Ethiopia was revealed to the international community (October 1984, see Chapter I) and for several months following, the media were filled with several contradictory assertions about the causes of the disaster responsible for mass starvation. Each of these had different implications for the design of appropriate solutions. These assertions can be traced to three major sources: 1) the Ethiopian government, 2) scholars and specialists on food supply and famine conditions, and 3) liberation fronts operating in areas of Ethiopia not controlled by the government.

Ethiopian Government's Statements About the Causes of Famine

The most widely cited assertions regarding causes of the famine were primarily those that originated with the Ethiopian government. These included the lack of rainfall, drought, natural factors and the failure of the West to provide aid when there were no rains.

Lack of Rainfall, Drought, Natural Factors

> The action we have taken in resettling more than 200,000 compatriots—those who were affected by drought again and again and could not be rehabilitated in their own area due to its uselessness, those who could not live in peace and produce, and those who were suffering in many of our towns due to unemployment—cannot be seen as a small achievement.
>
> *Radio Addis Ababa,* 9 February 1985

Failure of West to Provide Aid When Rains Failed

> Bernahu Bayeh, who is one of the five most powerful members of Ethiopia's Politburo and the government's top official in charge of resettlement ... maintained that "it is because the necessary funds have not been available for development and for an increase in food production in traditional drought-prone areas that we are now witnesses to the current tragedy of death and starvation."
>
> *The Washington Post,* 12 December 1984

Senior Ethiopian officials said today that the Western nations involved in emergency relief efforts here are largely to blame for the extent of the famine devastating the people of this nation. . . .

The New York Times, 12 December 1984

On Tuesday . . . Ethiopian authorities blamed what they called a paltry Western response for the famine that is afflicting an estimated 8 million people. They also asked for substantial Western support for the government's proposed relocation effort. . . .

The head of Ethiopia's Relief and Rehabilitation Commission, Dawit Wolde Giorgis, told the conference on Tuesday that "days of indifference turned into months of apathy" as Ethiopia was "forgotten by a world glutted with a surplus of grain."

He said that only "at a very late stage, generosity was shown by the donor community in a burst of activity."

The Boston Globe, 13 December 1984

Lieut. Col. Mengistu Haile Mariam, the Ethiopian leader, accused the West today of failing to provide adequate long-term aid to Africa.

"The lack of political will on the part of developed countries is the main obstacle to finding solutions to these problems."

The New York Times, 11 July 1985

Scholars' and Specialists' Statements About the Causes of Famine

Other causes of the crises given by scholars and specialists included long-term deterioration of productive capacity and inappropriate agrarian policies for level of technology including pricing policies, disproportionate investment and land distribution.

Long-term Deterioration of Productive Capacity

A report on energy prospects issued by the World Bank last July asserted that crop yields were being reduced by more than 1 million tons of grain a year because of a growing scarcity of firewood and the diversion of natural fertilizers for use in fireplaces. The report said forested land, 40 percent at the turn of the century, had been reduced to about 3 percent.

"If no more than the present level of replanting is undertaken, in 20 to 30 years all but the least accessible pockets of forest will have gone and large parts of the north will be uninhabitable: subject to persistent drought, crop failure, famine and outmigration," the report concluded.

The New York Times, 8 October 1984

The Ethiopian government is following a policy of collectivizing farmland that gives evidence of lowering still further, rather than raising, the nation's agricultural production.

International Daily News, 30 October 1984

Food production per head had declined by about 5 percent over the six years preceding the drought.

The Guardian, 9 November 1984

The famine in Ethiopia is caused not by the lack of rain that triggered it, the [Earthscan] report said, but by agricultural practices and deforestation that produced soil erosion, by population growth and by political decisions such as an emphasis on cash crops and a failure to develop adequate distribution systems. . . .

The New York Times, 18 November 1984

Foreign agricultural specialists here say the drought-seared land has been ruined, probably for decades, by deforestation, erosion, overpopulation and destructive farm practices. There is no way, these specialists say, that the highlands can feed the 7 million or so people who now live there.

The Washington Post, 3 January 1985

... forests now cover only about 3 percent of Ethiopia's terrain.

Denuded soil erodes rapidly and gives up its moisture easily. . . .

... the authorities only allocated plots to farmers, with the Government becoming, in effect, the landlord.

The Ethiopian peasant, never certain that the property he works this year will be his to work next year as well, has had little incentive to undertake long-term improvements, development specialists say. . . .

The hiring of laborers and the stocking of grain reserves as a hedge against hard times have also been condemned as counter-revolutionary.

An even bigger disincentive to productivity has been the low, fixed prices farmers have been paid by the Government.

"In some cases," said Dr. Joseph Collins of the San Francisco-based Institute for Food and Development Policy, "the prices farmers have been forced to accept are actually less than their costs."

"Why? Because the Government wants to keep food prices low for the army, the civil service bureaucracy and a potentially volatile urban population."

The New York Times, 23 May 1985

Ethiopia's farm policy, driven by the same Marxist rigidities that have made Russian agriculture such an abysmal failure, discourages farmers from raising any more than they need to feed their families. They won't make enough in the government-controlled market for entrepreneurship to be worth their while.

The Christian Science Monitor, 2 July 1985

Liberation Fronts' Statements About the Causes of Famine

The least visible assertions for the causes of the food crisis were those of the liberation fronts. They included such factors as destroying traditional production systems and confiscating production to break down resistance to the government, directing the war to eliminate food supply and suppliers, and misusing and misappropriating aid given for relief and development.

Destruction of Traditional Production Systems

... the Ethiopian regime is using the food aid meant for drought-stricken people as a means of enhancing its armed offensive. . . . The Dergue government, after an arms-purchasing spree, is forcing the emaciated youth and elderly people to join its army by giving them wheat that was provided to them by donor organizations. Those who refused to join the army, who preferred a peaceful life, are being refused aid along with their families.

Eritrean Peoples' Liberation Front (EPLF) Radio, 29 October 1984

[The present junta] diverted all resources to strengthen its security and military machinery at the expense of famine [the famine of 1973-74] and to avert its recurrence. On the contrary it took steps that further deteriorated agricultural production throughout the country by perpetrating truly colossal destruction of human and material resources in order to perpetuate its . . . rule.

[The junta] normally destroys crops and cattle in its efforts to subdue peoples that openly defy its dictatorial rule. After creating food shortages in this manner it appeals to the international community for food assistance with the primary intention of sustaining and expanding its large . . . armed force.

Joint Statement by the TPLF and OLF, 29 November 1984

Directing War to Eliminate Food Supply and Suppliers

... The Dergue regime is aggravating the situation by carrying out air raids and ground attacks, burning the property, and destroying the agricultural products of innocent people, thus worsening the drought and forcing the people to move from their homes to other areas controlled by its forces.

Eritrean Peoples' Liberation Front (EPLF) Radio, 29 October 1984

Guerrillas from the Tigre People's Liberation Front said in a statement issued in Khartoum and London the aircraft attacked the refugees Dec. 3 near the village of Shelair, inside rebel-controlled areas of Ethiopia....

The rebels said the victims had been fleeing an Ethiopian government resettlement program, which is expected to relocate up to 2.4 million people mostly from the rebellious provinces of Tigre and Eritrea to government-controlled southern areas within the next year.

The Boston Globe, 8 December 1984

Major Research Issues Addressed

In order to examine assertions by the various parties and to test them systematically among those to be interviewed, we designed the investigation to address the following research issues (presented here in a question format):

1. What are the dimensions of the current famine in Ethiopia?
2. What are the major causes (long- and short-term) of the famine crisis?
3. What are the most important considerations in the formulation of immediate relief and longer term development programs directed at alleviating famine in this region?
    - How do the solutions presently under review by international agencies specifically address the causes of the famine?
    - How should the resettlement program and other solutions for which the Ethiopian Government is seeking international support be considered?
    - How should the development programs for which the liberation fronts operating in affected areas are seeking international support be evaluated?
4. What are the perceptions of affected peoples with respect to specific causes and proposals for solution of the crisis?

The above questions were evaluated according to the kinds of information required to answer them satisfactorily. This most often required that the assertions made by the range of commentators cited above be rephrased in terms of a set of hypotheses. From these hypotheses emerged specific data components necessary to determine which assertions had more validity or to bring forth new assertions.

The assertions on which we drew up the hypotheses were taken from 1) a close monitoring of the famine coverage in the media as the story broke in the Western and Ethiopian press, 2) discussions with governmental and non-governmental agency personnel who are designing and directing programs in the area, 3) the published statements of liberation fronts operating in areas beyond the control of the Ethiopian government, and 4) available literature on the general topic of famine and the specific region of the Horn of Africa with which the planners were acquainted due to long familiarity with the subject and the area.

The following categories of information to be derived from famine victims were identified as essential for evaluating the current working assumptions regarding the causes of the famine crisis in Ethiopia as well as the proposed or implemented programs intended to alleviate famine. Our questions to refugees were designed to examine commonly advanced and commonly held assumptions regarding each research issue. The complete general survey questionnaire is attached as Appendix A; Appendices B, C, D and E contain summaries of four other, more intensive questionnaires on, respectively, long-term causes of famine/socioeconomic history, immediate flight/displacement factors, repatriation and the mechanisms of resettlement. The general survey was designed to generate data that would shed light on the four general questions outlined at the beginning of this section. It required 30 minutes for response. The intensive questionnaires on specific topics were seen as follow-up interviews that would allow a more accurate analysis of the information collected in the general survey questionnaire. These would take as long as one and a half to two hours to administer.

Dimensions of the Famine

Is there a pattern to who is starving and who is not — according to region, ethnic group, religion, urban/rural residence, gender, military/nonmilitary status, participants in state-run programs versus nonparticipants, members in good standing of local peasant associations or *kebeles* versus members not in good standing or nonmembers?

Where do the the 4 million to 10 million people live who are said to be affected by the famine (see Map 9)? What is the basis for the figure, the discrepancy?

Is there a geographical variation in the famine crisis in Ethiopia? If so, why?

What measures do the peasants use to assess change in the current natural/ecological conditions as compared to the past?

Who is crossing international borders? Do they belong to specific ethnic or political groups? Who is internally displaced? Why do some people leave the country and others stay behind?

Causes of the Famine

Is lack of rainfall the primary cause of famine?

Are there plant or animal pests that contribute to the famine?

Is warfare between resistance movements and regular government forces a factor in the creation of the famine? To what extent does warfare divert labor or resources from agricultural production? What is the specific evidence that acts of war destroy the productive capacity of the country, e.g., destruction of houses, irrigation systems, terraces, crops, animals, water sources, fallow fields, communication networks, markets?

Has there been a long-term deterioration of the productive capacity of the famine-affected regions? Has the soil declined in fertility? Is there a reliable source of water? Has the fallow cycle shortened? Do respondents think their condition is better or worse than that of their parents? Have people changed basic production strategies? Do they supplement income from one source (e.g., agriculture) with income from others (e.g., wage labor, trading)? Did their parents? Are family members able to help with production or are they required to be someplace else during crucial periods of the agricultural cycle? Is wage labor available in all areas? How much of the crop is normally sold? To whom? For what price? Do farmers have to donate produce or labor for state-sponsored activities? Do they use fertilizers, pesticides, improved seed varieties? How do they obtain them?

Have government programs or policies affected agricultural production? Do increased taxes, fees or voluntary contributions hamper local investment in agriculture? Is state investment in agriculture disproportionately applied to commercial production over subsistence production, to state farms over peasant farms? Do mandatory literacy programs and political meetings disrupt work patterns? Has collectivization of agriculture encouraged investment in permanent assets to increase production? Is land allocation fair? Does one get the same plot of land each year? Are producers required to work on communal plots? Do they receive any compensation for this work? Does the conscription of young men into the military seriously affect agricultural production? What kinds of people are conscripted? Is there any way to prevent someone from being conscripted?

Emergency Assistance and Long-term Development Assistance

How do the affected people evaluate the possibilities of returning to their homes and rehabilitation to a productive life? What do they see as their greatest needs? How aware are they of the assistance programs offered by the Ethiopian government, the liberation fronts and the international community? How do they assess their options? Do they have access to the programs of which they are aware? If not, why not? Do any of the parties that deliver aid discriminate against recipients? What are the guidelines of discrimination? What is the evidence of manipulation of assistance programs for political ends on the part of those offering aid? How do the victims believe assistance programs can be designed so that they actually reach them?

Solutions to the Famine

Do the peoples affected by the famine endorse any particular solution to the problems that caused their dilemma? Do the affected peoples (refugees or displaced people living in feeding centers or resettlement areas) have plans to return to their homelands? Are their plans to return based on specific, recent information from their regions? What are the prospects for finding long-term solutions to the current crisis in the host regions to which the refugees and displaced persons have relocated?

Research Methods

From these questions we developed a series of hypotheses about the famine in Ethiopia that were sent to more than 20 US-based humanitarian assistance agencies for comment. Two agencies replied to these hypotheses. We then designed our questionnaires and sent them for review to the US-based agencies raising funds for famine assistance in Ethiopia. We asked them to review the questionnaires and to make specific suggestions as to how they could be improved so as to address more directly the assumptions on which the agencies' own programs were based. Three agencies responded with suggestions. In one case, by adopting the suggested change in the questionnaire (to withdraw the question asking the nationality of the interviewee) we lost what we later came to regard as extremely important information concerning identity. Nevertheless, the suggestions as well as additional information that had appeared in the press were incorporated into the questionnaires, which were then printed.

The information that was collected in Sudan is analyzed in Chapters IV-IX. Three researchers undertook the surveys of people who had fled to Sudan as a result of famine and/or government programs intended to alleviate it (see Map 13). Jason Clay went to three camps in eastern Sudan to interview Tigrayans who fled their homelands to Sudan. Peter Niggli and Bonnie Holcomb went to a holding camp near Damazine where they interviewed people from Tigray, Wollo, northern Shoa and Addis Ababa who had been resettled and then escaped from the sites and walked to Sudan. Bonnie Holcomb traveled farther south and interviewed people from Wollo and Tigray who had escaped from resettlement sites and were encountered in or near Kirmuk. Bonnie Holcomb also interviewed people indigenous to the resettlement areas who had been displaced from their homes by the new settlers and had fled to the Kirmuk and Yabuus areas.

Translators were hired in Khartoum to work with each interviewer in order to decrease the possibility of mistranslation by locally affiliated, more politically aligned individuals. Bonnie Holcomb also speaks Oromo. Many general interviews were recorded randomly, and most intensive interviews were recorded. Random, recorded interviews were independently translated in the United States so that they could be certain that the field translations were accurate.

Each interviewer selected randomly a sample of at least 20 people from each site where refugees from Ethiopia were interviewed. The sample of 20 people per site allowed statistically reliable inferences at the .05 level and allowed us to undertake non-parametric analyses. In the planned settlements the random sample was drawn mathematically by counting rows of houses. In the spontaneous settlements, the sample was drawn by dividing the area to be surveyed into quadrants and selecting individuals more or less evenly spaced from each quadrant. The number of people interviewed at each location is indicated below. Randomly and non-randomly selected people for interviews are listed; the non-random interviews have been kept in separate chapters (VI and VIII) or included in the more general analysis found in Chapter IX.

PEOPLE INTERVIEWED AT EACH LOCATION

Cultural Survival Interview Site	Random Interviews	Non-Random Interviews
Khartoum	0	7
Tawawa	20	4
Fau II	20	8
Wad Kauli	20	10*
Gedaref	0	6
Damazine	65	20
Kirmuk	0	38
Yabuus	45	14
Total	170	107

*In addition, 119 individuals were each asked about the timing of agricultural inputs they needed if they were to return to Tigray to plant their crops in 1985.

Map 13

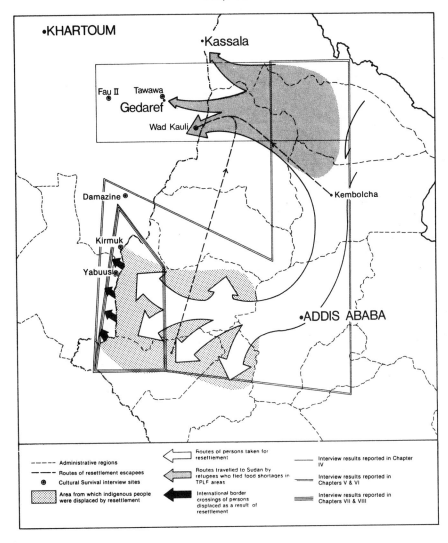

- •KHARTOUM
- •Kassala
- Fau II
- Tawawa
- Gedaref
- Wad Kauli
- Damazine
- Kembolcha
- Kirmuk
- Yabuus
- •ADDIS ABABA

– – – – Administrative regions	Routes of persons taken for resettlement
– – – – Routes of resettlement escapees	Routes travelled to Sudan by refugees who fled food shortages in TPLF areas
◉ Cultural Survival interview sites	International border crossings of persons displaced as a result of resettlement
Area from which indigenous people were displaced by resettlement	

Interview results reported in Chapter IV

Interview results reported in Chapters V & VI

Interview results reported in Chapters VII & VIII

GROUPS OF PERSONS INTERVIEWED BY CULTURAL SURVIVAL
REGARDING CAUSES OF (AND SOLUTIONS TO) FOOD
SHORTAGES IN ETHIOPIA

Chapter IV

CAUSES OF FAMINE IN THE TIGRAY REGION: TESTIMONY OF VICTIMS OF FOOD SHORTAGES WHO FLED WESTWARD FROM TIGRAY INTO SUDAN

Tigrayan refugees present in eastern Sudan in March 1985 were interviewed in three different camps: Tawawa, Fau II and Wad Kauli (see Map 14). These camps were selected because the residents at each came to Sudan at different times and therefore represent a chronological sequence of events with regard to the current famine in northern Ethiopia. The conditions that precipitated the flight of each of the populations vary and were considered significant for understanding the cumulative causes of the refugees' present predicament and future prospects in Sudan or in Tigray.

Refugees in Eastern Sudan

Flight of refugees from northern Ethiopia dates to the period when Ethiopia annexed Eritrea in the early 1960s and refugees from that disputed region began to flee across the border to eastern Sudan. Under the rule of Haile Selassie, the exodus was made up almost entirely of Eritreans. Not until the military took power in 1974 and began to institute major reforms such as the land nationalization program did Tigrayans begin to enter Sudan as well, primarily from Humara.

According to refugees interviewed in Tawawa who had been in Sudan for the longest period of those interviewed — having entered sometime between the 1960s and the early 1970s, many poor Tigrayans migrated seasonally from within Tigray to the Humara region of northern Gondar Province to work in large farms as agricultural laborers. Some even settled in the area. They cleared forested lands for large landowners and were allowed to plant subsistence crops for one season before moving on to other forested areas. In this leapfrog manner, much of the forested land in the area was gradually turned into large agricultural estates. Some Tigrayans eventually acquired their own land in the region; others continued to work for large landowners as manual laborers or even at such skilled jobs as tractor drivers. During the 1960s and 1970s private and public investors from many countries financed commercial agricultural schemes in eastern Sudan. Although much of the investment was in mechanized, capital-intensive production systems, serious labor shortages still plagued most of eastern Sudan.

As a result, during the agricultural off-season in the Humara, Ethiopia area, some Tigrayan wage laborers living in the area as well as some seasonal workers from the northern and western highlands went to work in eastern Sudan. When the military government took power in Ethiopia, their land reforms were resisted by people in the Humara region. According to refugees living in that area at the time, they challenged the authority of the new government longer than residents in any other area in Ethiopia. According to the refugees, their resistance, which lasted nearly two years, endured for three reasons. First, many royalists fled to the area and quickly

Map 14

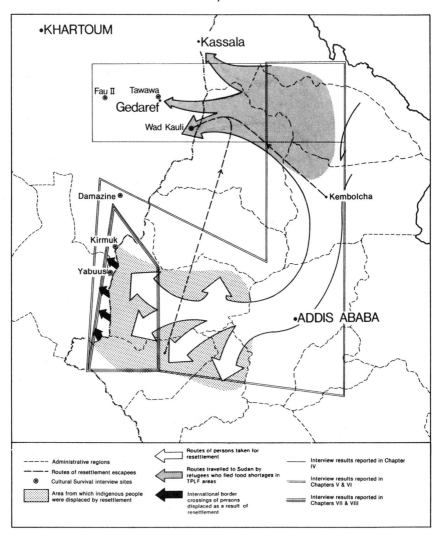

•KHARTOUM

•Kassala

Fau II   Tawawa
Gedaref

Wad Kauli

Damazine

Kembolcha

Kirmuk

Yabuus

•ADDIS ABABA

– – – – – Administrative regions	Routes of persons taken for resettlement
– – – Routes of resettlement escapees	Routes travelled to Sudan by refugees who fled food shortages in TPLF areas
⊚ Cultural Survival interview sites	International border crossings of persons displaced as a result of resettlement
Area from which indigenous people were displaced by resettlement	

Interview results reported in Chapter IV

Interview results reported in Chapters V & VI

Interview results reported in Chapters VII & VIII

GROUPS OF PERSONS INTERVIEWED BY CULTURAL SURVIVAL
REGARDING CAUSES OF (AND SOLUTIONS TO) FOOD
SHORTAGES IN ETHIOPIA

formalized opposition to the central government by organizing an army to defend the area. Second, many residents who had recently established modern farms in the area saw that they stood to lose these farms under the new government. Finally, because the Humara region was relatively isolated from the rest of the empire, it was difficult for the central government to move troops into the region.

Following the defeat of this opposition, the Dergue government suspected many Humara residents of supporting counterrevolutionaries (most often cited to be the EDU, Ethiopian Democratic Union). Whether or not this was the case, many residents were accused and fled to Sudan to avoid reprisals. The government also confiscated many large estates and turned them into state farms. At that time, given the choice of working on the farms at what they described as "forced labor," additional Tigrayans fled to eastern Sudan. In the late 1970s and early 1980s labor was so short for the Ethiopian state farms that the Dergue began to capture and to forcibly transport vagrants and people considered undesirable from cities to work on these state farms. The Anti-Slavery Society of London described work conditions at that time as "slave-like" (1979).

Most of the early refugees who arrived in Sudan from Gondar and Tigray were forced by the Sudanese to settle in refugee camps that became notorious for supplying cheap labor to neighboring agricultural schemes in eastern Sudan. They have consequently been widely referred to as labor camps. Refugees in these camps were expected to work for nearby Sudanese farmers, and it was projected that they would become "self-sufficient" from the wages they earned there. After 1979 some 20,000 of these refugees were forcibly relocated by the Sudanese government to the Tawawa camp, which became in essence a labor camp about six km northwest of Gedaref.

During the year 1984-85, an additional 5,000 refugees spontaneously settled in Tawawa, attempting to avoid the "famine" camps nearer the border where newly arrived refugees are given assistance but officially not allowed to work for wages. Nearly 1,000 of the new arrivals were Ethiopian Jews who had been moved to the camp from the border before being secretly airlifted from Sudan to Israel in late March. The remaining 4,000 new refugees were individuals with some marketable skills who either already had friends or relatives living in Tawawa or who wanted to earn money quickly working as wage laborers in order to assist their destitute families in Tigray.

Victims of food shortages in Tigray began to arrive in eastern Sudan in October 1984. By the end of the year, the TPLF had assisted approximately 100,000 refugees who arrived in the Kassala area (see Map 15). The Sudan government then decided to move the majority of these refugees to three camps that were to be created near Fau, a recently established Sudanese village for agricultural laborers in a region of irrigated, commercial agriculture.

By the end of 1984 the TPLF, in consultation with Sudanese, United Nations High Commissioner for Refugees (UNHCR) and EPLF officials, changed the route they were using to escort refugees from Tigray to Sudan. The new route brought the refugees to Wad Kauli, a small settlement about 100 km southeast of Gedaref and 11 km from the border of Ethiopia. By the end of March 1985 the TPLF guided another 100,000 refugees to Wad Kauli,

Map 15

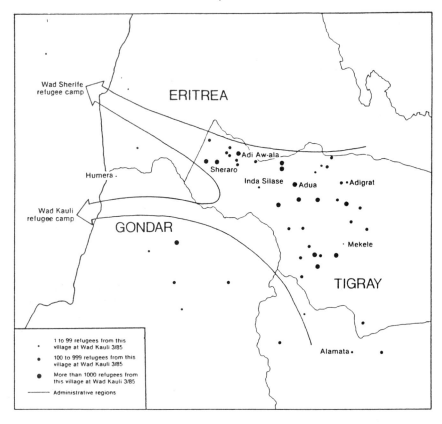

ROUTES TRAVELLED TO SUDAN BY REFUGEES FLEEING FOOD
SHORTAGES IN NORTHERN ETHIOPIA (11/84 TO 2/85)

many of whom had already been resettled from Wad Kauli to nearby sites
because of water shortages and resulting deterioration of sanitation levels in
the camps.

Below is a comparison of information collected from refugees interviewed
randomly — 20 in each of the three camps. Detailed information gathered in
intensive interviews with approximately 10 people in each of the camps ex-
pands and underscores these data.

Personal History of Respondents (see Table No. 1)

Men were predominant among those randomly interviewed in all three
locations. A number of factors appear to be responsible for this. First, in
contrast to most refugee populations in the world, the camps in eastern
Sudan have a larger number of adult men than women. Second, since the
random selection was made of tents rather than individuals, women
residents of the home where the interview was being conducted were often
absent during the daytime hours, usually attending to the needs of at least

one child who was enrolled in an intensive or supplementary feeding program. Third, when both men and women were present during an interview men spoke, even when questions were directed to women only. Only occasionally did they defer to women on specific questions. The interviewer and translator were males.

There were notable differences between refugees in Tawawa and refugees in Fau II and Wad Kauli. Those surveyed in Wad Kauli and Fau II averaged 42 years of age while those from Tawawa averaged only 32 years. Most Tawawa residents had come to the Sudan to escape military duty and/or to find economic opportunities. Most had worked in Humara as young, single wage laborers when the government changed in Ethiopia and had decided to go to Sudan rather than return to their homes.

All those interviewed in the three camps were Coptic Christians who came to Sudan from villages located in the administrative unit of Tigray. All the refugees interviewed in the three camps spoke Tigrinya, but an overwhelming number of the more recent arrivals in Fau II and Wad Kauli spoke only Tigrinya while 75 percent of the residents in Tawawa spoke more than one language. Similarly, most Tawawa residents were literate in at least one language while most refugees in the other two camps were illiterate.

Nearly all those interviewed in Wad Kauli and Fau II lived in areas that were controlled, at least nominally, by the TPLF. The people living in Tawawa were usually unaware of who controlled their area, but most stated that they saw no more reason to trust the TPLF than the Dergue. While none of those interviewed in Fau II and Tawawa said they had immediate family members active in the TPLF, 15 percent of those interviewed in Wad Kauli did. Virtually all of those interviewed claimed that as a result of the past year's events, they were now much more willing to assist the TPLF in whatever way they could.

No one reported that the TPLF had taken anything from them or had forced them to give or sell materials. "I have never paid anything to the TPLF; if anything, the TPLF helps us," said one refugee. Some indicated that in the past when there were crop surpluses they sold them to the TPLF. These views are in stark contrast with those toward the Dergue (see below, "The Impact of Army Activities and Government Policies on Agricultural Production in Tigray").

Table No. 1
PERSONAL HISTORY OF RESPONDENTS

	Wad Kauli	Fau II	Tawawa
Sex of Respondent			
Male	90.0%	95.0%	85.0%
Female	10.0%	5.0%	15.0%
Average Age	42.2	42.2	32.4
Religion			
Coptic Christian	100.0%	100.0%	100.0%
Spoke Only Tigrinya	95.0%	90.0%	25.0%
Was Literate in Any Language	20.0%	32.0%	55.0%
Village Under TPLF Control	100.0%	95.0%	— —
Family Involved With the TPLF	15.0%	0.0%	0.0%

Family History of Respondents (see Table No. 2)

All those interviewed in the three sites had been born in the same villages as their fathers (see Map 16). Most were married, although there was a larger number of single people in Tawawa, a fact probably consistent with the younger average age there. The average age of marriage in all three groups is from 20 to 22 years. The number of years Wad Kauli and Fau II residents have been married is 40 percent greater than for the residents of Tawawa, and they have three times as many children as the residents of Tawawa. It is not clear whether the residents of Tawawa chose to have fewer children or if more of their children have died. Of those interviewed in Wad Kauli and Fau II, less than half of their immediate family had come to the Sudan. Of those in Tawawa, nearly 70 percent of the immediate family were living with them, reflecting, perhaps, the political, permanent nature of the flight of refugees in Tawawa. At the time of the interviews, 21 percent of interviewees from Wad Kauli and 40 percent in Fau II had siblings living in the Sudan.

Respondents living in Wad Kauli and Fau II reported that their families were virtually the same size as those of their parents. Those living in Tawawa, however, had, on average, 16 percent more siblings than those interviewed in Wad Kauli and 35 percent more than in Fau II; yet they had on-

Table No. 2
FAMILY HISTORY OF RESPONDENTS

	Wad Kauli	Fau II	Tawawa
Respondent's Birthplace Same as Father's	100.0%	100.0%	100.0%
Birthplace Same as Father's Father	100.0%	100.0%	100.0%
Percent of Respondents Married	90.0%	95.0%	75.0%
Average Number of Years Married	20.6	19.6	`12.4
Average Number of Children For Those Married	5.5	5.7	1.8
Average Number From Nuclear Family in Sudan	3.3	3.8	2.6
Percent of Respondents With Death in Nuclear Family Since October 1984	5.0%	20.0%	0.0%
Average Number of Siblings Per Respondent	4.9	4.2	5.7
Percent of Respondents With Siblings in Sudan	21.0%	40.0%	25%

Map 16

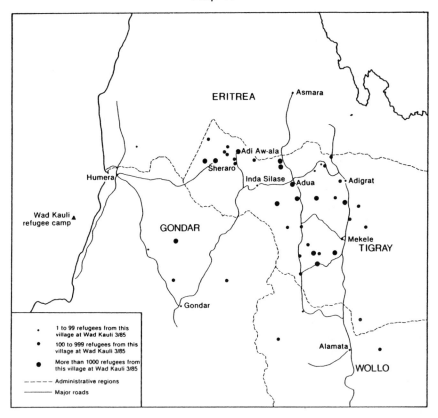

ERITREA

Asmara

Adi Aw-ala

Sheraro

Humera

Inda Silase

Adua

Adigrat

Wad Kauli
refugee camp

GONDAR

Mekele
TIGRAY

Gondar

•   1 to 99 refugees from this
    village at Wad Kauli 3/85

●   100 to 999 refugees from this
    village at Wad Kauli 3/85

⬤   More than 1000 refugees from
    this village at Wad Kauli 3/85

– – – – Administrative regions

——— Major roads

Alamata

WOLLO

HOME VILLAGES OF WAD KAULI REFUGEES

ly 30 percent as many children. Few Tawawa or Wad Kauli residents reported deaths in their immediate family since October 1984. Twenty percent in Fau II, however, reported deaths, indicating perhaps that their condition at the onset of this period was more precarious.

Economic Background of Respondents (see Tables 3 and 4)

All interviewees were farmers; their fathers had been farmers too. Similar to their fathers, most kept livestock; but in addition, more worked as traders or for wages than their fathers. Most indicated, however, that they had fewer animals, and in general, fewer assets, than their fathers. Most stated that their fathers never had to work for wages, but that they had had to do so due to food shortages. It was not, they insisted, merely a question of wage labor being more readily available than before.

Those who had livestock five years ago reported, on average, that they had about six or seven large animals (oxen, cows, mules, donkeys). As one man reported, "During a good year, agriculture gives better than livestock; but during a bad year, the animals keep us alive." Another farmer reported that because there is less grass, he is "worse off than his father."

By the time the respondents left Tigray only 15 percent of those farmers in Wad Kauli had a pair of oxen to use for plowing and none of those in Fau II had a team of oxen. Large animals had been sold to buy food, died, been eaten or been taken by the army.

Some 30 percent of those interviewed reported owning, on average, 16 small animals — goats or sheep — five years before. At the time of the interviews, only five percent of those from Wad Kauli had any small animals. Small animals, interviewees explained, are important because they are more divisible than large animals. Once killed, they provide a meat supply that can be consumed before it spoils or that can be sold and used to purchase small amounts of grain for planting. One man summed up the condition of his herd.

> Four years ago, I had 10 cows, four oxen and 40 sheep and goats. When I left, there were five cows, two oxen and 10 sheep and goats. I left them with a neighbor who couldn't make the trip. They won't be alive when I go back. I tried to sell them, but no one wants to buy animals; they're afraid they'll die. We killed some of the goats to eat.

Some 97 percent of those interviewed were from TPLF villages. They indicated that the TPLF had undertaken its own land reform in their villages. As one respondent explained, "Land ownership is completely changed under the TPLF. Land is shared communally according to need. Most land before was in the hands of rich landlords. Now the tenants have enough land to plow, to live on."

All those interviewed reported that land is allocated equally but that it isn't reallocated every year as under the Dergue. They explained that this meant that they could plant trees or make improvements without fearing that someone else would be using the land the next year.

No one reported having paid taxes to the TPLF. Some indicated that they sold surplus grain to the TPLF, but that was all. Others reported that when the TPLF took over their areas, the government granaries were opened and distributed to local peasants.

Table No. 3
ECONOMIC ACTIVITIES OF RESPONDENTS

	Wad Kauli	Fau II
Farmer		
Father	100.0%	100.0%
Respondent	100.0%	100.0%
Herder		
Father	85.0%	85.0%
Respondent	75.0%	85.0%
Trader		
Father	10.0%	5.0%
Respondent	15.0%	10.0%
Wage Laborer		
Father	10.0%	0.0%
Respondent	55.0%	40.0%

Table No. 4
ANIMALS OWNED BY RESPONDENTS, 1980 AND 1984

	Wad Kauli	Fau II
Number of Large Animals Respondent Owned 1980	7.6	5.7
Respondents With Oxen When Left For Sudan	15.0%	0.0%
Number of Goats or Sheep 1980	16.4	17.0
Number of Respondents With Goats or Sheep 1980	30.0%	30.0%
Respondents With Goats or Sheep When Left For Sudan	5.0%	0.0%

Agricultural Production (see Table No. 5)

The refugees explained that the average amount of food needed by a family of six is 1,500 kg per year. About 1,200 kg are consumed by the family; the rest is sold so that necessities that cannot be produced can be purchased. One man said it took more for his family because his children were older: "It takes 25 donkey loads of produce [1,625 kg] to keep my family [of six]. That's for food, clothes and everything."

Another man, who also earns money from trading, indicated that he needed less: "In 1982, I had 10 donkey loads of produce [650 kg for a family of six] and I was satisfied. Last year I produced 200 kg and borrowed from friends and neighbors. I had no harvest this year."

Those interviewed in Wad Kauli and Fau II, however, indicated that in even the best year in memory, they have produced only 13 to 26 percent above their minimal needs. In 1983, Wad Kauli respondents claimed to have produced, on average, only 28 percent of their total needs while those interviewed in Fau II produced 43 percent of their subsistence needs. In 1984, Fau II interviewees did not have any harvest while those in Wad Kauli produced, on average, 22.5 kg of grain per family. Total seed needs, per family, were estimated at 150 kg in Wad Kauli and 210 kg in Fau II. Most farmers insist that because their land is not fertile, they must use more seed (in part for replanting) and yet total production continues to decline.

Farmers often utilize a number of small fields with different soils and drainage systems on which different crops are planted. It is not clear if this is a remnant of an inheritance-based land-tenure system and/or an ecological adaptation that reduces risk of total crop failure. One man described his situation as follows:

I plant teff, wheat, lentils, sorghum, peas and corn. I use seven different pieces of land, some big, some small, some better for certain crops than others. But the land is not fertile. If I leave it fallow, however, the weeds take over.

Another man described the basic farming system in Adua, Tigray, as follows.

Some farmers share oxen in my area [Asai, Adua]. We work on one field at a time when each is ready to be planted. But only close relatives usually do this, as you might miss the season entirely. It is more common to work communally for weeding and harvesting.

In the lowlands they plow before the rains. In the highlands, however, we plow after the rain softens the land.

My land takes at least 40 days to plow with a pair of oxen, but that is spread over four or five months. We plant millet first in March and April. Then we plant sorghum in May, barley, pulses and wheat in the end of May and June. Teff, lentils and sunflowers are planted last. Often we replant areas throughout the growing season.

Depending on the rains any given year, millet can provide from 10 to 25 percent of all produce. Barley is our main crop. If it rains early, I plant corn at the same time as sorghum; otherwise, I don't plant it at all.

Where I live, one donkey [load] of sorghum seed yields four donkeys of produce. Barley and wheat are better. Peas are good too, especially when there are insects. Next year I'll plant more peas.

My land is infertile so it takes more seed to get a stand, yet it produces less.

Many interviewees indicated that they had sold or eaten their animals in the 1983-84 agricultural year to compensate for the poor harvest. However, between 1982 and 1984, grain prices rose from approximately E$.20 per small tin to E$2 per tin. Because so many people were selling livestock (usually to merchants, traders or peasant association officials) to buy food and because few potential buyers had adequate pasture for animals until the next rainy season, the average value of an oxen fell from E$300 to E$60. While grain prices increased tenfold, the value of oxen decreased by 80 percent. Thus, crop failure for two years in a row left most of those interviewed destitute.

Many attempted to supplement their own produce with income from working as wage laborers or by trading. This proved to be difficult, however. Few local residents had money to hire laborers, so would-be workers had to travel long distances to find work. Government bombing raids on daytime markets in TPLF-held areas forced many markets to be held at night and, consequently, restricted many potential traders' travel.

Oxen have long been a critical variable for agricultural production in Tigray. In the past, there have been shortages, but over the last five years the number of people without oxen, at least in TPLF areas, has increased dramatically. One respondent said,

In my village only one-quarter of the farmers own a pair of oxen. They plow their own land first. I don't have oxen, so I give my land on a 50/50 share. The owner of the oxen provides half the seed and half the weeding. In 1982, my share was 12 donkeys; last year [1983] it was eight; this year it was none.

Various arrangements, which differ from region to region, have evolved which allow farmers to gain access to the oxen needed for plowing their fields. In some cases, neighbors, each with a single ox, will join their animals together to plow their fields. Those interviewed indicated that this was common in the Adua area. People without oxen have been able to borrow a pair of oxen from their neighbors in return for the use of the straw and stubble after the harvest. A landowner can let another farm his land, without even providing seed or labor, and still receive a portion of the harvest. The portion varies tremendously, however. Typical respondents' reports follow.

> I give my land to those with oxen. They get two-thirds of the produce; I get one-third. We share all labor and seed requirements.

> There are many in my village who had oxen taken by the Dergue. These people often join the TPLF. Their farms will be done on a 50/50 share by their families.

> I would use my oxen to farm other people's land. I was able to keep one-quarter of what we produced. Our area became TPLF six years ago, and this practice is not common now.

Most of those interviewed indicated that the most common arrangement for using other people's oxen was on a 50/50 share of the harvest. The owner of the land and the owner of the oxen each provided 50 percent of the seed and the labor for planting, weeding and harvesting and then each received half the harvest.

Most people observed that the problem with getting oxen from other people is that they always work on their own land first. This means that they arrive to plow other people's land after the optimal times for plowing and planting have passed. In fact, many pointed out that traditionally people would communally weed and harvest together, but never plant together because "you miss the best season."

A number of people indicated that they have not had enough seed to plant their crops. Normally people sell goats, sheep, a cow or even honey to buy seed. This year many were forced to borrow seed. One man explained the system, "If I borrow one donkey load of seed, I have to pay back one and a half donkey loads. If the farmer who lends the seed plows the land, he gets his seed plus half again and then 50 percent of the rest of the crop."

Table No. 5
AGRICULTURAL PRODUCTION INFORMATION FROM RESPONDENTS
Average, Best, 1983, 1984, Average Seed Needs

	Wad Kauli	Fau II
Amount of Produce Needed For Family of Six	1,500.0 kg	1,500.0 kg
Production in Best Year Since 1974	1,695.0 kg	1,896.0 kg
Total Production in 1983	420.0 kg	648.0 kg
Total Production in 1984	22.5 kg	0.0 kg
Total Seed Needed (All Kinds)	150.0 kg	210.0 kg

The Impact of Army Activities and Government Policies on Agricultural Production in Tigray—Causes of Famine (See Tables 6, 7 and 8)

When asked directly why there were food shortages in their village, refugees indicated, in order of importance, that insects, drought and the army were responsible. Through follow-up intensive interviews, substantial factors emerged that cast these responses in a new light — government policies severely curb farmers' ability to curtail drought- and insect-related production declines.

Our questionnaires (see Appendices A, B, C, D and E) did not specify quantitative detail about how the army's specific activities affected production. This information came to light through intensive interviews. Consequently, the interviewees were not all asked the same specific follow-up questions about how the Dergue's activities specifically affected production. In some cases, the interview took a different turn and the information was not collected. Even so, the figures below represent the percentage of all respondents interviewed who mentioned specific army or government activities. These figures are, therefore, only a minimal estimate since it remains possible that the rest of the people not questioned about these topics could have responded with additional detail.

Most interviewees reported that over the last three years the army had burned houses in their village as well as crops standing in the field, piled ready for threshing or stored in granaries or houses (see Map 17). Some of the respondents' reports follow.

The Dergue is one of the reasons people are hungry. He is the main reason over the last four years. I can't even remember all the people who have had their crops burned. The government always comes during harvest.

The army took 500 cows and oxen from my village, they burned people's houses and took honey, butter and anything made of leather. They even took old clothes. They didn't bother to carry the grain; they just burned it. The militia, they're farmers from the area, they take our tools so that they can use them. They all take salt and coffee. The army burned my grain in 1983 and they took 24 tins of honey which were worth E$7 each. They eat as much as they can and then sell what's left. In 1982, the army came through our village and forced me to pay E$400. I had to borrow the money from a neighbor. Because of the money that I had to pay the army and the grain that they burned I had to sell all my animals in 1984. Now I have nothing. That's why I am here.

Table No. 6
CAUSES OF HUNGER
(Short-Term)

	Wad Kauli	Fau II
Insects (Armyworm)	39.0%	83.0%
Insects/Drought	28.0%	11.0%
Drought	22.0%	6.0%
Ethiopian Army	11.0%	

In 1984, the army came to our village. That was the last time they took anything. They got one of my oxen. I ran away then; if they had caught me, they would have killed me. It is not now [as a result of drought] that we lost our animals. Soldiers took things when they wanted it. One of my neighbors had 17 cows taken a year ago, the same time I lost my ox. Another day the villagers were hiding from the army. He [the Dergue] found and killed a woman and her two kids. The army is now in my area taking all the property of those who left and many who didn't.

The Dergue has attacked my village six times. The sixth time the Dergue destroyed much, even more, than the armyworms. He [the Dergue] took money and animals.

They took all of some people's oxen and made them pay E$200 to E$300. They also destroyed crops. In 1981, they took pepper and corn still green, directly from the land.

When they came in 1981, I ran away with my cattle, but my brother stayed and was captured by the Dergue. He had to pay E$350. My brother was imprisoned and all my other brothers sold an ox to pay for his release. This was in 1981.

Since 1981, there have been many attacks. The army would come at night and take people. Some were taken to the army; some were allowed to return home when their relatives paid money for them — E$200 to E$400. In 1981, the Dergue took control of our village and stayed for about a year.

They started a peasant association then. The Dergue appointed all the officials. The remote areas never accepted the peasant associations, but in the town the residents were forced to pay more than E$200 for taxes and various contributions.

Map 17

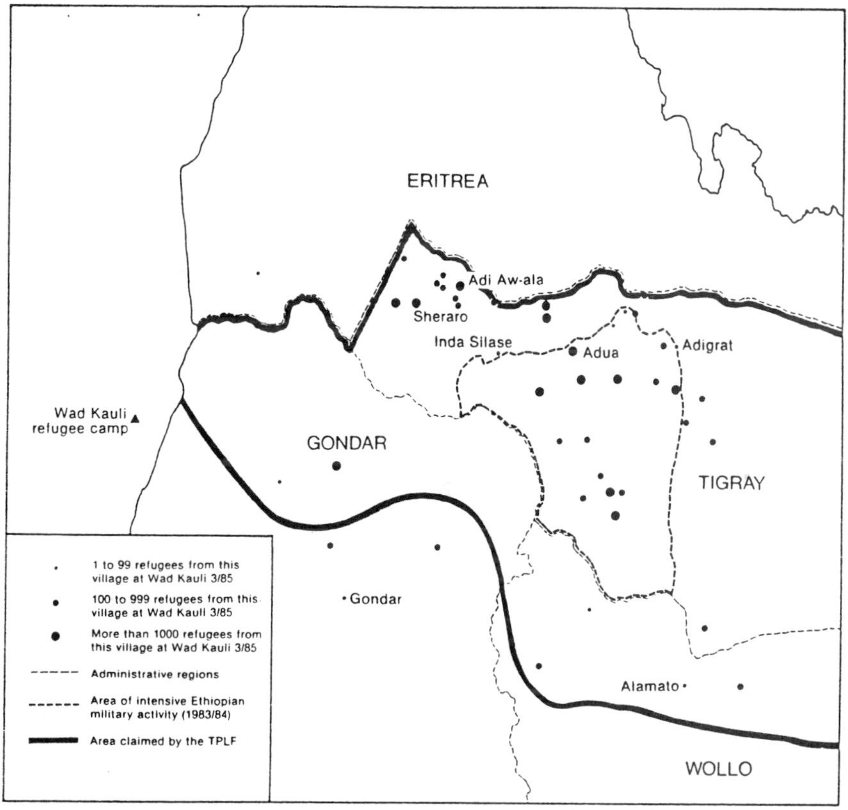

Map legend:
- . 1 to 99 refugees from this village at Wad Kauli 3/85
- • 100 to 999 refugees from this village at Wad Kauli 3/85
- ● More than 1000 refugees from this village at Wad Kauli 3/85
- - - - - Administrative regions
- — — — Area of intensive Ethiopian military activity (1983/84)
- ▬▬ Area claimed by the TPLF

Map labels: ERITREA, Adi Aw-ala, Sheraro, Inda Silase, Adua, Adigrat, Wad Kauli refugee camp, GONDAR, TIGRAY, Gondar, Alamato, WOLLO

HOME VILLAGES OF WAD KAULI REFUGEES (3/1985) AND THE MOST CONCENTRATED ETHIOPIAN MILITARY ACTIVITIES (1983/84)

On October 9, 1984, people in my village were killed when the Dergue bombed it. The army took my possessions last May [1984]. All the leather is used to make shoes. Some things the military keep; others are sold in town for money to buy drinks. They sold my plow for E$15 and bought liquor with the money. They also took grain, boards, even woven bowls. They burned the grass and straw that we had gathered for our livestock for a whole season.

The army has destroyed crops in my area [Tsedia] by burning it when it is stacked to be threshed. He [the Dergue] burned lumber and houses, killed people without even thinking, destroyed food and other materials in the houses.

In Tsedia the army has taken 200 oxen and 300 donkeys and horses. They took many more goats and sheep than that.

The army is still taking animals and bombing villages.

One market day, he [the Dergue] came, surrounded the village and forced everyone to pay five to seven years back taxes. I paid E$70. That's all I had. I received no paper showing I had paid anything.

They took our cattle, burned our houses and killed kids in the village. When they killed the kids, the army forced the mothers to dance around their bodies. At this time they also burned the crops. We ran away to a cave in the mountains.

In 1982, our property was destroyed by the government. Houses were bombed by airplanes and burned and some people were killed in the market. Some people were killed when they were at church and seven were burned to death in their field when their crops were burned.

In July 1984, there was fighting in my village [Hintalo]. People were killed, churches were destroyed and so were corn and houses. Oxen were taken; my sister lost two. Men were taken for the army by force. There were many oxen taken from an area, maybe 1,000 altogether.

The army took 16 tins of honey [E$5 per tin], butter, leather thongs and three oxen from me; they killed and ate seven or eight goats and sheep. They used my plow to make a fire and then roasted the small animals. They ate anything they found in my house.

In 1982, he [the Dergue] took donkeys from me and oxen from my neighbors. But he hasn't come since then because he got his [suffered the] consequences.

My area has been under the control of the TPLF for 10 years, but the Dergue can come when he wants. Many farmers have been killed by the Dergue; I can't count them all.

Three of my relatives were taken for the army in 1983. Young men are preferred, but many are taken.

Men give money to get people out of prison, but women who try to buy men out are taken for training.

We are forced to pay an ox, even money [E$50] and almost one donkey load of grain as taxes and contributions to the army when it comes to the village.

I left from the village, but all I had had already been taken by the army. For example, they took butter, they killed my oxen and my house was destroyed. During one night the army dumped chemicals in the water. The next day when people and animals drank it, they died. Such things happen, especially during planting and harvesting. While people are working in the fields, they are taken; 100 farmers were taken from our village.

When the army comes and takes our equipment — plows, harnesses, seed bags — everything must be replaced. We don't have the money to buy it so it all has to be made by hand. This slows our planting.

The matter-of-fact manner in which government activities were reported in interviews was astounding and the interviewees' attitudes indicated that such events were normal under the present government. Single sentences were used to sum up events that must have been as emotionally traumatic as they were economically disastrous.

In 1984, the government arrived at night, burned my house and took three cows.

In 1981, our harvest was burned by the government and our cattle were taken and killed [eaten] by them too. When the army burns our crops, other villages help us. When the market at Howzen was bombed, a lot of people died.

Many of my neighbors were forced to pay money at the same time my four cows and oxen were taken.

Most also said that their villages had been bombed. Churches, markets, funerals and schools — places where large groups gathered — were the principal targets. As one man said,

The Amhara [Dergue] have attacked and bombed our village for four years. Crops that were harvested to be threshed were burned. Mine, by chance, weren't burned, but my neighbors' were. Some of them are here [in Sudan].

The military killed young people in the village, but the village has an armed guard that watches all the time and warns the people when the army is on its way.

Sometimes the cattle don't go "voluntarily" when they are captured by the army. So they kill them.

They took nothing from me. They never got to my house; it is three hours from the nearest village.

Another farmer pointed out,

The Dergue bombs local markets so that merchants won't travel to them any more. This makes prices even higher. It is because of the Dergue that we are now in Sudan. Under normal conditions, even with the drought, we would have been able to trade and make a living. But now that markets are bombed, most are held at night and it's hard for us to travel to them.

Most of those people interviewed expected the army to retaliate against them for leaving Ethiopia. They believed that the army would go to their villages and loot and burn everything they left behind. As one respondent said, "Everything I left behind when I came to Sudan will be taken or destroyed."

Even though interviewees (with one exception) were from TPLF-held areas, most reported that young men were captured and forced into the Ethiopian army. One respondent explained, "My town is a three-hour journey from him [the Dergue]. But he comes and takes too many young men. Many that I know. Many are killed. Sometimes he just takes people to the edge of the village, kills them and leaves."

One woman reported that her 17-year-old son was taken by force to join the Ethiopian army in Adua. After a month there he escaped and returned home. The army went to the village, prompting the woman, her daughter and the son to flee to the forests with their only oxen. The oxen soon died. They moved to a new village for two months. After that, there was nothing to eat, so they came to Sudan.

One of every four people interviewed said that the army had stolen farm equipment and food from them and in addition captured and held them until their families could pay a ransom to obtain their release. One respondent reported,

> My village hasn't lost any animals to the army. We have lookouts, and when we see them coming, we hide our stuff in the forest so they can't get them.
>
> People in my village have had to pay up to E$500 to get relatives from prison, though.
>
> In 1982, I paid E$80 in taxes. In 1976, it was E$7, then E$20, then E$80, then E$100 per year. All by force. If a man is arrested, his wife pays. I was arrested in 1982 and held until my wife paid E$80. Many people here in this camp have been arrested.

Twenty percent of all interviewees reported that civilians had been killed and insisted that the purpose of the attacks was to destroy food and commerce and to terrify local residents. For the most part, government attacks were unrelated to specific TPLF activities.

Refugees reported several kinds of atrocities inflicted by the Ethiopian army upon the civilian population. Those in eastern Sudan consistently mentioned that the army killed, maimed or abused people in their villages. People were most incensed that the army publicly raped women in the village, in particular the wives of priests. Those interviewed said they thought this was done to humiliate them and to teach them a lesson. The army also was reported to have killed pregnant women. Two men in different camps reported that the army had cut the right hand off some of the boys in their villages. Others said that the army often killed young boys and then forced their mothers to dance near the bodies. As cited previously, one man reported that in 1981, the army poisoned the only water source near the village of Redaga Arbi. Many animals and some people died.

Only 35 percent of those sampled had ever paid taxes to the Dergue's government, but the taxes that they collectively reported to have paid had increased substantially between 1977 and 1984 — the same period during which the government had reduced services to rural areas in general and particularly those areas suspected of being sympathetic to the liberation fronts. Taxes were not given voluntarily. One respondent reported,

> Nothing is given willingly to the Dergue, but much is taken by force. He always takes honey and butter to eat.
>
> The government imprisons people until their families pay more than E$120 to have them released.

The following scenario was often reported to us.

> The army came to my area [a contested area] to collect back taxes. All the men in the village, along with the oxen, were arrested. They were not given water or food so that E$117 would be collected quickly before the animals died. Women had to beg for money from relatives and neighbors.

Recently, the army and militia have stepped up their sweeps through the TPLF areas, forcing residents who did not escape in time to pay back taxes for a number of years. Many people indicated that they paid taxes for programs that they never benefited from. One interviewee said, "We paid a special tax for such things as education and health, but we don't have education or health programs. The school we built under Haile Selassie was bombed by this government."

Table No. 7
ARMY ACTIVITIES AND GOVERNMENT POLICIES THAT
CONTRIBUTE TO FAMINE

	Wad Kauli	Fau II
Army Burned Houses in the Village	50.0%	60.0%
Army Burned Crops in the Village	60.0%	95.0%
Army Bombed the Village	60.0%	70.0%
Army Took Livestock From the Village	65.0%	70.0%
Young Men Were Conscripted Into the Army	65.0%	60.0%
Village Civilians Killed by Army	20.0%	20.0%
Respondents Imprisoned and Held For Ransom	25.0%	25.0%
Army Confiscated Respondent's Farm Equipment	20.0%	35.0%
People Resettled From the Village by Ethiopian Government	35.0%	10.0%
People From the Village Who Went to the Government Feeding Centers	15.0%	10.0%
Respondents Who Had Paid Taxes to the Dergue	35.0%	35.0%
Average "Contribution" to Dergue	E$116.70	E$176.70
Annual Peasant Association Fees		
Cash	E$10.00	E$10.00
Grain (Wheat or Teff)	30 tins	30 tins
Labor	Varied	Varied

NOTE: It must be noted here that this information comes from the same people whose presenting complaints were drought and pests yet each answered with great detail regarding government actions that have severely decreased food supplies and productive capacity. This contradiction is discussed in our concluding chapters.

Table No. 8
AVERAGE TAXES PAID (E$ PER YEAR)*

	1977	1978	1979	1980	1981	1982	1983	1984
Wad Kauli	12		20	30			40	100
Fau II	50	70			170	80	117	

*For some years, those interviewed either did not pay taxes or could not remember the amounts paid.

Many people claimed that they had been forced to make contributions to various government programs including peasant associations, literacy campaigns, women's and children's associations and special campaigns such as "Call to the Motherland." Those interviewed reported that contributions, taken collectively, were much larger than annual taxes. While many contributions were collected for specific programs, others were reportedly used by army personnel to increase their income. Not one person interviewed reported receiving a receipt that acknowledged any of their contributions. Some respondents reported that they had also been forced to make contributions to local schools. Often, however, the schools were constructed in government-held cities where rural residents would not let their children attend. As one respondent explained,

> The school in our area was built close to the town, so that people had to go there to it. For people from the TPLF areas, this meant going to areas where they could be arrested for not having peasant association cards.
> The peasant associations oversee the schools. Fees for the literacy campaign are collected from peasant association members. The peasant associations are in charge of the literacy program.

Respondents pointed out that when schools were built in rural areas, the army bombed them.

Reasons Given for Fleeing Homeland Areas (see Table No. 9)

As the table below illustrates, those refugees from Tigray who left prior to October 1984 indicated that they left primarily for reasons other than famine. Wad Kauli and Fau II residents, by comparison, indicated that drought, or food shortages brought on by other factors (the respondents emphasized the distinction between the two), were the main reasons they left Tigray.

Table No. 9
REASONS FOR FLEEING HOMELANDS

	Wad Kauli	Fau II	Tawawa
Drought	47.0%	13.0%	20.0%
Food Shortage	26.0%	53.0%	
Drought/Food Shortage	5.0%		
Food Shortage/Insects		20.0%	
Insects	11.0%	13.0%	5.0%
Conscription Into the Army	5.0%		10.0%
Political Persecution	5.0%		25.0%
War (EDU/Dergue)			10.0%
Land Taken by the Dergue			10.0%
Start a New Life			5.0%
To Make Money			15.0%

The data presented in the rest of the report cover only the recently arrived refugees living in Fau II and Wad Kauli. Information from those at Tawawa, while interesting in and of itself, does not shed much light on recent events surrounding the famine in Tigray. The testimony of the refugees indicates that food shortages were the main reasons for going to Sudan.

The rains don't continue to the end of the growing season; they stop in the middle. There is nothing to eat.

I left because insects and drought destroyed our crops. There was drought and nothing to eat. Instead of dying at home, I decided to come to Sudan. I knew that the people were different but that there was food here. We thought we could work here. People from my area had come to work in Sudan. We even met some of them returning as we came here. They told us the birr [E$1 = $.50] had more value so what one earned in Sudan was not great. The TPLF gave me information. There were lots of planes, so we traveled at night, we couldn't even cook during the day. We got our food from the TPLF. There were rivers, so each night we got water for the next day. But it will be hard to go back to plant because many of these rivers are dry.

Others interviewed intensively indicated interconnections among complex causes for their flight and the strategies they had tried before deciding to leave Tigray.

I decided to leave home because of the drought and our enemy [the Dergue].

Insects and the lack of rain were equally important, but the government caused the famine too.

We were able to survive by trading and selling animals and farming equipment. We sold to traders from the towns. They took everything to the town. Now the government disrupts trading so we can't get by anymore.

It is because of the Dergue that we are here. Under normal conditions, even with drought, we would have been able to trade and make it through. But with markets being bombed, many are only held at night. The enemy [Dergue] made it difficult to trade. . . .

The lack of rain is the most important cause of the drought, but the reason we are in Sudan is because of the Dergue.

Before, I had 10 cows and oxen. Last year the Dergue took three cows and one ox. I sold one cow for E$66; it should have been worth E$300. Four animals died. One cow was alive when I left. Many from my village were captured and forced to pay money, but I escaped. They got my animals, though. It's all the same thing, isn't it?

In 1982, I produced 30 donkey loads [one donkey load equals about 65 kg, but can range from 50 to 70 kg] of crops with six donkey loads of seed. In 1983, I borrowed E$300 from a rich farmer to get seed. I paid him back E$400. If you borrow E$100, for instance, you pay E$5 per month interest.

Many of the respondents indicated they had worked as agricultural laborers as a way to earn money to buy food for their families.

I lived in Tsedia until October 1984, then I went to Tsalimbitia. I thought I might be able to get work or food. My wife stayed in Tsedia; I haven't seen her or our five children since October.

My village has had drought for six years. Two years ago I started working in Sudan, for three months. Last year I worked more. Now it's hard to work in Sudan at all, so I came as a refugee.

In May 1984, I left Arz'bi with my wife and five children and went to Adi Abu. I worked there as a farm laborer for E$1.50 to E$2 per day. My wife and two children went home after we saved a little money. I came to Sudan directly from Adi Abu. I haven't seen my wife or two children since.

Some of those interviewed thought they would be able to work in Sudan.

I heard there was lots of agriculture in Sudan with lots of production. I thought I could work, but I haven't been able to.

I have been here three months. I haven't worked here [in Sudan], but some people in the camp [Wad Kauli] have.

Attempts to Receive Food at Government-Run Feeding Centers

Not one of the people interviewed felt that they could safely go to the government feeding centers and receive food. As one man said, summing up the experience of many from Tigray, "All the ways to food are closed by the Dergue. We have free access only to Sudan." Another man reported, "Neighboring villages went to government feeding centers. They were controlled by the Dergue, however. I couldn't go to the feeding centers because I am from a TPLF area." As another stated,

Some from my area went to a government feeding center. Some got a little bit of food. This caused more to go to the center, and many were then taken to the south. Many went to the feeding centers who were sympathetic to the TPLF. The government claimed it would give food to the starving even from the TPLF areas, but they didn't. They just tricked them.

Those interviewed cited numerous examples of people who had gone and either been turned away or taken away for resettlement. One man said, "Everyone [in a nearby village] was told that assistance was in Mekele. They all went there to a big hall. Then the army came and took them away to be resettled." Others said that in neighboring villages, those closer to the feeding centers, a few individuals, had been given small amounts of grain and encouraged to go home and bring everyone from their village the next day. On the following day, the entire village would show up and everyone would be put in a holding camp to determine who would be resettled. The refugees in Sudan saw the feeding centers as government bait in a trap to lure people into government-controlled areas so that the young and able-bodied could be resettled to other areas of the country.

In November 1984, I went to Adua to get some food. The government rounded us up — there were 800 men and some women and children too. We were taken from Adua to Axum. There were nine or 10 trucks to take us.

I escaped from Axum with my friend here; the rest were taken to Mekele, Addis Ababa and on to Wollega. Military and militia both guarded us. Most of them spoke Amhara, not Tigrinya.

I went to Axum to get assistance for my family. I had to register four times for the aid and each time tell them my name, my father's name and my grandfather's name. I was not given aid; instead they arrested me. I escaped, returned to my home in Nadir and then came to Sudan. I brought two of my children. The other four are with my wife, who is pregnant and couldn't travel. I left three goats with her as well as some money from the sale of a cow.

A number of respondents were quick to point out that resettlement from their areas was not new. Their observations reflect many experiences shared with those who recently escaped from resettlement sites in southwest Ethiopia (see Chapters V and VI).

Resettlement has been the most common during the last four years. Maybe 3,000 people were taken from our area. I heard they went to Wollega. In other cases, [presumably in the Bale region] the resettlement sites were dangerous and those resettled fought with Somali. If settlers tried to escape, they were shot. This happened a few years ago. Some settlers were armed. Today, perhaps, they are fighting with the Somali Abo [Oromo]. He [the Dergue] trains the settlers to be armed.

More than three years ago, 300 farmers were taken for resettlement from our village. Sometimes it was women, sometimes men, sometimes husbands and wives. More than 400 were taken this year, just the same as before — sometimes women, etc.

A few of those resettled three years ago made their way back to the village. It took them four months to get back.

In February 1984, they took some people from Aragil [a neighboring village] to be resettled. The village was attacked first. Many were killed; 380 houses were destroyed. Some of the people ran away; others stayed behind. Those who stayed were caught and taken south. About 180 were taken from Aragil to Mekele and to Wollega, I think. But they were all taken by force.

In December, some of my neighbors went to the market in Howzen. They were captured, taken by force and resettled.

First the government bombed the area. Some 300 houses were burned and abandoned. Then the army arrived and took people for resettlement in Wollega. In a neighboring village they have taken 670 people.

Smaller numbers said that people had begun to be resettled from their villages, but that these moves began more than five years ago. A small percentage said that people from their village had gone to the government feeding centers. One man reported a close relationship between resettlement and feeding centers.

Resettlement from my area [Hintalo, Mekele] started with Mengistu; it has been continuous ever since. This year people were taken too. I don't think people were taken under Haile Selassie.

Most of the people in my village were resettled to the south this year. But some are still there and a few are here [in the refugee camp]. He [Dergue] told them there was food at Hintalo. Two or three went and got a little grain. They were told to bring back everyone in the village for food. When they went back with most of the village, soldiers surrounded them and took them for resettlement. This happened in October 1984. People were forced to walk under guard to Mekele. I escaped from Mekele. Many escaped, many are here. Some escaped even from the trucks as they were going south.

In spite of conditions in Tigray, those interviewed said that the TPLF in no way prevented them from going to government feeding centers. Those who went to Sudan did not trust the government. As one man said, "We have seen his [the Dergue's] face before." Another man said,

It is a six-hour journey to Mekele. Some entire villages that were closer were rounded up and taken to Mekele. Many were then taken south. The TPLF told us of these problems but didn't tell us not to go to Mekele to get food.

Why Parts of Families Stayed in Ethiopia Rather Than Travel to Sudan
On average those interviewed in Sudan had been accompanied by only 60 percent of their immediate families. The splitting up of families was voluntary and caused by the following considerations.

My wife was ill; she couldn't come. Our three youngest daughters were too small to travel so they stayed with her.

My wife is pregnant and the three children are too young to make the journey.

My wife and three youngest children are at home. They couldn't make the trip. The oldest child (nine years) is with me.

My wife stayed home to take care of her parents who are too old to make the trip.

My wife is with the TPLF.

My two oldest children stayed to take care of the remaining animals.

The Trip to Sudan (see Table No. 10)
After a survey of the 1984 harvest throughout the TPLF-held area, which was, according to the TPLF, an area comprising about 80 percent of the region occupied by Tigrayans, the TPLF (personal communication) decided that it would be impossible for many Tigrayans to survive if they stayed in the region. According to respondents, the TPLF explained to them that the organization knew that it could not get enough food for everyone, so it organized an exodus of those able-bodied people who were willing to go to Sudan. Most of the people in eastern Sudan were from TPLF-held areas. Surveys of Wad Kauli and Fau II, for example, found that only two and a half percent of all those surveyed admitted to being from Dergue, or government-held, areas.

More than 75 percent of those surveyed in Wad Kauli and Fau II indicated that the TPLF held a meeting in their villages to explain what they considered the people's options.

The TPLF organized us to come to the Sudan, even from our homes. All the information came from the TPLF, but I had heard of Sudan before. We came with many others from our village. We had a TPLF guide and on the way got assistance from REST [Relief Society of Tigray]. It took us three months to arrive.

We received orientation from the TPLF in our village. They told us about the drought and about how it was throughout the region. They said that we should prepare to go to Sudan before we got too weak because it is a difficult journey.

Many interviewed reported that they were told, "You can stay here and die for sure or go to Sudan where you will be able to get food." All those interviewed reported that they went voluntarily with the TPLF to Sudan. Most interviewees also said that they assumed, or at least hoped, that they would receive clothes, money, seed and oxen so that they could return to plant their crops. It seems that both TPLF officials and those who fled to the Sudan considered the move temporary. They assumed that the displaced would return to Tigray, beginning in April, to prepare their land and plant a crop. By July 1985, after our research was concluded, we received reports that perhaps 25 percent had returned.

The TPLF provided more than 85 percent of the refugees with a guide who accompanied them from their village to Sudan. The remaining refugees picked up a TPLF guide along the way. The route was set, and groups of villagers joined the procession along the way. Food and water was provided in the evening; the people were usually expected to cook with their own pans, or with ones provided by the TPLF or others traveling in the group. As two respondents explained:

Some 4,000 from my village came to Sudan in eight different groups. I started from the village with enough food for a few days; the trip took a month. On the way we got assistance from REST. They provided a guide, too, not from the village, though, although REST did help many villages.

REST gave us all our food after [leaving] Adagakebret. REST provided meals, but we had to cook it on our own utensils which we carried throughout the trip.

Much of the traveling was done at night. In November and December, refugees reported, their columns were attacked by the Ethiopian Air Force and some people were killed. One man stated, "Even when we were gathering to come to Sudan the army started to burn houses. On the way here, the planes killed 80 to 100 people." Another reported, "The government tried to capture us on the way to Sudan. They dropped bombs on us on the way. Some in our group died."

Many people were taken by the army when they were on their way to Sudan. As one respondent explained,

On the way here the army caught me and took me to the officers where they hit me with sticks. After that they asked me where I was going and where my pass paper was. I told them that last month I had gone to Adua to the feeding center to see if I could get food, but I hadn't received any. Now I was going to a different center to try again. They let me go. I continued on the journey, but only at night. We heard one group was bombed while they were cooking their meal and 80 or 100 died; others were wounded, so we walked at night.

In March, attacks by the Ethiopian Air Force on the refugee exodus were reported by the TPLF and humanitarian agencies in Khartoum. It took the refugees, on average, four to five weeks to make the journey. The refugees in Wad Kauli arrived in Sudan approximately one month later than those in Fau II.

Table No. 10
INFORMATION GIVEN ABOUT THE TRIP TO SUDAN

	Wad Kauli	Fau II
TPLF Orientation in Village	75.0%	84.0%
TPLF Guide From Village	85.0%	89.0%
TPLF Guide Into the Sudan	100.0%	100.0%
Length of Time It Took to Walk to Sudan	5 weeks	4 weeks
Total Time Spent in the Camps in Sudan	2.5 months	3.5 months

Plans for the Future (see Tables 11-16)

All but one person interviewed wanted to return to Tigray to plant a crop in 1985 (the sole exception was a 68-year-old man who said he wished to die in Sudan rather than walk back and try to start over). They did not see their residence in Sudan as permanent or even long-term. Few said that they wanted to work in Sudan. Their goals are to get seed and money for equipment, return to their homes and the rest of their families and plant a crop. As of May 1985, only about 25 percent had actually achieved these goals. The rest were still in refugee camps in Sudan. In February-March of 1985 the daily wage for agricultural laborers, as a result of the refugee influx, had already fallen to SL1.00 (US$.35) per day from an already low SL3.00 per day the previous fall.

Table No. 11
PLANS FOR THE FUTURE

	Wad Kauli	Fau II
Want to Return Home to Plant	95.0%	100.0%
Want to Work in the Sudan	15.0%	10.0%

In an effort to determine what would be required for these refugees to return to their homeland to plant their crops at the appropriate times, we devised a short questionnaire that was delivered to randomly selected representatives from 97 percent of the villages represented in the Wad Kauli refugee camp population. In each case, two to three farmers, aged 30 to 50 years, were asked the following questions:

- What village are you from?
- How long did it take you to come to Sudan?
- How long would it take those who do the planting to return?
- What is the order of planting of your crops?
- When do you plant each of them?
- How long does it take you to plow the land for the first crop?
- How much seed do you need to plant your crops?
- When do you need to leave Sudan in order to arrive in time to plant?

In one and a half days we were able to interview farmers from 58 villages in Wad Kauli (there were approximately 60,000 people in the camp at the time of the survey). A summary of the results is presented below (the complete report — "The Needs of Refugees in Eastern Sudan If They Are to Return to Tigray to Plant Their Crops" — can be obtained from Cultural Survival). It is our belief that given the number of refugees from Tigray who have remained in Sudan in 1985 as well as the number of displaced people in northern Ethiopia who need assistance to begin producing again, the information continues to be relevant to those attempting to supply input to people who want to plant crops.

Nearly 90 percent of people from the 58 villages polled stated that, if they were to walk to their homes, they would have to leave Sudan by April 1 in order to arrive in time to plant their first crops. For many of those interviewed, the first crops accounted for a sizeable proportion of their total annual yields (10 to 25 percent) during regular yields and even more during years when the rains stop early and/or the Ethiopian military attacks and delays planting. Departure dates are important if assistance is to be given to people which they will carry back to Tigray with them.

There are, however, indications that minor delays in the ideal departure dates could be tolerated. Some farmers, for instance, want to return in time to make agricultural equipment, including plows, so that they do not have to buy them. Plowing and planting are often done simultaneously over a period of four to six weeks for the first crop. Most farmers do not have oxen and will have to depend on those of relatives, friends or wealthier individuals. In such circumstances, they will need to be able to work whenever these animals are available. Finally, there are six religious holidays during the month of April on which devout Coptic Christians are not supposed to work.

Table No. 12
DEPARTURE DATES FROM WAD KAULI OF FARMERS IF THEY ARE
TO RETURN IN TIME TO PLANT THEIR FIRST CROPS

March 1	17.0%
March 3	50.7%
April 1	21.4%
April 15	2.9%
May 5	4.6%
May 15	3.2%

More than 75 percent of those interviewed estimated that they would need oxen in their villages by March 15 if they were to prepare the soil in a timely manner (some plow the land after the first rains, so the dates are not fixed). As was discussed above, only 15 percent of those interviewed in Wad Kauli had a pair of oxen at the time they left for Sudan. None of them expected their oxen to be alive when they returned home.

DATE OXEN NEEDED IN VILLAGES

March 1	46.5%
March 15	29.3%
April 1	5.6%
April 15	7.0%
May 1	4.2%
May 15	5.7%
June 1	1.7%

Some 43 percent of the villages needed seed for the first planting by April 15; another 43 percent of those interviewed reported that they needed seed for the first crops in their village by May 1.

Table No. 14
DATE SEED FIRST NEEDED IN VILLAGES

March 15	13.2%
April 1	16.9%
April 15	12.9%
May 1	43.3%
May 15	.5%
June 1	1.3%
June 15	.2%

Sorghum, millet and dagusa (a small, black millet) are the most common first crops planted in the villages represented in the Wad Kauli camp population. There is also a variety of teff that is planted early as it requires less moisture than the more common variety. Those interviewed insisted that they needed seeds for different crops so they could best use the diverse ecological niches on their farms as well as minimize their risks of total crop failure.

Table No. 15
MOST COMMON FIRST CROPS REPORTED BY WAD KAULI RESIDENTS

Sorghum	11.4%
Sorghum/Millet	13.3%
Sorghum/Teff	1.2%
Sorghum/Millet/Dagusa	19.1%
Sorghum/Dagusa	22.1%
Millet/Dagusa	20.1%
Dagusa	3.5%
Sorghum/Dagusa/Teff	.6%
Sorghum/Millet/Dagusa/Teff	4.4%
Sorghum/Millet/Maize	.8%
Sorghum/Maize	1.4%
Teff/Barley/Wheat	1.2%
Teff/Maize/Barley	.6%

THE MAIN CROPS PLANTED IN ALL VILLAGES

Sorghum	74.4%
Dagusa	69.9%
Millet	57.8%
Teff	8.0%
Maize	2.8%
Barley	1.8%
Wheat	1.4%

Most Tigrayans interviewed in Wad Kauli indicated that they would like to return to Tigray to plant their crops. Most, however, said that they could not return unless they received assistance from the TPLF, the UNHCR or international relief agencies. Most said that they would prefer to receive assistance in the form of cash since it is easier to transport and they could use it to purchase or rent the tools required to plant their crops. They insisted that they simply could not carry all the materials they needed. Perhaps the most common attitude refugees expressed when contemplating their return to Tigray was summed up by one man: "I have given the TPLF food and water in the past. When I go back, if there is rain, I will help the TPLF as much as I can. All in all, the farmers in my area feel the same. We will all help the TPLF even more."

Chapter V

CONDITIONS FACED BEFORE AND AFTER RESETTLEMENT: TESTIMONY FROM ESCAPEES OF THE ETHIOPIAN RESETTLEMENT CAMPS

Throughout the opening months of 1985, residents of the border regions of the Blue Nile and Upper Nile administrative provinces of Sudan were instructed to notify the Sudanese security of any refugees found crossing the Ethiopian-Sudanese border from the Ethiopian side. Beginning in January 1985 individuals and groups had been found wandering in those regions, unable to speak Arabic to the inhabitants, and uncertain whether or not they had crossed a border and reached Sudan or whether they were in areas still under the jurisdiction of the Ethiopian government. Such people, who were first encountered by relief workers of the Oromo Relief Association (ORA), the Relief Society of Tigray (REST), and local residents, usually turned out to be escapees from the Ethiopian resettlement program often reported in the Western press by journalists stationed in Addis Ababa (see Appendix F). Personnel from ORA and REST who were able to communicate with these refugees determined that they wished to return home to their native regions of Tigray and Wollo inside Ethiopia. They requested assistance in making the long trek home. Sudanese authorities, aware of the presence of these new refugees in Sudan, arranged for them to be brought to a makeshift camp on the outskirts of Damazine, the administrative capital of Blue Nile Province, located 525 km south of Khartoum until other arrangements could be made for them.

The resulting Sudanese policy was that once escapees from the Ethiopian resettlement sites found their way across the border to Sudan, they were collected by Sudanese citizens at various points along the border, transferred into the custody of Sudanese officials, and then transported by the Sudanese authorities to the holding area outside Damazine. The Sudanese had not constructed any permanent refugee camps in the southern part of Blue Nile Province at that time. The Damazine holding center, however, was run by the Sudan Commission of Refugees (COR) with the assistance of the Tigray People's Liberation Front (TPLF) and REST. The United Nations High Commissioner for Refugees (UNHCR) had no presence in the camp, although UNHCR officials had made brief visits (Smith 1985). The trickle of refugees that had begun in January had increased to the point that 997 people had been gathered in this temporary holding camp at Damazine in March 1985, the time that the Cultural Survival team arrived.

Earliest warnings and reports about this new type of refugee originally came from ORA and REST; then visitors to the Sudan began to be aware of the phenomenon of the arrival of escapees from resettlement. Gayle Smith, working as an independent journalist, traveled to Damazine in January and compiled the first investigative report (Smith 1985). A representative of Berliner Missionswerk visited the site near Damazine where the new refugees were being held and then he returned to Berlin intent upon enlisting someone to interview the escapees in depth about their experiences in resettlement. Jip Ketel, an Oxfam UK representative who was in Sudan, organized a small group to visit the Damazine camp in February and included his assessment in his report to Oxfam (Ketel 1985).

The Cultural Survival team was already prepared to conduct our research on the causes of the Ethiopian famine by interviewing refugees in Sudan when the news came to us that yet another group of people affected by famine in Ethiopia had arrived in Sudan. We immediately decided to arrange a way to include this new group of eyewitnesses to famine in our sample for research. Fortunately, we were able to read Gayle Smith's and Jip Ketel's reports before launching our own work, and we met Peter Niggli in Khartoum before he began his trip to Damazine. Niggli, a Swiss journalist with experience in the Horn of Africa, had been enlisted by the Berliner Missionswerk to investigate the scope and mechanisms of the 1984-85 resettlement program in Ethiopia. Through extensive discussions in Khartoum, we agreed to cooperate in our investigations.

The Interviews

Upon coordinating our work, Niggli and Holcomb conducted a mathematically calculated random sample survey of the Damazine camp and Niggli interviewed persons who had been selected according to that procedure. In addition to discussing in detail the participants' experiences during the Ethiopian resettlement process, which had been Niggli's original objective,* he administered the Cultural Survival questionnaires to each of the refugees he interviewed. He interviewed 50 refugees in this way. Bonnie Holcomb conducted 17 additional survey interviews in Damazine before going south to Kurmuk and Yabuus to talk to another category of refugees — those who had crossed the border from their homes in the Ethiopian administrative regions of Wollega and Illubabor (see Chapters VII, VIII and IX).

The data presented in this chapter were from individuals who had been taken from their homes to resettlement sites in Wollega or Kefa and then escaped and made their way to Sudan. We talked to them both about their experiences of famine in their home regions and also about what they had experienced during the resettlement process. The first part of the chapter presents the information concerning the causes of food shortages in the refugees' home regions collected by both Niggli and Holcomb. The second part of the chapter then recounts specific aspects of these peoples' experiences as participants in Ethiopian resettlement.

This information represents the experience of people present in Damazine in March 1985. Escapees from Ethiopian resettlement who had entered Sudan in the previous six to eight weeks had been gathered by the Sudanese officials into a holding area five km out of town. The process of selecting

---

* Niggli has subsequently produced a separate detailed narrative account of the 1984-1985 Ethiopian resettlement program based on his intensive interviews with the escapees on this topic. This has been published in German (Niggli 1985), and has been translated into English both by Cultural Survival (Niggli 1985a) and by Berliner Missionswerk (Niggli 1985b). We strongly recommend his superbly written report. This account of the internal workings of the resettlement program may be obtained from Cultural Survival in either German or English.

people to be interviewed was one of random selection. The holding center was first mapped and surveyed to account for all the sections in which people were present; then out of the residents present in every vicinity, every 15th person was interviewed. When children were selected, information was taken from the supervising adult present in the camp. (This presented no problem since in no case had a child found his/her way to the camp without the assistance of an adult.) All persons were willing to be interviewed except one woman who was too debilitated. People were interviewed individually away from the administrators of the camp, relief officials, or, in most cases, other refugees.

Most of the refugees in the Damazine holding center perceived themselves to be en route to their homes (see Map 18). (In fact, during our research the Sudanese began to erect a semi-permanent health clinic; the refugees reacted with alarm and resistance thinking that they were going to be retained there against their will.) Shedding light on this matter, observers who visited the area in June 1985 reported that the escapees who had been present in the Damazine holding center at the time of our interviews in March had already been transferred to the camp at Wad Kauli. From there the refugees were allowed to return to their home areas. Of the 1,500 people transported to Wad Kauli, about 250 reportedly decided to remain behind in Sudan (see Chapters XI and XIII for discussion of the fate of these refugees.)

Personal Background of the Escapees† (see Table No. 1.)

We found that the refugees thus randomly selected from the camp were originally from the Ethiopian administrative regions of Tigray, Wollo, Gondar and northern Shoa. Sixty percent were from Tigray; forty percent were from Wollo, Gondar and northern Shoa. For the purposes of presenting our findings clearly and for purposes of analysis, the responses are presented in these two broad categories, i.e., according to the administrative regions of origin of the respondents. The 40 people from Tigray are grouped together and those from Wollo, Gondar and Shoa are classified together under the rubric "Wollo, etc." Twenty-five people were from Wollo; one interviewee each was from Shoa and Gondar. Since those two persons were from places that closely bordered Wollo, we saw no useful purpose in continually listing their data in separate columns in the accompanying tables.

Most of the refugees interviewed at Damazine were male. Those Tigray were nearly 20 years older than the other people who had escaped from the resettlement sites.* Virtually all of those interviewed had lived all their lives in the same villages in Tigray and Wollo prior to their move to the resettlement sites. The Tigrayans were all Coptic Christians; 95 percent from the Wollo region were Moslem while only five percent were Christian. Three

---

† Additional detailed information from resettlement escapees was obtained by Holcomb as she travelled south in Sudan en route to the Sudanese border. Since these were not part of the random sample, the information from these interviews is not calculated as part of the statistical report given in this chapter. What was learned from those refugees, however, is presented separately in the following chapter. Information from these people confirms, reinforces, and elaborates much of what we found from the camp population (see Chapter VI).

*9 Supplementary interviews Bonnie Holcomb conducted (see Chapter VI) also indicated that the Tigrayans (42 years) were on average twice as old as those from Wollo (21.6 years).

Map 18

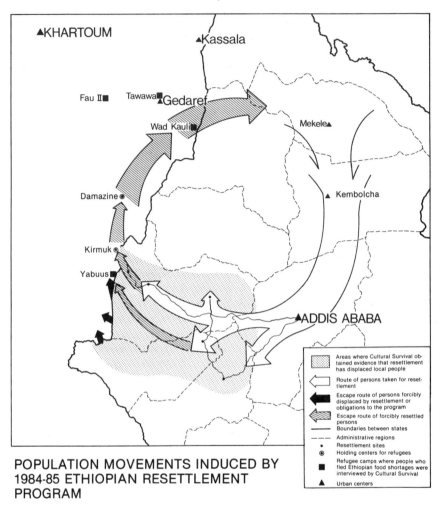

POPULATION MOVEMENTS INDUCED BY 1984-85 ETHIOPIAN RESETTLEMENT PROGRAM

quarters of those from Tigray could speak only Tigrinya. One quarter could also speak Amharic. About 86 percent of the other refugees could speak only Amharic; the remainder spoke Oromo. Many of the other refugees, particularly those from Wollo, referred to themselves as "the people who have forgotten even our language [Oromo]." They appear to be of Oromo background (see "The Case of Wollo" in Chapter II).

One third of the Tigrayans were literate while nearly two thirds of the other refugees were literate. Most literate Tigrayans were literate only in Tigrinya, while most of the others were literate in Amharic.

PERSONAL BACKGROUND OF RESPONDENTS

	Tigray	Wollo, etc.
Number Interviewed	40	27
Geographic Origin	60.0%	40.0%
Interviewee is Male	89.3%	82.0%
Age (years)	43.3	24.7
Religion		
Coptic Christian	100.0%	
Christian		5.0%
Moslem		95.0%
Languages Spoken		
Tigrinya	78.6%	
Tigrinya and Amharic	21.4%	
Tigrinya and Saho	3.7%	
Amharic		86.0%
Oromo		14.0%
Total Literate	35.7%	68.0%
in Tigrinya	25.0%	
in Tigrinya and Amharic	10.7%	
in Amharic		45.5%
in Amharic and Arabic		9.1%
in Oromo and Amharic		4.5%
in Arabic		9.1%

Family History of Respondents (see Table No. 2)

Persons interviewed in the Damazine holding center had been born in the same village as their fathers and their fathers' fathers. Nearly fifty percent of those from Tigray reported that they were from TPLF-held areas. Half of those from Tigray were from the Adua district — the two figures are not mutually exclusive. Nearly 90 percent of those from Tigray were married and had been married, on average, for 21 years. They had approximately 5.36 children each. Fewer than one third had been resettled with any of their immediate family; only eight percent had been resettled with their entire family.

Those interviewed from Wollo, Shoa and Gondar were much younger on average. Consequently, 36 percent were single; those who were married had been married only seven years on average and had an average of 1.4 children each. Slightly more than half of this group had been resettled with some of their family but only 18 percent had been resettled with their entire families. It is likely that nearly twice as many of this group were resettled with their families intact only because the families were much smaller.

The people interviewed, regardless of area of origin, had just over four siblings each. This meant their parents' family numbered approximately seven. About twice as m.. y people from Tigray knew of siblings who had been resettled in Ethiopia. People from Tigray appeared to have more knowledge of events affecting their immediate families. A small but equal percentage of those interviewed in both groups had siblings who were refugees in the Sudan or who were in the Ethiopian army. A small percentage of those from Tigray indicated that they had siblings in prison or fighting with the TPLF.

FAMILY HISTORY OF RESPONDENTS

	Tigray	Wollo, etc.
Father Born in Same Village	100.0%	95.0%
Father's Father Born in Same Village	96.5%	100.0%
Married	89.3%	64.0%
Average Number of Years Married	21.2	7.0
Number of Children	5.4	1.4
Resettlement		
Resettled Alone	67.8%	46.0%
Resettled With Some Family Members	24.0%	36.0%
Resettled With Entire Family	8.2%	18.0%
Total Number With Siblings	4.6	4.2
Percent Resettled With Siblings	17.8%	9.1%
Percent With Siblings Living in Sudan	7.0%	4.5%
Percent With Siblings in Ethiopian Army	7.0%	4.5
Percent With Siblings in Prison	3.6%	
Percent With Siblings in TPLF	7.0%	

Economic Background of Respondents (see Table No. 3)

Most of those interviewed in Damazine were farmers whose fathers had also been farmers. A number of young interviewees had continued to farm with their fathers. In some cases, they were studying and not farming at all. In both groups of people interviewed, virtually all those who farmed had livestock. On average the farmers from Tigray owned 22.6 head of large and small animals while the group of respondents from Wollo, etc., owned 16.3 head of animals. About 87 percent of those from Tigray had owned a pair of oxen (necessary for plowing) five years ago. All the others interviewed who owned livestock had owned a pair of oxen five years ago. More than three quarters of all respondents had had a pair of oxen at the time that they were resettled, although about 20 percent in each interview group noted that they would have had to sell the animals to buy food or seed before the next harvest. In this aspect, resettled farmers appear to have had far more assets at the time of resettlement than those famine victims who fled west from Tigray into Sudan in 1984-85 (see Chapter IV).

Those interviewed from Tigray showed a marked increase over their fathers' generation in working as traders or for wages to supplement on-farm income. Those from Wollo, etc., showed much less inclination to work as traders or wage laborers even though a larger percentage earned income from these sources than had their fathers.

Agricultural Production

Depending on the location, 1981, 1982 and 1983 appear to have been the best years for agricultural production in Tigray since the current government took power. More than one quarter of the group who were not from Tigray reported that production had been higher before the present government. Farmers who reported production yields for their best years reported an average of 2,000 kg. This is about one third more than needed for food and seed (1,200 kg) and other necessities (300 kg) for a family of six in an average year.

The 1984 production for the two groups differed. For those from Tigray who harvested their crops in 1984, 14 percent had no harvest, 38 percent

ECONOMIC BACKGROUND OF RESPONDENTS	Tigray	Wollo, etc.
Agriculture		
Father Was a Farmer	96.4%	95.5%
Farmed With Father	10.7%	18.2%
Farmed Alone	89.3%	59.1%
Did Not Farm		22.7%
Livestock		
Father Had Livestock	92.9%	95.5%
Had Livestock With Father	7.1%	13.6%
Had Livestock of His Own	85.8%	63.7%
Had No Livestock	7.1%	22.7%
Respondents With Livestock		
Average Number of Animals (Large and Small)	22.6	16.3
Percent With a Pair of Oxen Five Years Ago	87.5%	100.0%
Percent With a Pair of Oxen When Resettled	75.0%	84.6%
Percent Who Would Have to Sell Oxen to Buy Food or Seed Before the Next Harvest	20.8%	21.4%
Trading		
Father Worked as Trader	7.0%	13.6%
Respondent Worked as Trader	39.0%	22.7%
Wage Labor		
Father Worked for Wages	0.0%	0.0%
Respondent Worked for Wages	17.9%	4.5%

had a small harvest, 35.5 percent an average harvest and 14 percent a good one. About 20 percent of those interviewed had crops but were not allowed to harvest them before they were forcibly resettled. Others had been captured and hence were not allowed to thresh the grain that they had already cut. Those who did harvest their crops, however, reported average yields of nearly three quarters of subsistence needs. In addition to the grain, most of

Table No. 4
AGRICULTURAL PRODUCTION
Year of Best Yield and Yield in 1984

	Tigray	Wollo, etc.
Year of Best Agricultural Production		
Not Asked	3.5%	4.5%
Before 1976	10.7%	27.2%
1979		9.1%
1980	7.1%	9.1%
1981	7.1%	22.7%
1982	25.0%	13.6%
1983	46.4%	9.1%
Yield in Best Year	1,960 kg	2,110 kg
Yield in 1984 (of Those Who Harvested)	891 kg	240 kg

those interviewed had a number of livestock that could be eaten or sold to make up the difference in their families' food needs.

Individuals from Wollo, etc., had less produce (240 kg) and fewer reserve animals. About 20 percent of all those interviewed reported a small harvest and five percent an average harvest. Most of these farmers, however, had also been resettled before they had harvested. While production was certainly low for this group, so were overall food needs. One third of this group was single. In addition, the married individuals who had families averaged only 3.4 people so their food needs would have been about half those of the people from Tigray (700 kg).

Causes of Production Declines (see Tables 5, 6 and 7)
People from Tigray cited insects and drought as the main causes of hunger in 1984. Those from Wollo, etc., indicated that drought was the main problem but that government policies were also an important factor.*
Many indicated that the policies of land distribution in areas held by the government posed a major problem for survival. They explained that the amount of land assigned to a peasant association is fixed, but the number of people who qualify for it increases. Each year women, widows and newly married couples are added. Land had been redistributed several times and this distribution was not equitable.

> The chairman of the peasant union, whose decisions in these matters are final, gave relatives and friends of the members of the executive board the largest and most fertile pieces of land. Those who used bribery could be promoted into this privileged "group of friends" (Niggli 1985a:14).

Interviews with resettled farmers from Tigray indicated that 38 percent complained about irregular or nonexistent rains, 28 percent claimed that armyworms were the cause of a terrible harvest and 24 percent said that without armyworms they would have had a good harvest.
All of the people who commented on their area's soil quality indicated that it was either average or fertile.

Table No. 5
CAUSES OF HUNGER IN 1984

	Tigray	Wollo, etc.
Insects (Armyworm)	30.0%	
Drought	30.0%	68.4%
Insects/Drought	30.0%	
Frost/Drought	3.7%	
Land Reform	3.7%	
Drought/Dergue		13.6%
Government Policies		18.0%

Table No. 6
SOIL QUALITY IN HOMELAND AS REPORTED BY RESPONDENTS

	Tigray	Wollo, etc.
Fertile	57.0%	64.0%
Average	7.0%	
Not Asked	36.0%	36.0%

*When interviewed in detail, the same persons who responded to the survey questions saying that drought and insects had caused their production declines painted a picture that indicated that policy measures had left them vulnerable to these factors where they had not been previously (see Chapters VI and X).

Ethiopian Army and Government Actions in the Respondents' Villages
(see Table No. 7)

More than one third of the persons from Tigray reported that young men had been forcibly conscripted from their villages, crops and houses burned, oxen stolen and civilians killed. One quarter of those from Tigray interviewed reported that the army burned the straw fed to the animals in the dry season. Seven percent also reported that their villages had been bombed. Since every interviewee was not asked each of these questions, these figures should be interpreted as minimal estimates of the army's activities.

Table No. 7
ETHIOPIAN ARMY AND GOVERNMENT ACTIONS
IN THE RESPONDENTS' VILLAGES

	Tigray	Wollo, etc.
Men Forcibly Conscripted Into the Army		
From the Village	35.0%	64.0%
Village Bombed	7.0%	
Crops Burned Near Village	39.3%	
Civilians Killed in Village	35.0%	
Houses Burned in Village	35.0%	
Straw Burned in Village	25.0%	
Oxen and Other Large Animals Stolen From		
Village	39.3%	
Respondent Tortured	4.5%	
Respondent Imprisoned	4.5%	

Nearly two thirds of the people from Wollo, etc., reported that people from their village had been forcibly conscripted. In addition, a few said that they had been tortured or imprisoned. One man from Wollo described how he had been imprisoned and fined E$25 when his father fled to Sudan.

Participants' Accounts of Ethiopian Resettlement: Abduction
and Resettlement Coercion Methods (see Tables 8 and 9)

None of the people interviewed in Demazine had volunteered to resettle. Those from Tigray insisted that they had been captured (their term) for resettlement when (in order of importance):
• Soldiers surrounded their village.
• They went to the feeding centers to get food for their families.
• They were working in their fields.
• They were buying or selling items at the market.
• They were taking their children to the health clinic.
• They were trying to find family members who had disappeared.

A number of those interviewed from Tigray strongly asserted that they had been captured for resettlement when involved in economic activities — working in their fields, threshing grain, selling produce, trading livestock or having their cattle vaccinated. A man from Abi 'Adi (Ahsaa Worreda) reported that his village had received orders from district officials to take their cattle to Adua town to be vaccinated. He reported that some 750 cattle from the area were brought to Adua on the appointed day. The men who brought them were then taken for resettlement by soldiers. He did not know what happened to the cattle that were left behind.

Tigrayan farming families, for the most part, consider it risky to come into contact with the government. They attempt to minimize all contact.

Many of those interviewed said that usually only women or old men were sent to the cities when it was absolutely necessary. It was thought that such people would be less suspect of having cooperated with the TPLF. Furthermore, such people were not normally taken for service in the army.

For the most part, the people from Wollo, Gondar and Shoa reported that they were captured for resettlement when their peasant association sent them to nearby cities to collect food. Later, when peasant association officials came to the cities and did nothing to obtain their release, it became clear that each peasant association was responsible for "nominating" a number of people to be resettled. In the holding camp at Mersa, for example, those interviewed reported that people "nominated" by 38 different peasant associations were being held for resettlement.

Joseph Collins (personal communication) reported that relief workers in Wollo indicated that the peasant association was required to fill its quota of people resettled before it was given famine assistance to distribute locally. In Korem, Collins also witnessed women and children being denied food at two feeding centers. Expatriate relief workers were told by local Ethiopian officials that these women's husbands had escaped from the resettlement camps the week before and that, consequently, they and their children would no longer receive food.

A number of people from Wollo, etc., had been arrested on the road while walking. People from Wollo said they were told, "If you are not willing to go voluntarily, you will be resettled at gunpoint." As one person put it, "Anyone who opposed resettlement in front of the group was taken out and beaten with sticks and guns."

Even among the people from Wollo, where food production among those resettled had been far less than among the Tigrayans, famine appears to be only one of several motives for resettlement. In the relatively productive

Table No. 8
WHERE RESPONDENTS WERE TAKEN FOR RESETTLEMENT

	Tigray	Wollo, etc.
At Home		
Village Surrounded by Soldiers	21.4%	
Working in His Fields	10.7%	
Arrested on Suspicion of Crime		4.5%
	32.1	4.5
Away From Home For Personal Reasons		
Working or Seeking Work	7.2%	4.5%
Trading Between Villages	7.2%	
At a Local Market	10.7%	4.5%
Traveling to Find Children	10.7%	
Traveling		4.5%
Seeking Medical Treatment	3.6%	4.5%
Traveling and Mistaken For Peasant		4.5%
	39.4	22.5
Away From Home at Government's Suggestion		
Attending a Required Meeting	3.6%	
Going to Get Government Food	7.8%	72.7%
Taking Cattle to Be Vaccinated	7.2%	
	18.6	72.7

area of Kobo-Alemata (Raya Kobo), some 20,000 of 160,000 farmers were resettled even though famine was not prevalent in the area (Joseph Collins, personal communication). Kobo-Alemata, however, borders on Tigray and is suspected of having a larger following for the TPLF than other areas of Wollo. Respondents described their area as "TPLF by night and Dergue by day."

Peter Niggli has speculated that the government has resettled a large number of assimilated Oromo from Wollo in order to undermine the OLF's position in southwestern Ethiopia (1985:11). Few of those from Wollo who fled the resettlement camps and were interviewed expressed any allegiance to the government; they saw themselves as its victims.

All those interviewed insisted that they had been captured by government troops and forced to resettle and that considerable coercion was used by the government to force individuals to take part in the program. All those interviewed also reported that armed government troops guarded the "volunteers" from the point of their capture until they arrived at the resettlement sites. Those interviewed insisted that even when they were traveling in enclosed buses, they were accompanied by soldiers. A large portion reported that they were beaten and/or imprisoned after they were captured. Others said that they knew people who had been beaten or imprisoned between the time they were captured and the time they escaped to Sudan. Finally, approximately 10 percent of all those interviewed reported that they saw people killed who tried to escape. Others said that when people tried to escape from the resettlement sites their arms or legs were broken.

Table No. 9
COERCION DURING THE RESETTLEMENT PROCESS

	Tigray	Wollo, etc.
Imprisonment		
1 Time	53.6%	9.1%
2 Times	3.6%	4.5%
3 Times	3.6%	
Not Asked	39.2%	86.4%
Beatings		
Was Beaten	53.6%	27.0%
Witnessed Beatings	14.3%	27.0%
Not Asked	32.1%	46.0%
Saw People Beaten to Death	21.4%	
Saw People Killed Who Tried to Escape	10.7%	9.1%
Not Asked the Question	89.3%	90.9%

Holding Camp Conditions

Many of those captured for resettlement said that they were held in regular prisons with common criminals or in military barracks until transport was arranged. In other cases those to be resettled were placed in holding areas that were usually only a few miles from government feeding centers. Individuals were regularly transferred from feeding centers to holding camps.

Those captured said that local party officials registered them and asked their names and the names of their parents and other family members as well as their residences. Roll calls were held throughout the day to ensure that no one had escaped. In some holding camps, people were called by name and number to be taken on the next leg of the journey, but other camps were less tightly organized.

The names of the dead were deleted from the lists. Anyone that had not died and was not present was placed on a fugitive list. Such lists were used to punish families by denying relatives food at the feeding centers.

People from cities who had been abducted by mistake as well as young children, women past child-bearing age and older men were generally released or transferred to feeding centers. Some interviewees reported that students with identification were also freed. In Tigray, the government selected experienced farmers and women of child-bearing age. Tigrayans captured in Eritrea reported that the government went from house to house searching for Tigrayans who lived and worked in the area. According to the Tigrayans' reports, the government later released any Eritreans they had accidentally captured during these searches.

In Wollo, Shoa and Gondar, generally younger people were captured for resettlement. Some had lived in cities but had no permanent roots there. Most of those taken from Wollo were ethnically Oromo although they no longer spoke the language. They referred to themselves as the "people who have lost even our language."

Many of those resettled had been "nominated" by local peasant association officials. It is not unlikely, therefore, that resettlement became a pretext for such officials to increase their authority by eliminating people who had challenged or might challenge their authority or who were simply different. Most from Wollo, etc., were young men who might have become tempted to support or even join the TPLF. It must be noted that while Wollo is not an exclusively Moslem region, most who are Moslem have Oromo backgrounds (see Chapter II). Those in our sample who were resettled from the area were Moslems.

The government, it appears, also uses the resettlement program to rid the cities of vagrants and new migrants. Some of those from Wollo captured in Addis Ababa, for example, were told that they could return home if they had the cost of transport, E$25. Even though they did not have the money, they were skeptical that they would have been allowed to go home even if they had the money. They saw no one released.

Those captured for resettlement received very little food, "usually one or two (rolls of bread) per day." Some reported, however, that they did not get any food for three days prior to the journey to the resettlement sites. A number of those interviewed who had been at the holding camps nearest their homes reported that family members who knew their location begged officials to let them give food to their relatives. The soldiers refused and even beat many of those who brought food for relatives in the holding camps. Those interviewed stated the opinion that the government wanted to weaken them so that they would not try to escape en route to the resettlement camps.

In addition to the lack of food, there was often little water, although conditions varied from holding site to holding site. In Mai Daero (near Mekele), where some 4,000 to 8,000 people were kept at any point in time, there were two barrels for water distribution. One was for the soldiers' personal use and the other was for washing the soldiers' clothes and for drinking water for those to be resettled. The line for water formed hours before water was even available for distribution. As people attempted to draw a handful of water to drink, they were pushed out of the way by the other people in line.

In general, the distribution of scarce supplies of both food and water pitted people against one another, each fighting for their own or their family's needs. Often, women and children who were not with able-bodied men were denied food and water.

Most holding camps had no latrines. In Mekele, for example, people had to defecate in an open field; they were expected to step over fresh excrement. Camp prisoners were told to cover the feces with dirt each day. In Entichio, detainees were forced to defecate and urinate where they slept. In most holding camps men and women reported being outraged that there was not enough space for them to perform even the most intimate bodily functions in private.

Some people had signs of malnutrition at the time they were taken for resettlement; others experienced hunger for the first time during the resettlement process. The unhygienic conditions compounded the effect of malnourishment. Many of those to be resettled grew weak and became sick in the holding camps. Diarrhea and vomiting were common in the holding centers and en route to the resettlement camps. The sick were rarely separated from the rest of the camp population. Only in Mekele, it appears, were special tents erected for the sick. Those interviewed indicated that in some camps women who gave birth were driven to nearby towns, but this appears to have varied considerably from camp to camp; other women were not given even a piece of cloth.

Many of those interviewed reported that large numbers of people died in the holding camps while waiting to be resettled. In November 1984, when the Mersa camp had nearly 5,000 people, from 25 to 50 people died each day. By December, when the camp's population had grown to between 20,000 and 30,000 people, those interviewed who were in the camp at the time reported that nearly 100 died each day. Most people who passed through the camp at Mekele reported that about five out of every 1,000 died each day. Those interviewed had passed through Mekele from early November until the end of December. Individuals who were captured at the same time as many others from their village reported that as many as 20 percent of those captured from their village during November and December 1984 died in the holding camps before even arriving at the resettlement camps. Bodies of the deceased were evacuated by truck or were buried by people near the holding camps. Often, only the bodies of people who had relatives in the camp were buried. It is not clear from the reports whether the captured individuals' malnourished states or the camp conditions (sleeping outside, little food or water) contributed more to the deaths.

Travel Conditions to the Resettlement Sites (see Tables 10 and 11)

People arrived at the resettlement sites via different routes. Those taken from Tigray and Eritrea were either captured in a city or were forced to walk to the nearest one (see Map 19). There they were taken by helicopter to the nearest city with an airport. From this city they were flown to Addis Ababa, where they were transferred to buses for the three-day journey to the resettlement sites. All buses traveled in convoys and followed the same route and most stopped overnight at the same locations. Helicopters and

Map 19

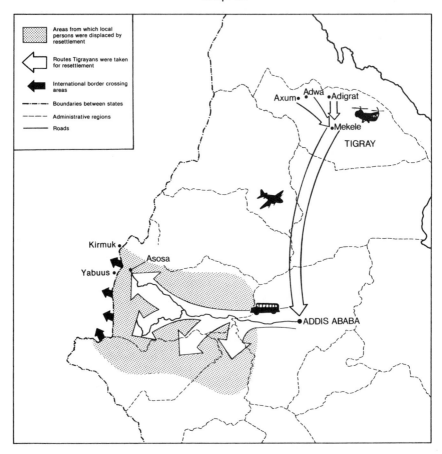

ROUTES OF PERSONS TAKEN FOR RESTTLEMENT FROM TIGRAY

During the 1984-85 Ethiopian Resettlement Program, persons from Tigray were forcibly taken from locations often only marginally controlled by the Ethiopian government. Captives were shuttled from northern holding centers by helicopter to Mekele. From there they were loaded onto Soviet-made Antonov cargo planes and flown to Addis Ababa Bole airport. Here, they were immediately transferred to buses with locked and boarded-up windows and military escorts to begin a three-day journey to resettlement sites. Details of the capture and transfer from interviewed escapees matched whether they had fled from sites in Kefa, Illubabor or Wollega. Those resettled were placed in locations previously inhabited by Oromo, Berta or Anuak agricultural and agro-pastoral peoples. In a few cases, settlers and displaced local residents escaped to Sudan together despite language differences.

airplanes flew many trips per day; truck and bus convoys, of from 30 to more than 100 vehicles, traveled continuously between Addis Ababa or Wollo and the resettlement camps. People detained in the collecting centers in the north could wait for a week or more between parts of the journey. Once the people were transported beyond Addis Ababa, however, they were taken directly to the resettlement camps, stopping only overnight for food and rest before moving on early the next morning. Some resettlement convoys traveled at night; most did not. (Niggli 1985b:15-17).

People were tightly packed onto the various transport vehicles. On average, helicopters carried about 35 people each trip; airplanes 340 people and microbuses about 66 people. About 60 percent of the Tigrayans said that they saw people die during the trip to the resettlement camps. (The remainder were not asked this question. Thus, everyone asked the question had seen people die en route.)

The most serious crowding was on the airplanes. Soviet-made Antonovs, with a 3-by-14-meter carrying space, were designed to carry, at most, 50 paratroopers. Interviewees reported that most of the planes had no seats and that people were lined up across the fuselage and pushed forward, row by row, with a stick. People unfortunate enough to be on the sides of the plane were forced to hang onto an overhead bar so that even the curved floor space underneath them could be used. Interviewees also reported that men standing at the door and sitting on the plane above the door used prods to force as many on the plane as possible. Children were held aloft so that they would not be crushed during takeoff or landing. A number of pregnant women miscarried during or shortly after the trip and when the load shifted during the trip, people were crushed to death.

Those transporting the people by air had another problem to resolve—the door of the Antonov had to be closed from the inside. Apparently none of those responsible for making sure that the maximum number of people was on each plane wanted to travel "packed like a sardine" with the passengers. Eventually, a special seat was attached to the ceiling of the plane so that the one whose job was to close the door could be separated from the other occupants. These people, it was reported, often used their prods to make sure that the occupants did not come too close to them. Only after hearing the descriptions from those who flew on the plane is it possible to understand how people could die in an hour-long plane ride. There was a great deal of suffocation and miscarriage. One woman reported that she had been standing on a person throughout the journey and could not move to get off of him. She expressed great concern that she would never know if he had been dead or alive.

All airplanes landed at Bole airport in Addis Ababa where people with stretchers met the planes to carry those dead and crushed away. Such preparations reveal that officials were aware that stretchers would be needed. This knowledge did not lead to the alteration of travel conditions. Upon arrival, those who disembarked from the plane received a cup of water, which, as one man reported, "was too small even to wash the vomit from the mouth." According to one observer water was not in short supply. Each plane was thoroughly rinsed out with equipment from the Addis Ababa fire department (cited in Niggli 1985a:14). Those who walked away from the airplanes were immediately loaded onto waiting buses. One Tigrayan woman reported caring for another woman who had miscarried on board but who was not allowed to stay overnight in Addis Ababa.

While people waited to be transported further along on their journey to the resettlement camp, they were held in barracks, prison yards, courtyards of official buildings or in bare fields. During the day they were, for the most part, left in areas unprotected from the sun or rain. At night they were left in the open, usually without blankets. Only a few people reported that tents existed at the holding sites for those being resettled.

People from Wollo, Shoa and Gondar were transported by truck and bus for the entire trip (see Map 20). One of those resettled was transported on a new Magirus-Deutz donated to the Ethiopian government for food transport to the famine areas (Niggli 1985a:12). Neither the trucks nor the buses stopped in Addis Ababa. The respondents reported that each truck was used to transport more than 50 people and each bus, more than 70 people. Fifty-nine percent reported that they saw people die en route to the resettlement camps; the remainder were not asked this question.

At Jimma, those to be resettled in Kefa were separated from those going to Illubabor. At both Jimma and Wolkite, remnants of families that had thus far managed to stay together were reported to have been deliberately separated.

During the resettlement process, meticulous lists were maintained of the occupants' names in each vehicle. At the end of each segment of the trip, the dead were deleted from the list. Roll calls were taken in the evening and the morning. People who had escaped were listed as fugitives, a classification that not only affected their own status in Ethiopia, but resulted in their families' being denied food in the feeding centers.

Table No. 10
AVERAGE NUMBER OF PEOPLE PER VEHICLE DURING RESETTLEMENT

	Tigray	Wollo, etc.
Helicopter	35.6	
Airplane	342.0	
Bus	66.2	73.0
Truck	51.8	

Table No. 11
RESPONDENTS WHO WITNESSED DEATHS DURING THE
RESETTLEMENT JOURNEY

	Tigray	Wollo, etc.
Saw People Die En Route to Resettlement Site	60.7%	59.0%
Reported That No One Died En Route to Resettlement Site	0.0%	0.0%
Not Asked This Question (see Chapter III for explanation)	39.3%	41.0%

Westerners and the Resettlement Scheme

While many of those interviewed reported that the holding camps were located in out-of-the-way places, others reported that they were held, initially at least, in feeding centers. Only later were they removed to locations that were distant from the feeding centers. The place one was destined for the resettlement program appears to be the most significant factor in where

Map 20

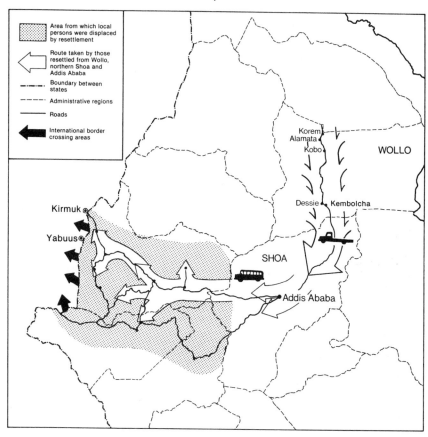

Area from which local persons were displaced by resettlement

Route taken by those resettled from Wollo, northern Shoa and Addis Ababa

Boundary between states

Administrative regions

Roads

International border crossing areas

Korem
Alamata
Kobo
WOLLO
Dessie
Kembolcha
Kirmuk
Yabuus
SHOA
Addis Ababa

ROUTES OF PERSONS TAKEN FOR RESETTLEMENT FROM WOLLO, NORTHERN SHOA AND ADDIS ABABA

Persons taken for the Ethiopian resettlement program in 1984-85 from Wollo Administrative Region were primarily individuals sent ("nominated") by their peasant associations because they had 1) failed to pay taxes for the previous year, 2) had no oxen for cultivation, or 3) volunteered to carry internationally donated grain from distribution centers back to their villages and were informed of their impending resettlement when they asked for the food. In some cases, the entire peasant association was taken for resettlement. A few reported that they had responded to government-sponsored appeals for nominees which emphasized greatly improved standards of living in the resettlement sites. Persons taken from Addis Ababa were captured (their term) as vagrants while seeking employment and assistance in the capital city. From Wollo and Shoa, settlers were transported in trucks and buses to areas formally occupied by indigenous Oromo, Berta and Anuak agriculturalists and agro-pastoralists. The journey generally took three to five days.

one was initially held; those captured at the feeding centers were usually held there for some time, while those captured near their homes were often taken to military barracks or jails.

At the time people were captured for resettlement they often believed there must have been a mistake. They selected spokesmen from among themselves and wrote petitions to local officials. It soon became clear, however, that there was no mistake. Those who opposed resettlement were beaten. Outspoken resisters were moved far away from the area where Westerners were allowed. In some cases, they were locked up in buildings. Only the meek, quiet people were allowed to see Western journalists or agency officials. When those to be resettled were allowed to talk to the Westerners, cadre officials instructed them to say that they were moving voluntarily. One cadre official, Agadon, was reported to have said,

> White guests are coming, you have to say, "We have come because of famine and drought. We are voluntary. We want to be resettled in the west." Whether you speak positively or negatively now, we will tell the journalists you are saying you want to be resettled.

When the spokesmen of one group openly declared in Tigrinya, in front of Western journalists, that the people were not voluntarily relocating, the journalists could not understand. Later, the spokesmen were beaten and put in prison.

Individuals from Wollo also said that they were not able to talk freely with whites who came to visit them at the holding camps. According to one man,

> ... 10 whites took pictures of us in Kembolcha and then left on a helicopter without talking to us. At Kembolcha, other white people took pictures and gave blankets and cups. They were Dominicans. They couldn't speak to us; they were too far away and we were surrounded by soldiers. . . . In Asosa, we were told, "If white people are asking you what are your problems, you say, 'There are no problems.' If not, we will punish you."

One man reported that at the end of December, almost all of those in the Mekele holding camp were moved to a remote valley.

> Only some 100 people from Raya Azebo remained back in the camp. Most of them had suffered from a terrible drought and were more or less prepared to be resettled since they saw no other hope. My friend and I thought the Raya were being rewarded for their good conduct and so we remained in the camp to receive the same reward. Then the soldiers took off their uniforms and put on old, used clothes and put pistols under their belts. In these costumes they mixed in with us.
>
> In the distance a pair of white trucks with red crosses painted on the sides drove up. First a band from Mekele played some music, then the administrator spoke, probably about how we were starving and wanted to be resettled. Then an old person protested, a very old man from Enderta. He cried out in Tigrinya that no one wants to be resettled and these poor people here are only a fraction of all the people normally in this camp waiting for their forced resettlement. Laughing, the party official went up to the old man, took him by the hand, and said, "What are you crying about? You are much too old. Do you really think we would resettle you? No, we will give you food to eat and drive you back to your village. Come, sit here near me on this chair. Your place is not among those people who want to be resettled." . . . When the delegation had gone away, the man was beaten and later resettled.

Interviewees reported a number of forms of punishment for resisters which ranged from killings to lesser forms of physical abuse to humiliation. The following forms of punishment were reported in the holding camps:
• killings
• torturing in prisons
• beatings with rifle butts and rods and sticks
• running over thorns or lying or rolling in thorn bushes
• crawling on hands and knees for long periods of time
• throwing water on the victim and then making him roll in the dirt
• tying two people together and forcing them to roll in the dirt
Victims were, in the end, freed, but they were not given water to wash themselves or their clothes. Most punishments were performed in front of the other camp residents to serve as a warning to them. However, in Adua, the local administrator became so enraged when most camp residents refused to be resettled that he sent 1,000 to prison. Here they were made to "walk" back and forth across the prison courtyard on their knees. The most severe punishments, however, were reserved for those who attempted to escape.

Conditions in the Asosa Resettlement Sites

Interviewees who had been sent to Asosa were shocked by the conditions at the resettlement sites. One respondent explained,

> When I saw Asosa, I realized that I had been cheated. I thought about committing suicide; I don't understand much about government matters, but I thought it would be better to die than to live under such a government. Then, I wanted to escape at any cost.

As another interviewee described it, Asosa was like a "veritable hell." Another explained, "Around us grew grass and bamboo as tall as men. I felt like garbage that one had dropped in the middle of nowhere" (Niggli 1985a:18).

The city of Asosa is the capital of the most western district of Wollega administrative region. The district was traditionally inhabited by a small population of Bertha except in the south where Oromo agriculturalists prevail. By 1979, about 1,000 Bertha fled the area as government troops prepared for the first resettlement in the regime. From 1979 to 1980, about 20,000 to 25,000 people were transported to the region and resettled in the area by the Ethiopian government (see Dines 1982). Eshetu and Teshome (1984) report that in 1983, the RRC estimated that there were about 7,200 families in the Asosa camps. Given that people also resettled in the area from 1982 to 1983, it is likely that a number either died or fled the camps.

According to current RRC plans, more than 100,000 people are to be settled in Asosa from Tigray and Wollo. By January 1985, about 42,000 had already been transported there (according to an interview by Niggli with Fikre Selassie Warre, an RRC administrator in Asosa who had defected and fled to Damazine, Sudan). The 1985 resettlement initially occurred on the 1,700-meter plateau to the north and south of Asosa. As it proved easy for people to escape to Sudan from these locations, resettlement camps were relocated to the east in the lowlands from Dabus-Tals to Bambesi in camps that were as far as 50 km east of Asosa.

Each settlement of 500 families is intended to cultivate 2,500 hectares of land (Radio Addis Ababa, 19 January 1985). According to Fikre Selassie Warre, more than 100 such sites are planned for Asosa alone. If these plans are implemented, 250,000 hectares will be cleared in Asosa, an area that is more than twice the size of all resettlement sites in Ethiopia in 1982 combined (Eshetu and Teshome 1984). Forest experts in the Asosa area, who have not been given any role in the resettlement, are worried about the effects of such massive clearing. According to former workers in the Ministry of Agriculture in Asosa, specialists in the area have already recommended reforestation measures. One of the ironies of the presentation of resettlement as a solution to famine is that the program is quite likely to cause problems similar to those it was said to be solving — deforestation and soil erosion. An Oromo man who had seen settlers come to the Angar settlement in heavily forested northern Wollega commented, "The land in Tigray and Wollo is dry. If those people come here our land will also be dry. We loved it and saved it, but settlers cleared the forest [in Angar River area settlement] and the rains stopped."

A much-publicized aspect of the resettlement scheme in Asosa was the proposed irrigation system that would enable producers to harvest two or three crops per year. This has been promoted internationally and was cited by government officials in their attempts to convince people to move to the sites. Asosa has very limited irrigated agriculture. The former RRC official now in Sudan told Niggli that recent studies indicate that the required amounts of water for irrigated agriculture in the region are not available from rivers or underground sources on a year-round basis.

Interviewees reported that more than 40 different *ambas* (the Amharic word for resettlement villages) in the Asosa region already exist, but those interviewed only represented about a dozen. Each site was eventually to serve as a new village with its own mills, schools, clinics and stores and about 6,000 to 9,000 people. While many people had been moved to resettlement sites that had names, no infrastructure existed except on paper. *Ambas* are divided into sites that included about 500 colonists. Each site was divided, in turn, into work squads of 25 people. All planning and work was based on these units.

Members of the political cadres ran these resettlement villages and were responsible for the camp organization and work structure. According to one interviewee, each *amba* had 14 cadre members armed with pistols. Each site within the *amba* also had about five militiamen armed with rifles or machine guns.

It appears from the interviews that people from Wollo, Shoa and Gondar arrived first in Asosa. Nearly 60 percent of this group reported that there were no houses when they arrived; another 10 percent reported that there were not enough houses. These first settlers built houses where there were none or where the number was insufficient. They also dug latrines. The first priority at new sites was to build houses and beds for the militia. Those resettling in the area slept in the open until large collective houses could be constructed, which held 200 to 300 people. Many would have preferred to sleep in the open air rather than the overcrowded group houses, but that was not allowed. This is in contrast to the holding camps, where people had to sleep outside. They observed that it was easier for the militia to guard the settlers when they were all in a single house.

Those who arrived first "moved like locusts" through the environment. They were ordered to cut all the grass and bamboo they could find. They also gathered grass and cut bamboo poles that were trucked to other sites for house construction. When the houses on one site were completed, the first settlers were moved to another where they began the process again. In order for settlers to be closely guarded, the houses were constructed so close together that they often posed serious fire hazards. Hundreds of huts reportedly burned, the few possessions of many people were lost and scores of people died in these fires — particularly the people who were sick or near death due to starvation and could not escape.

Upon their arrival in resettlement sites, colonists, alone or in groups, were given a machete and hoe as well as some other basic farming and household equipment. Much of the equipment, which was in short supply, was second hand, indicating it had come from other farmers — probably ones already living in the area. Pans and metal sheets used for cooking were so limited that the colonist had to use them in shifts, beginning at 2 a.m., in order to finish cooking the day's meals before leaving for work at 6 a.m. Usually there was one cooking pan for 25 people, but in some cases there was only one pan for 100 people. Some settlers were forced to use shovels as cooking utensils.

Persistent Food Shortages at the Resettlement Sites

Interviewees were outraged by the small amount of food that they received at the settlements after they arrived. Each person, they said, was given a supply of whole corn or wheat flour that they were told was to last a month. These monthly grain rations varied from five kg per month per adult to a maximum of 25 kg per month. Even the largest rations reported were woefully inadequate for a population working 12 hours per day six and a half days per week. The food needs of some of the population in the camps were even higher than might normally have been expected because of their malnourished state at the time of their resettlement, due both to the withholding of food during the resettlement process and to the hard labor required of them.

It is not clear why there appear to have been such differences in the amount of food given to residents of the different camps. No doubt, food was always in short supply. In addition, many camp administrators did not know of the arrival of new settlers until they saw the buses approach. Often convoys of buses contained 2,000 to 3,000 people who had be be fed and sheltered.

The grain distributed was usually packed in sacks on which was written, "Food Aid of the European Economic Community to the People of Ethiopia." Some of those who had escaped to Damazine made clothes of such sacks (we saw many of these among refugees in Demazine). Officials in the camp explained to those asking for more food that the government had requested more food assistance from a number of countries, but that they had to be patient because it had not arrived yet. One man reported that a cadre official in his camp said, "Don't eat your rations at once, just savor the taste and smell of the grain in case you don't have any more at the end of the month and there will be nothing left to eat but dirt" (Niggli 1985a:21).

Only one man reported being paid for work in the resettlement sites — picking coffee — although a number said that they had been told that the amount of food they received was based on the amount of work they did. Productivity was rewarded, in some sites at least, with extra rations of oil and salt while poor work performances could result in the reduction of food rations. The work performances of the sick or malnourished often meant that their rations were reduced even though they needed them more than other camp residents. A black market for food existed in many resettlement sites. New arrivals often had to spend whatever money they brought with them on purchases of food until they received their rations. If they had food, then they often had to use some of it to "rent" pans in which to cook it. Even the military guards got involved in the food black market, demanding that settlers give them personally the rations which would have gone to those who died or to those who had escaped from the camps. Often the military demanded the return of far larger food rations for "missing" people than anyone in the camp had ever been given, but to protest brought beatings.

Perhaps the best indication of the lack of food in the camps is that priests for the old settlers as well as the new no longer advise their followers to observe fasts, an especially important Coptic Christian belief.

In addition to food, those interviewed reported other needs (clothes, soap, etc.) but no income with which to buy such things. Some interviewees reported that they cut firewood without permission, made their way to Asosa town and sold it to make money for food and other essentials. However, officials and guards attempted to limit these activities. One man said he was imprisoned for selling some of his tools to buy cigarettes:

> Some of the previous settlers in the area instructed us [the newcomers] to 'work hard and improve your life.' But they walk around like very poor people. They get only a share of their harvest. Some still seem to be in the same clothes they arrived in three years ago.

Reports from the people who escaped from the resettlement sites indicate that some of the previous settlers, who were living in some sites at the time of the 1985 settlement, were required to give their entire harvest (teff, sorghum, maize, wheat, peppers, tomatoes, potatoes, onions) to the government. In return for the more valuable crops they had raised, they received maize for their subsistence needs.

Others who had been resettled to the areas prior to 1984 explained a different system. They indicated that, for example, their site's produce filled seven graneries — five went to the government and two were reserved for the use of the settlers. Settlers received no payment for the crops that they produced which were taken by the government. The amount of food the settlers were allowed to retain did not meet their subsistence needs. Similarly, those interviewed reported that previous settlers were allowed to raise sheep but could only keep five for themselves. The rest went uncompensated to the government. The government's explanations are not clear to the settlers. Settlers point out, however, that in the present system they are forced to work without compensation as slaves.

The Collectivization of Agriculture

The resettlement sites are technically under the direction of the RRC, but, in fact, the program seems to be directed by the local political cadres; the RRC affiliation is designed to make it more acceptable to potential Western donors. While those who were resettled were originally told by government officials that they would be private landowners in the south, each site about which we have first-hand information is organized into a producers' cooperative. Legally, members of such cooperatives are entitled to rights of property and the disposal of their products.

The Cost of the Resettlement Program

The Ethiopian cost of any resettlement program is staggering; however, as of January 1985, the government had not budgeted any existing funds for resettlement. Those resettled prior to 1983 cost the government approximately E$1,400 per person (for clothing, food, housing and household materials). For the slightly more than 100,000 people who were resettled, the total cost would have reached about E$150 million. To move the 1.5 million people scheduled for relocation in 1985 even at the pre-1983 rates, would cost about E$2.1 billion (the entire Ethiopian budget was only E$2.9 billion in 1982). These figures do not include transportation, perhaps the most costly item of all.

Joseph Collins (personal communication) reported that in Addis Ababa in January 1985, the figure of E$5,000 per person was estimated to be the actual cost of the resettlement program excluding transportation. In addition to the fundamental question about less expensive, better programs that might be undertaken in the homelands of those being resettled, is the basic question of who is paying for the program. There are three possible answers — the Ethiopian government transferred funds from other programs (even perhaps famine assistance), other countries have financed the program, or the previous residents in the resettlement areas have had to provide for the newcomers. Radio Addis Ababa reported that, "Citizens who live in the area who have been chosen for resettlement, must help to contribute to the realization of the resettlement action, they must give whatever support is considered necessary" (7 December 1984). The impact of the resettlement program on indigenous peoples of the targeted areas is discussed in Chapters VII and IX but is taken up specifically in Chapter VIII.

In the coffee-producing area of Metu, Illubabor, three peasant associations were required to build and equip houses for the new settlers and to provide them with food for the first three days. Tigrayans report that Oromo farmers in the area were forced to transport even the government-provided grain to the resettlement sites. In the resettlement sites near Giba, Begi Wollega administrative unit, the local Oromo peasant associations were required to build 800 houses, provide 36 kg of grain per settler and bring oxen for the settlers. In addition each farmer had to contribute E$5 for the program.

Peter Niggli writes that approximately 15 percent (that would be 225,000 people) of those to be resettled in the southwest and west are destined to live in existing villages and join directly local peasant associations. Such an arrangement would call for a direct implementation of what has been a generally applied formula, i.e., each 12 households in a peasant association build and provision three new houses for the settlers. The local population provides colonists with food and the tools necessary to set up their houses and farm in that proportion. Since the land available to peasant associations is reportedly fixed in size the implications of an overnight change in land distribution are clear. (This issue is taken up in Chapter VIII).

Work Conditions in the Resettlement Sites

RRC officials' projections for the producers' cooperatives in the Asosa area are that they will attain financial independence after three years. However, 10-year-old resettlement sites have yet to become financially independent (Eshetu and Teshome 1984), so it is unlikely that the new ones will do so in such a short time. Warre, the RRC defector whom Niggli interviewed, suggested that it would take 10 years or longer for settlers to achieve food self-sufficiency (1985a:35).

According to a refugee who had been settled in Asosa in the early 1980s, some work in the older settlements is mechanized; for example, plowing, sowing and some cultivating is done by tractor. Most of the harvesting, weeding and threshing is done by hand. About 100 tractors were supplied to the Asosa resettlement sites in January 1985. The drivers and mechanics were recruited from among the settlers and trained in Asosa. These workers, who could be considered an elite of sorts among the work force at the resettlement site, receive 25 kg each of corn and sorghum per month as well as two cups of peppers and a half liter of oil. If they sold all their grain in the Asosa market they would recieve E$20 for it. By way of comparison, manual agricultural laborers in Tigray receive E$1.5 to E$3 per day; office boys, houseboys or cleaners in Addis Ababa receive about E$95 per month. Yet, "privileged, trained" workers in Asosa receive much less for their work and, in addition, have to barter away some of their grain every month to acquire other essential food items (onions, salt, sugar, tea) as well as many non-food items (clothes, tools, medicine).

In the resettlement sites, work is undertaken by teams. As soon as work gangs receive their instructions, they begin their tasks. Settlers recounted that often they had to walk six km to get to the fields. They had to arise at 2 a.m. in order to cook the amount of food required on the limited cooking equipment. They left at 6 a.m. and worked until 2 p.m. They took one hour off at which time they consumed the cold lunch that they had arisen to prepare. Then they worked again until 6 p.m. When the people returned home from their work, they were required to bury the dead before they could prepare their evening meal. Many reported that not a single day passed without burials. (These people were able to provide detailed accounts of the numbers of deaths occurring in the camps.) People in the camps were required to work six and a half days per week. On Sunday afternoons and evenings, meetings were held at each site with local cadre officials who discussed the past week's work performance and outlined goals for the coming week.

While the settlers were told in the orientation meetings prior to their resettlement that they would get their own farm land, in Asosa they found that they were expected to work communally and that the farms they were establishing would be run communally. Some of the new colonists reported that they were forced to harvest corn and teff on neighboring state farms without payment.

Some settlers reported harvesting crops from fields that officials told them were now government lands. They reported that they never saw the ones who had planted or tended the crops. One man reported that members of his site worked for a month harvesting coffee, and that they were paid E$.50 per day (the average daily wage for agricultural labor in Tigray at the time these settlers were captured was E$1.5 to E$3.00 per day). No one else reported receiving any payment for their labor. For the most part, people were put to work clearing fields and preparing them for planting. A few of those interviewed reported that at their sites there was no organized work. There were few oxen or plows available to the colonists, so most clearing and preparing of land was done by hand with hoes. It appears that different sites were designated for different crops. Colonists at some sites prepared land for planting corn, others for planting potatoes. None of the sites, it appears, were intended to produce a wide range of food crops or even to be self-sufficient in food production.

Mortality Rates in the Resettlement Camps

We did not anticipate that the refugees would have witnessed such consistently high death rates and therefore did not prepare the research design to uniformly ask the refugees about the details of their observations in such a way that we could compare them systematically. Yet virtually all interviewees reported that many people died at different stages of the journey to the resettlement camps as well as in the camps. Following are some of their specific observations, which do not include the deaths that took place in the holding centers reported above.

- In one site of 6,000 people, 92 people died in one day.
- In a site of 500 people, 13 to 14 people died each day.
- In another resettlement village of 6,000 people, 20 to 25 people died each day.
- At another site of 500 people, 40 to 50 people died of natural causes in the first week; another 10 were beaten to death.
- At a different site of 500, 50 people died and 10 were beaten to death.
- In *Amba* (settlement site) 15, 30 to 50 people died each day.
- In *Amba* 9, about 500 people, out of an estimated total of 6,000 to 7,000, died during the first two and a half months.
- In one camp, 1,500 people out of 7,000 died in the first two and a half months.
- There were 50 deaths reported in 500 families in one month.
- There were numerous reports of 10, 20 to 25, or 30 to 40 deaths daily in their immediate vicinity. [The total population was unclear.]
- One 65 year old man reported that he was responsible for burials and they often took a full day to complete.
- Many said that they had to bury people every night after work.

Two observations included deaths at the holding centers as well as at the resettlement sites.

- Of 40 people resettled from Raya Azoba, seven died by the time one man fled for Sudan.
- Of 32 people resettled from Agame and Eucheta, seven died.

In one site near Asosa, people from Wollo who had been resettled in the area three years before had died in great numbers, but the government had used the site again anyway. New people were brought in to replace those who died, and the site continued to experience high death rates.

The death rates reported by the refugees ranged from 33 deaths per 10,000 people per day to 270 deaths per 10,000 people per day. These rates are extremely high given that the camp populations were composed almost entirely of adults. Such figures were consistently reported from a number of different refugees from different areas. Furthermore, they were relayed by people who did not know each other. Some of the resettled people were undoubtedly malnourished as a result of declining agricultural production in their homelands, but many had not experienced famine until they were captured for resettlement. In attempting to explain the high death rate, perhaps it is more important to note that the settlers received miniscule amounts of food for as long as a month before they arrived in the resettlement camps and then were expected to work 11 hours each day for six and a half days each week. In addition, many of the settlers were forced to sleep in open fields for up to a month until their houses were constructed. Finally, there were probably a number of diseases that would account for high death rates in the resettlement sites to which colonists had little or no resistance.

Although these estimates of the death rate must be treated with caution, they are the best data to date. Given the serious implications of these figures, independent corroboration should be sought immediately. These figures raise, among other issues, the question of how many of the 400,000 people who were resettled by June of 1985 are still alive. If even the most conservative estimates of the death rate (33 per 10,000 per day) are reduced by half to allow for possible exaggeration or error and then reduced by half again to allow for decline in the rate of mortality (i.e., reduced by 75 percent), then 50,000 to 100,000 of those resettled in this massive program may have already been dead by July 1985. Clearly such findings demand further investigation. Refugees, however, when asked about the future of resettlement repeatedly insisted that "Everyone will be dead or gone by next year."

Security in the Resettlement Sites

The Ethiopian Workers Party has recruited more than 500 cadre members who are politically responsible for the camps in Asosa alone. Each cadre member is equipped with a pistol, an item that has become a standard, ubiquitous feature of their uniform. It is treated as a sign of prestige and authority. Cadre members — who live in nearly all the sites — live separately from the colonists and even from the militia. The newly arrived settlers had to build separate huts for cadre and militia in each site. These huts usually had corrugated iron roofs and sometimes were even made of stone, not grass and bamboo, which were used for the colonists' huts. Women and girls among the new settlers had to carry water and prepare food, which was often brought from the nearest towns for the cadre and militia. The militia received extra rations and were the first to get oil, onions, milk and eggs.

The cadre members are charged with organizing camp security and the colonists' work. As one escapee reported, "The cadres organize the militia who organize us." According to the refugees, the cadres exhibited no basic knowledge in agriculture, plants, soils, forests or any associated expertise.

This observation was also made by journalists and then international visitors who were taken by bus to Asosa in January 1985.

"Where are the agronomists and foresters?" asked one embassy official on the tour. "Where are the agricultural extension officers, the water engineers, the public health officials and the ecologists to explain to us how they're going to prevent the kind of environmental catastrophe that took place in the north from occurring here?"

"It looks like it's the party bureaucrats and not the technocrats who are running this show and I'm not at all convinced they know what they're doing," the embassy officials said.... (*The New York Times*, 21 January 1985).

Some of those resettled reported that cadre officials forbade the settlers to show provincial administrators or visitors from Addis Ababa around the sites. The militia enforced this command. The cadre, refugees believed, did not want the conditions in the camp to be held against them personally and affect their future in Ethiopia. So they told all visitors that those resettled were well fed and in good condition. In this way, visitors did not have to be confronted with the reality of the sites or figure out who was to blame. There appeared to be a tacit agreement not even to raise the issue.

During the past five years, the Asosa area was used to resettle people who were mostly from Wollo (see Chapter IX). The new colonists, those settled in 1984-85, were not allowed to interact with previous settlers. New settlers reported that the militia guarded them. Trusted individuals from previous groups of settlers filled the militia ranks—interviewees indicated that most spoke Amhara and/or were from Wollo, although there were reports of some Tigrays, Oromos and Kunamas serving in the militia. The ratio of militia in each site varied from one per 12 colonists to one per 100 colonists. This ratio depended on how close the site was to the Sudan border.

The militia knew that the benefits they received as a result of their role in the camps (better food, housing and freedom of movement) would be rescinded if they did not do their job well. In some cases, militia were beaten in front of the camp residents in order to make this point clear. One escapee reported that three militia in his site accused of letting colonists escape were publicly hung. The militia took such examples to heart. "The main job of the militia is to kick us," explained one escapee. Or as another put it, "Militia are forced to beat us, otherwise they will be killed or forced to join us in the hard work. When they have beaten us, they sometimes hide, even cry."

In the resettlement sites, approximately 10 young men from each group of 500 reportedly will be selected to train for the militia. Some new settlers from Wollo explained that members of the militia told them that they would later be militia, but for the time being, they were to work in the fields as farmers and form cooperative farms. It was those chosen on good behavior who lived in better housing, received weapons, ate oil, onions, eggs and milk, and were allowed freedom of movement.

Each site of 500 people was ordered to choose "leaders." These leaders were supposed to report to the camp militia and cadre members on behalf of the entire group. One man described the implications of this system: "We didn't want to elect leaders. Those people would be personally responsible for all who escaped. So, the government had to appoint leaders."

Many of the non-Wollo settlers complained about the old and new settlers from Wollo. One said, "All the youngsters from Wollo are militias. They enjoy giving orders." Others reported that "the Wollos" were settled to the west of the Tigrayans, putting them between the Tigrayans and the Sudan border. Tigrayans said that it was people from Wollo who reported when other settlers tried to escape. As one man from Tigray explained, "Wollos would always say that they came voluntarily. In return, they get salt, oil and flour. They were trusted. They always informed on us." Those from Wollo who escaped reported that most Wollo colonists were amazed at the Tigrayan settlers' courage. On occasion those from Wollo would comment on the Tigrays as a group.

> The Tigrayans were quite different from us. They would refuse to touch a tool. They fled as soon as they reached the camp, but we were herded like sheep to the workplace. I have seen 450 Tigrayans brought to the Asosa prison for refusing to do even minimal work. They are tough.

People who did not follow the cadre's or militia's orders or the camp rules were beaten and sometimes imprisoned. Beatings occurred, for example, when people urinated without permission or defecated in the wrong place. People were also beaten if they slowed the rate of work in the fields. One woman said she was beaten when she tried to rest. In one site, 450 Tigrayans who refused to work were all imprisoned in Asosa.

Escape from the Resettlement Sites

Most interviewees said they had thought about escape since the day of their capture. Some escaped immediately; others spent more than two months waiting for the right time to leave for Sudan. Most of those from Wollo, Shoa and Gondar escaped in small groups of seven or eight people. Usually everyone in these groups made it safely to Sudan. People from Tigray usually attempted to escape en masse. Their groups averaged more than 80 people; only about three quarters ever arrived in Sudan. Many died, were left on the way to die or were captured by local residents or militia.

Plans for the Future (see Table No. 12)

Virtually all the interviewees said that they wanted to return to their villages and families. Those from Tigray wanted to return with the assistance of the TPLF. Most of the others wanted to return with the UNHCR's assistance. More than a quarter of the others, however, wanted to return only when the government had changed. When asked what the best solution would be to their problem, all the Tigrayans interviewed said a change in government. Likewise, all but one from the Wollo area gave the same reply.

Table No. 12
PLANS FOR THE FUTURE

	Tigray	Wollo, etc.
Total Who Want to Return	96.4%	95.5%
Yes	21.4%	31.8%
Yes, With the TPLF	71.4%	4.5%
Yes, With the TPLF and the UNHCR	3.6%	
Yes, With the UNHCR		31.8%
Yes, If the Government Changes		27.3%
Not Asked	3.6%	4.5%
Best Solution to Predicament		
Rainfall		4.5%
Change the Government	63.3%	45.4%
Not Asked the Question	35.7%	50.1%

Chapter VI

CONDITIONS FACED BEFORE AND AFTER RESETTLEMENT: SUPPLEMENTARY DATA FROM PERSONS INTERVIEWED WHILE IN TRANSIT TO DAMAZINE HOLDING CAMP

Although our research design called for the random sampling of camp populations of refugees from Ethiopia currently in Sudan, the decision was made to also interview refugees present in Sudan but not found in a camp setting and to present their data separately (see Map 21). This chapter (and Chapter VIII) presents the results of such encounters. These interviews fell into two groups.

The first category of people interviewed had been segregated by the Sudanese authorities and were held in a small building in Kirmuk waiting to be sent north to Damazine to join the refugee population in that holding camp. These people had escaped from resettlement sites in Ethiopia and had expressed a desire to return home. They consisted of nine individuals from Wollo traveling together, and six more who arrived later.

The second category of refugees reported in this section is a group of 14 Tigrayans who had been taken as settlers to Illubabor and had escaped and walked to Sudan. They were en route to Kirmuk, where they would be registered and sent on to the Damazine holding camp for refugees from the resettlement camps. They wanted to return to the north of Sudan and trek home. We interviewed this group in Yabuus the day they crossed the border.

The information from these two different sets of resettlement escapees provides a check on the validity of the data acquired from the refugees interviewed through a random sample of the Damazine camp population. It is highly unlikely that the Sudanese, TPLF or anyone else in Sudan could have affected the testimony of these new arrivals as they theoretically might have been able to do in the camps.

Interviewing transients presents a methodological challenge. Even under the best of circumstances random sampling can be a time-consuming enterprise entailing surveys of regions or camps, and controlled selection of the interviewees if done in a scientific fashion. In this section data were collected from all escapees as they were encountered and as time (their leaving for another location or our catching transport) permitted. In some cases interviews could not be completed, and in other instances, individuals arrived as we were leaving.

While the 15 individuals from Wollo were being interviewed, 14 others arrived who could not be surveyed due to time and logistical constraints. Thirty other people resettled from Tigray had left Kirmuk for the Damazine holding camp only hours before our arrival. They had been sent in a merchant truck hired by Sudanese authorities. Those from Wollo were to be sent to Damazine eventually but the Tigrayans had been given priority due to a problem: although starving — one had died — the Tigrayans refused to

Map 21

MOVEMENT OF RESETTLEMENT ESCAPEES AND PERSONS
DISPLACED BY RESETTLEMENT FROM WHOM CULTURAL
SURVIVAL OBTAINED EYEWITNESS ACCOUNTS

eat meat killed by the Moslems in Sudan due to their Orthodox Christian
religious beliefs. The exasperated Sudanese had arranged to transport them
to Damazine where the TPLF-managed camp could accommodate their
needs.

Our objective in talking to transient refugees in Kirmuk and Yabuus was
to compare the general accounts given by these people with those given by
refugees sampled in camps. The interviews resulted in both confirmation of
some information and discovery of new factors and perspectives. It also
revealed some new areas and topics to be investigated by further research.

TRANSIENT SETTLERS FROM WOLLO INTERVIEWED IN KIRMUK

The 15 refugees who fled the resettlement camps in Wollega and were interviewed en route through Kirmuk were physically weak and their clothes
were in tatters. Only four carried small bundles of possessions; the re-

mainder were empty-handed. One man drank water from a gourd and remarked that he had carried this with him in Addis Ababa when he was captured for resettlement. He said that he had managed to hold onto the gourd even in the camps, though none of the others had containers in which to carry water—"They had to go to the river each time they needed to drink." One woman carried an eight-month-old child on her hip. There were no other children.

Personal History of Respondents (see Tables 1, 2 and 3)

The average age of the 15 refugees in this group was 20.5 years (excluding the child). While all were from the Wollo administrative region, 14 were from Yejju and one from Raya Kobo. All of them said that their fathers and grandfathers were from the same place. They were all Moslem—although one man said that he had been Christian at home. He had changed his affiliation when it had become problematic in the preceding few days to obtain food properly slaughtered and prepared according to Orthodox Christian procedures. Unlike the Tigrayans who had been sent on to Damazine by truck that morning, he had not refused to eat what was brought to him by Moslems. In his opinion, and that of the others as well, that made him a Moslem and he identified himself as such. His family, he noted, was not Moslem.

All of the refugees spoke Amharic; one spoke Oromo as a first language and Amharic as a second. The others who were interviewed in Kirmuk—nine of the total—launched into a discussion about language and identity. They pointed out that although they spoke Amharic, they were not Amhara. "We are people who have forgotten our own language," they said, referring to Oromo. Their fathers' and grandfathers' names were more

Table No. 1
PERSONAL HISTORY OF RESPONDENTS FROM WOLLO
(via Wollega)
INTERVIEWED IN KIRMUK

Average Age	20.5 years
Sex of Respondent	
Male	93.3%
Female	6.7%
Geographical Origin	
Yejju, Wollo	93.3%
Raya Kobo, Wollo	6.7%
Religion	
Moslem	93.3%
Christian-Moslem	6.7%
Languages Spoken	
Amharic	93.3%
Oromo Amharic	6.7%
Literacy Rate of Respondents	13.3%
Amharic	13.3%
Literacy Program	6.7%
School	6.7%

often than not Oromo names, and their language contained a large number of Oromo words. Two from this group were literate in Amharic; one had attended formal school and one had learned in the Dergue's literacy program. The remainder were illiterate.

There were 14 men and one woman in this group. Five of the men reported being married with a wife and children at home who had no idea what had happened to them. The only woman in the group had been taken for resettlement with her husband when their entire peasant association was taken, but the husband had been sent to another place. Through the assistance of neighbors from home who had been taken at the same time and resettled in the same site, the woman was able to escape with her baby.

Table No. 2
FAMILY HISTORY OF RESPONDENTS

Born in Same Village as Father and Father's Father	100.0%
Marital Status	
Married	33.0%
Single	67.0%
Average Number of Children	3.8
Average Number of Children in Sudan	.2

Table No. 3
HOW THOSE INTERVIEWED WERE CAPTURED FOR RESETTLEMENT

Entire Peasant Association Taken	40.0%
While Looking For Work in Addis Ababa	60.0%

Economic Background of Respondents (see Table 4)

Six of those interviewed (40 percent) claimed to have been farmers at home but said that they were unable to live on what they produced. In the past few years they had taken up activities such as preparing and selling charcoal—though they saw this as an activity within the range of what a farmer would do. In other words, they did not identify themselves as wage earners or traders, though they had not been able to survive on farming per se during the preceding two years. Comparing their answers relating to occupation with the information they gave concerning their attempts to provide for themselves and their families, it appears that "farming" was given more as an identity than as a description of recent work performed to fulfill and sustain their needs. Seven of these people said they had been farmers who had to leave home in order to look for work. Two identified themselves as wage earners; one spent several years on a government-run state farm. Only three said that their fathers had worked for wages.

Table No. 4
ECONOMIC BACKGROUND OF RESPONDENTS

Occupation	
Farmer	40.0%
Farmer/Wage Earner	47.0%
Wage Earner	13.0%
Father's Occupation	
Farmer	80.0%
Farmer/Wage Laborer	20.0%

Causes of Famine

The intensive interview with nine of these refugees was conducted as a group discussion. In response to a question about the causes of famine in their regions, one man would answer at length and those listening were invited to add more detail to his account or to supply contradictory or contrasting information from their experiences if appropriate. All had been surveyed.

When asked to explain the causes of famine in their home regions, these refugees from Wollo reported that they had not had adequate rain in the past two years to grow their food. They also said armyworms attacked crops that managed to grow. Yet when questioned in depth, those interviewed went on to explain that neither of these factors was the main reason for the problem they faced.* The rains, they said, are very uncertain in their country. Throughout the time of their fathers and in their own lifetimes, there have been periodic rainfall shortages. In the past, they planned for such periods by storing surplus grain from bumper harvests to be used during periods of poor harvests. Respondents also said that they live from animals and animal products during drier years. They had known difficult times, but things always improved when the rains returned.

At this time, however, they explained, people from Wollo are unable to survive. First, because of current government programs, they are no longer allowed to produce enough extra grain for those years without rain. Second, because they are now forced, at gunpoint, to give all surplus grain to the government (for taxes and "voluntary" payments), they can no longer retain sufficient food for periods without harvests. And third, even in good years now, they have had to sell and slaughter their animals for food and taxes. Because their methods of defending themselves from the uncertain weather conditions had been undermined, these refugees explained, food shortages had led to the starvation of many members of their own families during the past two years.

With regard to being unable to produce enough for lean years, one man explained, "There are farmers in our area who can produce in one harvest enough food for seven years. But not any more. This is not because the land has changed but because the government takes it all." Those listening unanimously agreed. Another offered, "The more we produce large amounts of crops, the more the government will force us to contribute for some cause such as militias."

Forcible transfer of grain to the government emerged as a chief reason for the food crisis in Wollo. One man insisted that he wanted to correct the answers he had given to our initial survey question, "When you asked me the reason for our hunger, I answered you saying, 'drought,' but this is behind our problems. If the government had not taken our extra product, then we would not be in a crisis now." Another added,

We were also forced to pay tax in a secret way by selling to the government 50 kg of grain for E$25. The same amount that the Agricultural Marketing Corporation [AMC] buys from us for E$25 can be sold for E$80 to the town

---

*This discrepancy between answers given to survey questions regarding causes of famine and explanations given by the same respondents regarding the long-term negative effects of Ethiopian agrarian and military policies on food production is addressed in Chapter X.

population. We do not know what the government does with the grain of the AMC, but we heard that it is for the town population of Addis Ababa and Asmara who can afford to pay a high price.

Nobody likes this policy [the government serving as middleman] because the city dwellers and the peasants both want to buy from the peasants, but they cannot.

Another man suggested that the major reason they could not produce even enough to feed themselves, let alone surpluses for coming years, was that they were forced to attend "untimely" meetings and government work.

Overall, these meetings required by the government may reduce our food production two thirds in a year. At the time the meeting is called, we could not delay even to eat our food because the militia come around to force us to attend. Even if there is rain, we have to go. Also, during the time we should be working in the fields, whether we like it or not, we plow the militias' plot of land before ours. Even the women participate in this—those who have no husbands and do not have land work on the militias' plots.

Another suggested this with his own scenario:

Yes, these [policies] affect our production badly. This is why we are starving. One day we are told to farm for the militias and on another day for the regional peasant association chairman and on the other day or week [until finished] we plow for the Woreda peasant association representative, etc., etc., and on it goes. During this time our crops will be infested with weeds, and sometimes our teff will be reduced because it was not cut and harvested and collected when it was ready. Yes, this reduced the crop we were to eat by two parts out of three. We are left to survive on one part [one third] and we cannot, as you can see. We are forced to go to meetings by militia and they guard us during the discussion so that we can not leave.

You see, the government's plan and our plan are not the same. They call us and force us to [go to] meetings to explain why they are taking our grain, our money, our people, but we do not agree. Meetings are held when an order is given. For example, we will be gathered for the meetings when officials call, or for the national literacy program. We were forced to hold meetings for military recruitment. We also have to remain there until we contribute more money for youth association. Sometimes they call us just for the purpose of telling us why we have to give, and we will be sitting there by force.

Generally these meetings were held for the problems of military and militia provisions. For them this is important but not for us. But their plan must be followed and ours must be abandoned. Even the women are forced to prepare food provisions for militias for 15 days, leaving all other things. The peasants are forced to go to their own farm land without food and can hardly work. Even when a peasant tries to ask for his morning [mid-day] meal he is refused. When a woman is working for this government or ready to go to the government meeting she cannot cook for her family. If her husband himself is requiring her to break the government's plan for his family's need he is imprisoned or has to pay a large amount.

The farmer's protest of the capricious or even destructive collection of taxes and obligations is to throw caution to the wind. According to one farmer,

In order to collect taxes for the government plan, they take even our seed grain from us by force. We will be left with nothing. This year I had small hope that the rains would come. When the ground was wet, I put the seed in, in case there would be a crop, but it remained on the dry land and produced nothing.

*It would have been better for me if I had eaten it, but the government would
have taken all from me, so I took a chance that it would grow.*

For some time farmers sold their oxen to pay taxes and contributions,
even though their families were hungry. As one farmer explained, by 1984
the price for oxen was so low that it was better to ignore the taxes and eat
their animals and take their chances with the government.

*About three years ago everyone still had animals, but as the food problem
became worse and we had to pay taxes we sold the animals for money. But by
January 1984 the ox that sold for more than E$100 was selling for E$50. We used to sell our animals and hoped to buy them again when conditions improved. But recently we began to slaughter them to eat because the price is too low
for selling. At least we get the meat. I do not know where we will get oxen in
the future.*

The experience of the refugees, even from the same area (Yejju, Wollo),
differed with regard to the issue of government tax collection during periods
of food shortages.

*We had to pay taxes and dues for association meetings plus contributions for
militia even if there was no food for anyone in the family. Last year I produced
20 saffia [equivalent to a gerry can] of grain. Out of this I had to feed my family and pay E$21 for land tax, E$7 for peasant association, E$3 for REYA, E$6
for mother and father, plus contributions for militia. That is E$47 plus con-
tributions of grain. They told us if we did not pay our taxes, we would be
resettled.*

Another man noted that the situation was different in his peasant association.

*There was no payment of tax last year, but this year it was "rescheduled."
They said that the tax we did not pay last year was overdue and we must find
a way of paying both. If we cannot — they knew we could not — we must go for
resettlement. The officials told us that all those who do not pay tax will go for
this resettlement program.*

Other issues raised during the discussion of decline in productivity were
the effect of land redistribution on production in Wollo and the impact of
collective farming on overall productivity. Most of those interviewed were
young enough that they had been farming with their fathers at the time of
the land redistribution. While some reported that their fathers had
cultivated large plots that were reduced to a quarter of their original size,
others said that the overall amount of the land had been increased but that
the low fertility of plots meant that total production had declined.

*My father had 12 oxen-days [of plowing] of land before the revolution. When
he died, I continued to plow it. After the revolution they gave me four oxen-
days of land, at a completely different location, to feed the same number of
people.*

*Before the new government program came, we had a small amount of land;
after the new government we were given a plot as large as the others got, but it
was less fertile than our own piece. Before the revolution we could exist for
two years on one harvest; now our best harvest is not enough for six months.
We have to sell our animals and animal products such as butter to survive to
the next harvest. Where we were before we could get 40 to 50 barrels of grain
[amount not estimated in more detail] from a small plot of land and take addi-*

tional large quantities from other plots of land too. But these days, in the best years, we get only 15 barrels of grain from the whole plot we were given.

My father was a landlord who had a large plot of land and in addition had Galla land around Dessie. Generally he was able to get 200 quintals [20,000 kg] from that land. After the revolution we got 15 quintals [1,500 kg].

My father got 40 percent of his former land. At that time we had two pairs of oxen, three cows, a donkey and grain in storage that was reserved for the coming years. Since the revolution the number of animals was reduced for two reasons — we had to sell them in the market or slaughter them for food. Only two animals remained.

The consensus among these former farmers and farmers' sons was that during the land redistribution, fertile productive land had gone either to rich men who were peasant association officials or to those who could bribe them, or to collective farms. Two men commented on the system of bribery that exists.

After the revolution people were not given equal shares of land. They were not given equal shares because some people, those who had money, got to retain their former plot and also get an amount of good land in another peasant association. This was easily done by bribing the elected chairman and his colleagues in a different peasant association. For this reason the poor peasants did not get equal shares with them. Furthermore, there were some people who obtained land after the land proclamation who had never farmed during the former regime.

Those who have money can apply to the peasant association representatives and bribe them even to get land from a poor peasant's share. They complain that their family is large when the number of people is the same as in the family of the poor peasant to begin with.

Many pointed out that richer people bribe peasant association officials to keep their sons home from military service. These same farmers apply to take the land of the poor whose sons went by force to the military. Thus, the "larger family" takes the land from the "smaller family" even though those serving in the military are supposed to have plots cultivated for them by their local peasant association.

The rest of the most fertile land was set aside as an incentive for farmers to join collective farms.

People who gave all of their animals and tools for collective farming at the initial stages of the land reform were given the largest plots of the most fertile land. I did not participate in this, but I saw it operating. These farmers, however, were not allowed to grow just any variety of crop that they liked or that is good for that soil. The crop to be planted in that area was selected by the officials. Often it was not suitable for those soils, and the yield on the best land was nothing. The next year many of those farmers were discouraged and began to start farming privately.

Negative Impact of Government Policies on Agricultural Strategies and Production — Causes of Famine

Those government policies that had a negative impact on agricultural production include: a) required meetings that disrupt the agricultural work cycle; b) labor obligations; c) heavy taxes and contributions; and d) mandatory sale of produce at unfavorable government prices.

Despite the reduced size of their plots and their lack of access to plots in different ecological zones, which would minimize their risk of total crop failure and ensure production of different types of food crops, these farmers asserted that they would have been able to manage to produce their subsistence needs if they were able to control the timing of their work and cooperate in the use of their resources. However, mandatory government labor programs, such as farming the crops of peasant association officials, land designated for "militia" and communal plots, kept them away from their own fields. Compulsory meetings called for literacy teaching and lengthy explanations of government needs and programs culminating in various fund-raising appeals equally affected their harvest, reducing its output by an estimated two-thirds.

Out of their reduced production, farmers were required to pay onerous taxes under penalty of imprisonment or forced resettlement. Peasants explained that the government's confiscation of their harvest, which the Dergue called "surplus," was the factor that left them destitute when the rains were short or missing in poor years. Formerly storage from good years to cover bad years had allowed them to survive. Government taxation policy defined anyone as able to pay taxes or contributions if they retained any assets in their possession. Peasants were excused from taxes in some areas only when they were empty-handed. Such "excused" taxes were "rescheduled" and payable at the whim of authorities (local or otherwise), a ploy that made many peasants "legally" vulnerable to resettlement in 1984.

In searching for ways to meet their known obligations, farmers stated that their grain could be sold only to the government AMC, which paid E$25 for grain that would bring E$80 in cities. Low prices, in addition to unscheduled and unpredictable demands from the government for "voluntary" contributions for one crisis or the other — usually military — served as disincentives for farmers to produce larger amounts even when the land might have been capable of it.

Those from Wollo, who had been taken by force from their homelands for resettlement, delivered searing indictments against the Ethiopian government for claiming that they were victims of nature and collecting money internally and internationally in their name.

The six refugees encountered on the road to Kirmuk were from Yejju and said that their "entire peasant association" had been taken for resettlement. Upon asking for clarification, we learned that the greater proportion of their peasant association was sent — the criterion being that "all those without oxen" had to go. This intriguing bit of information reveals a great deal about the "nomination" process through which candidates were selected for transfer to resettlement sites, as well as its implications for restructuring society in those regions vacated by the "oxenless."

Plans for the Future

Plans for returning home differed among these refugees from Wollo depending on whether they had been captured in Addis Ababa as vagrants or sent by their peasant association officials. The difference lay in whether they had legally departed with permission papers signed by peasant association officials or not; that is, those the peasant associations officially sent could not legally return home while the others, those who were not officially sent by the peasant associations, calculated that they could still legally return home.

Several of those interviewed expressed an interest and a willingness to work in Sudan for the same reasons that they had gone to find work in Addis Ababa before they were captured there for resettlement, i.e., to enable them to buy food for their families. Having just arrived in Sudan, they were considering the opportunities for employment with Sudanese farmers around Kirmuk and evaluating information from other refugees in Kirmuk about work on the commercial farms in that area.

Yet all planned to return home eventually. All were determined to see their families again. Some stated, "If I can spend at least one night with my family again before they kill me for escaping from their program, it will be worth it." Another asserted, "If I see that it is dangerous for my family, I will take them to TPLF areas for safety." In addition to saving their lives, most had escaped from the resettlement sites in order to go home.

TRANSIENT SETTLERS FROM TIGRAY INTERVIEWED IN YABUUS

A second group of people whom were fleeing resettlement was interviewed in Yabuus. This group consisted of 14 males from Tigray who had been resettled in Illubabor and had managed to escape. Their journey to Sudan took more than one month. We encountered them the same day they arrived in Sudan, before they had talked to any Sudanese or TPLF/REST officials. They were being sent by Sudanese officials to Kirmuk and then on to the Damazine holding center. They wanted to return to the north of Sudan so that they could walk home from there.

Personal Background of Respondents (see Table No. 5)

This group of settlers was, on average, 44 years old. They had been born and lived in Tigray region in TPLF-controlled zones. Half came from Agamo and Agomito and the remainder from Adi Koro, Mofarso, Adi Amo, Dega Hamos or Zata. All of the respondents in this group were Coptic Christians.

All but one of the people in the group were married and they had, on average, five children each. None of them had any family with them in Sudan. Even the 14-year-old boy with them had been separated from both parents.

All of the respondents spoke Tigrinya, and, in addition, two persons (14.3 percent) spoke Amharic. Tigrinya was the first language of the entire group and everyone was literate in Tigrinya.

Economic Background of Respondents (see Table No. 6)

All these respondents were farmers who also kept livestock. In addition, two of them, 14.3 percent, were priests. These men reported that 1979 to 1981 were the best recent years of agricultural production. Average annual yields during the best year were 1,160 kg, although the range varied from 800 kg to 1,600 kg. In 1984, however, harvested grain averaged only 79 kg per farmer in the group. All of these farmers (100 percent) cited armyworms as the main cause of declining yields. It should be noted here that delays in planting dramatically affect the ability of armyworm to destroy crops (see discussion, Chapter X).

PERSONAL BACKGROUND OF RESPONDENTS

Average Age Range	44 years
0-15	7.1%
16-25	
26-35	
36-45	42.5%
46-55	50.0%
55+	
Geographical Origin (all villages in Tigray Region)	
Adi Koro	14.3%
Agamo	28.6%
Agomito	21.4%
Mofarso	7.1%
Adi Amo	14.3%
Dega Hamos	7.1%
Zata	7.1%
Religion	
Christian	100.0%
Marital Status	
Married	92.9%
Single	7.1%
Average Number of Children	5
Languages Known	
Tigrinya	85.7%
Tigrinya-Amharic	14.3%
First Language	
Tigrinya	100.0%
Literacy Rate	100.0%

Table No. 6
ECONOMIC BACKGROUND OF RESPONDENTS

Occupation of Respondents	
Farmer With Animals	85.7%
Farmer/Priest	14.3%
Respondents' Agricultural Production	
Years of Best Production	1979-81
Average Yield per Year in Best Year	1,160 kg
Range Reported For Best Year	1,600-800 kg
Average Production in 1984	79 kg
Range Reported For 1984	200-0 kg
Cause of Declining Yields	
Lack of Rain	0.0%
Armyworm	100.0%

Participants' Account of Resettlement in Metu, Illubabor

The refugees in this group were intensively interviewed regarding their experiences in resettlement. They had been taken by force to Illubabor, a region receiving a large proportion of settlers but one there had been relatively little information about. Their account, quoted here at length, sums up their predicament and sheds light on conditions faced by those resettled away from the massive Asosa-type schemes in smaller scale but widespread sites.

We were taken from Adua. We went there on the Dergue's announcement of assistance there. One had to apply to the Red Cross to get the food. The announcement was given at the district level. We lived in a TPLF area and thought that the food was only for those from the government-held areas. But then we heard that people from TPLF areas were getting food in Adigrat, Axuma and Adua. The first people who went to the distribution centers got small amounts of wheat flour and oil. Others heard about this and thought food would be given to everyone. We asked the TPLF for permission to go for this food and they said that was okay. It took us six hours to walk to the distribution center. A lot of people left families at home; some took their children; some even took donkeys to carry the grain. When I was captured, my donkeys were left tied up in the market. I don't know what happened to them. In Adua, a foreign man and woman gave each of us a blanket. They took our pictures with the blankets. We were put on a truck and told that we would get food in another place. Some in the group resisted. They were beaten unconscious and thrown onto the trucks like sacks of grain.

At the new place, the government then told us that we were going to be resettled. When everyone resisted with one voice, they told us we would have to give up the blankets if we didn't agree to go. Everyone gave up their blankets; not one person kept them. Then we were sent anyway.

Those from 17 to 45 years old were sent to settlements. Many resisted, saying, "If you want to feed us, feed us here." We selected spokespeople to tell the officials we did not want to be resettled; we were imprisoned for two weeks. Soldiers surrounded us and forced us to get into trucks without anything; we had nothing. In prison we were given two small breads per day and some water.

When we were in prison, waiting to be resettled, we saw the soldiers carrying bags of food. Two people went over to where the food was being carried to the soldiers' place of cooking. It was in bags just like these we are carrying [marked Canada, Federal Republic of Germany, European Economic Commission (EEC)].

Then they took us to Mekele and warned us that anybody who asked questions would be imprisoned. We were taken by helicopters. The drivers were not Ethiopians. They were white.

We stayed in Mekele two weeks. We were kept in an open field with no shade. If the sun was strong we burned up; at night we were cold. Out of several thousand people in the camp, only about 50 were given blankets. Many people got earaches and other ailments from the cold. We were given one piece of bread each per day, no other food. When prisoners' families from the local area brought them food, the officials refused to allow them to have it.

We were not allowed to leave the guarded field even to go to urinate or defecate. There were always armed soldiers surrounding the area where we were kept. During those two weeks many people got sick and we counted 72 who died out of the huge group, maybe it was even 10,000 people. The 72 were buried in a big open pit that was dug in the same area where we all stayed. There were all kinds of people in the camp — children and old people, men and women.

Many people tried to escape, but only one I knew of managed to get away. The others were wounded or killed. We all saw these things happen.

We talked to the other people at Mekele. We didn't find one person who was being resettled voluntarily. All the people resisted, whether they were from the Ethiopian or the TPLF areas.

We wrote a petition to the regional governor asking to be allowed to return to our homes. We wrote petitions in Adua and in Mekele and gave them to our elected representatives, who gave them to the soldiers. In both cases the soldiers returned with the news that we had to go for resettlement whether we liked it or not. I don't think the soldiers even delivered the messages; I think they just threw them away and told us that anyway.

One day officials came to the area with foreign guests. All of us [Tigrayans] were taken to another place and the foreigners talked only to those from Wollo and Raya Azebo. The Wollos told us that the foreigners interviewed them. We all think that they must have told them that they were going willingly since their area is so dry, but we weren't there and don't really know what was said.

At Mekele the political cadres came and told us we had to go for this program. Many people tried to escape. One man who tried to get away was shot in the legs. He had to be taken to the hospital.

They tried to convince us to be resettled. They told us that we could not survive in our home areas. They told us that there had been no rain in our area for four years, but we knew that was not so. The rains were fine, it was the armyworm that ate all the crops. They told us that there would be no more rains for four years. They said, "If you stay here in Tigray you are going to remain beggars. We are going to take you to a fertile land that will produce two times a year. We are going to farm with tractors for you for one year so that you will have plenty to eat. After that we will give you oxen so that you can produce your own food."

They asked us if we wanted to bring our families with us. Some people said yes because they did not want to be separated from their families. We did not ask for ours because we did not want to go away in the first place and did not want to stay there. Even those who asked for their families did not get them; they were taken anyway.

We were taken by plane from Mekele to Addis Ababa. There were at least 350 people standing in the airplane. Is was very crowded and hot in the airplane. A lot of people got sick and vomited. Many were sick, but there was no chance to clean up in Addis Ababa. We got a cup of water in Addis Ababa and were put immediately onto a bus. We each had a seat on the bus.

On the bus journey we slept outside at night. Once some people slept in a meeting house but there was not enough room for everyone. We ate only in the evening at which time we got a small amount of boiled wheat.

During the journey we had no contact with the local people. Food was brought to us when the bus stopped in the evening, but we didn't know where it came from.

Many people managed to escape en route. There were no soldiers guarding the buses, and no one guarded us while we slept at night. Some people even jumped from the moving buses, and many broke their arms and legs. We saw some people die when they jumped out of the bus.

Some who tried to escape from the sleeping areas were captured by the local people and then returned to the buses. It was Oromos who captured them. The local peasant associations had been told that if they saw the settlers trying to escape they should bring them back.

When we arrived in Illubabor, the district peasant association brought us bread and cooked corn and sorghum. The local people were ordered by the government not to speak to us or to interact with us in any way, but we could see from their faces that they did not like us.

When we first arrived in Illubabor, the peasant association leaders from the local residents called us together and made announcements. They spoke in Amharic. Our group was 350 people. They told us to form a peasant association. They told us we would get a literacy campaign. In two months we only met twice. At each meeting a district official came and gave us a speech.

We were given food each week.

There were a few militia around us, but they were not armed. There were armed police in the market, but not near us. There were some kulaks [rich peasants] who had guns, but they were private people.

There was no crime or other problems with our group, but we heard that one of the settlers went to pick coffee left on the tree after the harvest. The local people killed him.

We met some Tigrayans at the local market. They lived in town. They told us that the government will arm Tigrayans to fight against the enemies of the state [OLF]. They told us we would have no choice and that we should get out of the area before that happened.

I do not think the settlers and the local people can live in peace. The local people say that we brought them problems. "We are starving because of you," they say.

We tried to tell them that we had not come to their area voluntarily, but the Wollos and those from Raya Azebo had come voluntarily before us. The government told them that we, too, had come willingly. Finally we were able to convince them that that was not true. They advised us, however, as fathers and brothers, that there was no way to escape.

The Oromo faced several problems because of us. Since September 1984 they have been building houses for settlers. And they are ordered to feed us. They had to feed us from their own land and prepare all the food for the first three days. Then when we began to receive international wheat [at this point they showed the sacks this wheat had come in — from Canada, West German Red Cross and the EEC], these Oromo had to carry the wheat to us, but they could not eat it. They were ordered to bring the grain to us on their own donkeys. If they did not have donkeys, they had to carry the wheat on their own backs. Because of all this work for us, they could not watch their own crops. The wild animals finished all their own crops this year.

There was no organized labor for us to do at the resettlement sites. We were told to plant gardens around our houses, however. While there was plenty of food in our sites, there was little water and few cooking utensils. We had no pan to cook our food in so we had to use our shovel as a skillet over the fire to cook food at night and as a digging instrument by day.

Our settlement was located behind Metu. We escaped from it and passed the town around 3:00 a.m. There dogs barked at us and the chairman of the peasant association came and cried out to the other people in the village. They all came out and chased us. They had flashlights but no guns. The chairman had a gun but he did not shoot it. We went into tall grass and they followed us. At that time we were 28. They captured three. The 11 others got separated from us. The rest of us [14] came together by clapping our hands and whistling to each other. We discussed what to do about the others. We decided that nothing we could do would help the three that had been captured, and we could be imprisoned. We hoped we would run into the other 11 on the way to Sudan.

Fifteen other people had agreed to escape with us, but they never showed up so we decided to go on without them.

We had no idea how to get to Sudan. If we came upon a village during the day, we had to go to the forest and sleep there all day until we could travel again that night. Early in the morning if we found that we were near a village we lost the whole day. If we could figure out ways to avoid the villages we could travel the entire day and at night.

We quickly finished our food. The first day after we ate the last of it we ate the fruit of the oda tree, the second day the fruit of the kiltu. The third day we put our remaining salt in water and drank it. After that we put dirt in the water and drank it. Then we broke up some garlic that we had bought in the market before leaving the site and ate that.

Then we said to ourselves, "We have finished our food, what shall we do?" We decided three people should go to a local town to buy food for us. I was one of the ones to go. We saw two local people on the road and went to talk to them while the rest of the group hid. These two Oromo told us where to go to the nearest market.

After that we came to a big river and tried to find a shallow place to cross it. We all made it and entered a forest. There were buffalo, elephants, lions and other wild animals in that forest. We were terrified, but the animals ignored us and went on their own way.

Then came other little rivers that we crossed together. We came to a huge river. While we were trying to find a place to cross we ate most of the food we had purchased at the market. Finally we found a place to cross.

This brought us to Gidami. There we found a settlement [resettlement] area near there. There was one Wollo person in the forest. We asked him the way to Sudan. He said, "You cannot escape here, there are so many villages here and a huge river between here and Asosa." We asked what we could do and he said, "You must return to Illubabor. We have been here one month. There are so many militias they will find you. They are surrounding us."

When we heard this we said, "Okay, we'll return." But we had no intention of going back. We went back to the forest and went on by night.

After we left that place we found two local people, Oromo, who told us there was no hope for us to get to Sudan. "The militia will find you," they said. We told them that we were just looking for jobs.

When we found the river, it was being used for irrigation. It was a Thursday. We spent that entire day in the forest.

We discussed our lack of food and decided that we had to go to market on Saturday which is the day all Wollo settlers go into the local market so we thought we would not be detected.

At that time we had only a little money with us. We bought some corn and chickpeas in the market. Then we returned to the forest and began traveling at night. We found an Oromo who spoke Amharic. He cooperated with us and showed us the way. We were able to travel the entire night in the right direction with his help.

After that night we came to a forest where we could find no people—only wild animals, elephants, lions, etc. Finally we reached a river two days later. After crossing it we found Komo people who indicated to us in a few words and sign language the way to Sudan. They were organized under the OLF.

The next night we spotted the fires from a second village. There were only women and children there and they were afraid of us. We tried to make food with corn and chickpeas. Finally the men came; they had old guns and one Kalishnikov.

The men greeted us in sign language and assured us that we could get to the OLF. They gave us food and a place to sleep. The next morning they took us to another area, a village that had been organized into a peasant association under the Dergue but is now under the OLF.

The peasant association chairman took us to his house and fed us. He kept us there for the entire day and we were getting nervous about why we were being kept there. Finally we met our OLF brothers there. They asked us who we were and how we came to be there. We told them our story. They said, "Starting now you are free, no danger can come to you."

After that they took us to their nearest camp and they fed us well. We stayed for two days at that camp and then they took us to another and then another. After four camps we reached the border here.

Chapter VII

THE SPREAD OF FAMINE THROUGH POLICY: TESTIMONY FROM PEOPLES INDIGENOUS TO THE AREAS TARGETED FOR RESETTLEMENT

Refugees in the Yabuus Region

For nearly a decade there has been a continuous flow of refugees into the Yabuus camp on the Sudanese border as a result of the long-standing nature and cumulative effects of various Ethiopian government policies. Thus, those seeking refuge in the Yabuus area of Sudan have tended to arrive in a persistent flow despite a few large waves. The camp is located on the Yabuus (called Dabus in Ethiopia) River, which has water year round. The land set aside for the camp was given by the Sudanese government. The Oromo Relief Association (ORA) runs the camp. The UNHCR has no presence in the camp.

According to data kept by ORA 3,000 refugees lived in the immediate vicinity and are assisted at the Yabuus camp, but many more refugees than that are in the general area. The refugees that ORA assists consist of Oromo-, Dungula- and Gitaan-speaking people and are dispersed throughout the surrounding countryside, making it a challenge to draw a random sample from the total camp population. The center of the camp, from which food, medical, technical and educational assistance is distributed, is the most densely populated area. Faced with the decision of using our time in the area to walk or to talk with refugees, we decided that we should talk to as many people as possible. For the purposes of our research, then, we established an arbitrary boundary around this more densely populated area and proceeded to draw our random sample from that population. ORA representatives, refugees and two earlier reports from observers who traveled throughout the region (Mekuria 1983, Terfa 1982) reported that those refugees who lived in more dispersed settlements did not differ greatly from those who lived in more densely settled areas. Further, all refugees in the area were in regular contact.

Within the area from which our sample was drawn, we found 1,113 camp residents. The average age of those living in the sampled area was 22.5 years; 55 percent were children under 15. Some 44 percent of all those in the survey area were male, and 88 percent of the adults were married. Our initial survey of the sampled area indicated that "neighborhoods" tended to be inhabited by people who spoke the same first language and/or who fled Ethiopia at the same time. These categories overlapped significantly because specific Ethiopian government policies directed at groups of a particular nationality drove many of their members out of the country together.

About 54 percent of the total population was 16 years old or older, and it was this group from which we drew the random sample, interviewing 45 of the 601 adults in the camp. We decided that only adults would have the type of information concerning agricultural production and the impact of government policies that was necessary for our study.

Map 22

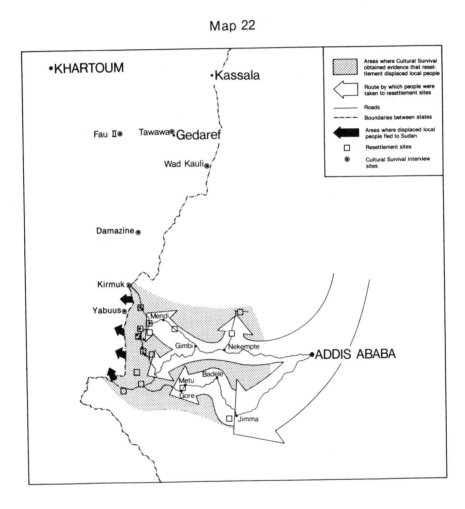

AREAS FROM WHICH LOCAL POPULATIONS ARE KNOWN TO HAVE BEEN DISPLACED BY RESETTLEMENT PROGRAM

Personal Background of Respondents (see Tables 1 and 2)

Most of those we interviewed in Yabuus were male.* The average age of respondents was 34.8 years. The vast majority of the people — 77.8 percent — were married; 92.9 percent of them were with some of their family in Sudan. Out of the 22.2 percent who were single, half had brothers, sisters and/or parents in the Sudan camps with them. These statistics confirm statements ORA officials made indicating that Yabuus is similar in composition to communities found on the other side of the Sudanese/Ethiopian border. The statistics also confirm statements the refugees made during the interviews that they came "in order to save our families" or "to raise our families in peace." The respondents' statements regarding the total number of their family members and those in Sudan also account for the large number of children in the camp.

More than 73 percent of the respondents were Moslem and 24 percent were Christian. A few had changed their religion from Christian to Moslem upon arrival in Sudan.

Table No. 1
PERSONAL BACKGROUND OF RESPONDENTS

Sex of Respondent	
Male	84.4%
Female	15.6%
Average Age of Respondent	34.8 years
Respondents Who Were Married	77.8%
Married Respondents With Some Family in Sudan	92.9%
Single Respondents With Some Family in Sudan	50.0%
Religion of Respondents	
Moslem	73.4%
Christian	24.4%

The respondents' first language was reflected by the "neighborhoods" they inhabited within the camp, and by their experiences in their homelands including the time they left those areas.

Over one quarter of the refugees used the term "Dungula" to refer to the language they first learned to speak as a child. When asked what language they used most often the refugees replied, "Oromo." Then when the issue of order of language learning was raised, they said "our language" was the first, but did not name it. When pushed for the name, they appeared uncomfortable but finally answered "Dungula." This term is used to refer to a specific group in Sudan related to the people on the Ethiopian side of the

*Females are not represented in this sample in proportion to their numbers in the camp. This discrepancy occurred in Yabuus primarily because women were not present in the camps in representative numbers at the time the random sample was conducted. They were extremely busy during the daylight hours with gathering firewood and water, grinding by hand the whole grain distributed by ORA (ORA's diesel-driven mill was out of operation during the period of this research and consequently the bulk of the onerous task of grinding this hardened grain fell on the women), and arranging for the numerous tasks involved in setting up their new households. They had arrived in camp only weeks earlier. When appointments were taken to interview women, they often had to be postponed due to the real burden of their work. Including the testimony of women refugees in this kind of setting needs to be seriously considered by future researchers and time and logistical adjustments made to accommodate them specifically (see Chapter III on methodology).

border whom Oromo and Sudanese in Sudan commonly designate "Berta." Since we had not included a direct question regarding nationality in our questionnaire, and therefore have no basis for determining whether the refugees call themselves Berta, Oromo, Dungula or some other term, they are referred to as "Dungula-speaking" in this report.

The same issue was raised with the refugees who alternatively referred to their first language as "our language," "Gitaan" and "Mao" but who indentified themselves as "Oromo" in the course of conversation. "Gitaan" is used here since it seemed to be preferred by them over "Mao." Most of the Gitaan speakers interviewed left their original homelands as early as 1977 or 1978, resettled in a region bordering the lands of the Komo and conducted trade with various Sudanese groups using Arabic as the lingua franca. This is reflected in the language acquisition patterns of those refugees who spoke Gitaan first. The men of this group, as well as the Dungula speakers, indicated that Oromo was the language used most. Women, however, said that although they spoke Gitaan and Oromo, they spoke Gitaan more often. Children learned both languages at home.

Table No. 2
LANGUAGES OF THE RESPONDENTS

Languages Spoken by the Respondents	
Oromo	97.8%
Arabic	37.8%
Amharic	17.7%
Gitaan	24.4%
Dungula	26.7%
Komo	11.1%
Order of Language Acquisition	
Dungula-Oromo-Arabic	26.6%
Dungula-Oromo	2.2%
Gitaan-Oromo-Arabic	4.4%
Gitaan-Oromo-Komo	8.9%
Gitaan-Oromo-Amharic	2.2%
Gitaan-Oromo-Komo-Amharic-Arabic	2.2%
Oromo only	24.6%
Oromo-Amharic	8.9%
Oromo-Amharic-Arabic	2.2%
Oromo-Arabic-Komo	2.2%
Oromo-Gitaan	11.1%
Komo only	2.2%
First Language of Respondents	
Dungula	26.6%
Gitaan	23.7%
Oromo	47.5%
Komo	2.2%
Language Most Used by Respondents	
Oromo	92.2%
Gitaan	5.2%
Komo	2.2%
Literacy Rate of Respondents	
Not Literate	64.4%
Literate in Some Language	35.6%
Oromo	15.6%
Arabic	2.2%
Amharic	17.8%

A majority of the respondents, 51 percent, indicated that they spoke Arabic. During intensive follow-up interviews, however, it became clear that several individuals had claimed a knowledge of Arabic when they really had acquired only such rudimentary skills as counting and exchanging greetings with local Sudanese around the camp, so this figure should be viewed with caution.

Only 35.6 percent of the refugees had had any literacy training. Of those, 42.8 percent had been taught in Oromo. Many began their training at the camp in Yabuus where ORA conducts a literacy program. Half of those who were already literate had been trained in Amharic either through the Ethiopian government's literacy campaign or through elementary schools in their homelands. Later we learned that three individuals who had been in the government literacy program and had indicated that they were literate in Amharic could only read and write their names. Clearly literacy claims in this context should be treated with caution as well.

All the refugees in Yabuus came from Wollega region: 26.7 percent from the Gitaan area, an equal percentage from the Kissan (Berta) area near Asosa (this is the Dungula-speaking group) and the remainder (the Oromo) came from primarily the Begi and Mendi areas.

Economic Background of Respondents (see Table No. 3)

To varying degrees all those interviewed in Yabuus had engaged in farming, trading and other subsistence activities before leaving their homes. [Among the respondents was a former *balabat* (local administrative official during the Haile Selassie period), as well as his children, each of whom had also farmed.] While 17.7 percent of the respondents' fathers had traded in addition to farming, 37.7 percent of respondents engaged in trade before leaving their homes — the figures here reflect the trading activities of Gitaan — and Dungula-speaking refugees during their stays near the Sudanese border. An increased need to supplement declining agricultural production with other income explains why more individuals engaged in trading.

Since taking refuge in Sudan, 55.5 percent of the respondents reported that they had engaged in trading while 40 percent had sought work as wage laborers. More than 86 percent of those interviewed expressed a desire to farm in Sudan. At the time of the interviews none of the refugees had successfully farmed in Sudan.

Table No. 3
ECONOMIC BACKGROUND OF RESPONDENTS

Occupation at Home	
Farmer With Animals	62.3%
Farmer/Trader	37.7%
Wage Earner	0.0%
Occupation in Sudan	
Wage Earner	40.0%
Trading	55.5%
Expressed Desire to Farm in Sudan	86.7%
Father's Occupation	
Farmer With Animals	73.5%
Balabat/Governor	8.8%
Farmer/Trader	17.7%
Wage Earner	0.0%

All but two of the Yabuus refugees had farmed in the same place as their fathers but there had been a history of direct and indirect displacement in their fathers' and grandfathers' time. Two older refugees reported that their fathers had been forced out of their homes in Qellem during the 1920s, when hundreds of Oromo farmers were displaced due to a widespread peasant revolt (see Triulzi 1983) against the demands of *neftanya* (literally, gun-carrying settler) Amhara landlords who had been given large sections of Qellem under Emperor Menelik. Three other refugees (one was 50 years old, another 75) said that "Amhara" had forced their fathers off their land. Farmers who refused to work for landlords on their own land met with reprisals from the state-backed settlers, so they moved "voluntarily" to the Begi highlands where their families lived in peace until the current wave of settlers arrived. The refugees emphatically compared the state-sponsored settlers who took their fathers' and grandfathers' land under earlier governments and the current wave of settlers who receive similar state support to take over their homelands.

Table No. 4

DISCREPANCY BETWEEN GEOGRAPHICAL ORIGIN
OF RESPONDENT AND FATHER/GRANDFATHER

Grandfather Forced to Move	4.4%
Father Had Moved	20.0%

Agricultural Production (see Table No. 5)

Farming in western Wollega includes in addition to agriculture, beekeeping, house and furniture construction and tool-making as well as breeding and raising large and small livestock (cattle, sheep, goats, donkeys, horses, mules) and fowl. All of the farmers interviewed owned livestock and had been plowing with their own oxen when they left their homes. In heated discussion and/or speculation over what had become of their livestock and other property they had to leave behind, these peasants concluded that all of their belongings had probably been taken over by the peasant association rather than passed to other family members (who they claimed would be punished for the refugee's departure).

All of those interviewed reported that their fathers at their age were better off than they. It was extremely difficult for respondents to remember and report precisely agricultural yields during their fathers' eras. Refugees were asked to try to remember the amounts their fathers harvested in an average year, but they tended to remember only the remarkable harvests, when the grain, pulses and coffee exceeded storage facilities. To specify amounts for each kind of crop produced — teff, corn, barley, sorghum, wheat, peas, beans, coffee, oil seeds, etc. — over two harvesting periods required more time and detailed cross-checking than our research allowed. Different agricultural practices, storage systems and measurements further complicated attempts to quantify agricultural produce. So many *gombisa* (a term literally meaning "roof" or "cover" which in this area is used to designate a locally made granary) was a common answer to the question "How much did your father produce?" *Gombisa* can vary in size from 50 to 500 quintals (5,000 to 50,000 kg). The respondents reported that during their fathers' lifetimes, grain was often stored "with its grass" and taken for threshing throughout the year. Threshed grain was divided in two portions, one to keep at home and the other to sell at the market. The amount of grain consumed also varied greatly from years when a household hosted large feasts such as for a wedding celebration to those when the family household expanded to include auxiliary members. Given all these provisos, we calculated from a wide variety of responses an estimate that their fathers' produce averaged 100 to 200 quintals (10,000 to 20,000 kg) per year for a family of six.

Farmers in the sample were asked what had been their best harvest since the Dergue's land redistribution took place. Most of the respondents, 64.3 percent, reported that they had had their best harvest in 1976. The other 35.7 percent of the respondents said that they had had their best harvest in 1975 and that conditions had continually deteriorated since then.

Table No. 5
AGRICULTURAL PRODUCTION UNDER THE DERGUE

Best Production Under Dergue (For Family of Six)	4,600 kg
Best Year 1976	64.3%
Best Year 1975	35.7%
Production in 1983-84	900 kg

Background to Land Reform and Peasant Associations

Oromo farmers pointed out that they had already reallocated land among themselves prior to implementation of the Dergue's land reform policy and prior, even, to the demise of Haile Selassie's government. Their testimony in this regard casts in a new light the current interpretations that the Dergue enjoyed widespread peasant support for its land reform and peasant association policies. In order to undermine landlords' and *balabats'* power, the local farmers had organized themselves in the late 1960s and early 1970s to claim the land. They had redistributed land, according to traditional Oromo principals of allocation, in many of the Oromo regions discussed in this report, as one man put it — "according to the *gada.*"

Those interviewed claimed that Oromo had formed their own associations "in order to isolate the landlord." The tenants agreed to contribute money for oxen in order to plow for themselves and to keep the produce or redistribute it according to their own agreement. One man explained,

> We contributed E$500 and bought a pair of oxen. We helped those who were sick and hungry. We also planted coffee and saw five to six stores of crops. We lent the money we had contributed without interest. This was for two years before the Dergue came. We planned this idea in order to help each other, for we cannot kill the landlord.

> We had a committee of five leaders. Our members were 80. We met to discuss and solve our problems but we did not call ourselves mahiber because it would be considered illegal and we would be fined. So we called the organization dado, an organization to help each other farm, especially harvest. Those who had oxen plowed the land for those who were sick, unable to work, etc. The women also worked.

> The landlord tried to disorganize our associations by giving bribes to the judge. But he [the landlord] was not able to succeed because we also gave bribes to the judge. When Haile Selassie fell this man was taken to Nekempte to prison.

> There were many organizations like this among Oromo in our area.

In 1974, when students representing the Dergue government arrived in the area following the change of government to instruct the Oromo peasants about new land reform policies, these local associations were already functioning. The students informed the peasants that the Dergue approved of and recognized as legal the Oromo farmers' principles of operation and that there would no longer be a tax or landlord's fee. The Oromo farmers were also told that the government was interested in helping the poor and dispossessed to work according to the principles of operation the farmers had already initiated throughout the area. Their land base was also expanded and measured in *gashas* (1 gasha = 40 hectares). Many of the officers of these locally formed organizations were elected to office within the new peasant associations.

For two years, until 1976, these farmers worked with minimum government involvement and reported an average yield of 46 quintals (4,600 kg). In 1976, however, when the Dergue began to consolidate power to create peasant associations, the Oromo's traditional democratic/participatory structures were outlawed and replaced with hand-picked officials and became attached to top-down organizations. The refugees referred to this action as the Dergue's "betrayal." They then gave details of their unrelieved decline in production and productive capacity since that time. The causes of their predicament lay in this reversal of policy.

Causes of Agricultural Production Declines (see Tables 6 and 7)

All those interviewed reported a decline in agricultural production since 1976. Compared to their average yield of 46 quintals (4,600 kg) in 1975-76, these farmers reported average yields of only 9 quintals (900 kg) on the same land in 1983-84. None of those interviewed said that decreases in rainfall were a major or even contributing cause of declining harvests in the region. The three groups of refugees who left their homelands in three

Table No. 6
CAUSES OF AGRICULTURAL PRODUCTION DECLINES
REPORTED BY RESPONDENTS
(Factors Mentioned in Combination)

Lack of Rain	0.0%
Government Programs Interfere With Food Production	
Work Required Four to Five Days a Week on Peasant Association Collective Plots	95.4%
Other Peasant Association Obligations	27.2%
Required Attendance at Peasant Association Meetings and Literacy Programs	73.4%
Disarming Populations	63.6%
Military Conscription	15.6%
Imprisonment Prevents Farm Work	86.3%
Government Policies Force Redistribution of Assets	
Land Redistribution	52.2%
Forced Sale of Oxen to Pay Taxes and "Voluntary" Contributions	41.0%
All Products Confiscated for Taxes (Including Seed Grain)	36.3%
Oxen and Tools Confiscated for Collectivization or Resettlement	13.6%
Oxen Given to Others in Peasant Association	6.8%
Government "Improvement" Programs Destroy Crops	
Government "Experts" Untrained in Farming	13.6%
Grass, for Erosion Control, Overtook Crops	9.0%

distinct periods — the first in 1977-78, the second in 1980-81 and the third in 1984-85 — all gave similar explanations for the causes of food shortages in their areas. Their explanations fall into two categories: decline in production and confiscation of produce. The relative differences among their explanations lay in the government's ability to enforce policies that the indigenous farmers resisted.

Work required on peasant association plots presented one of the biggest obstacles to food production in the home regions of these refugees. Ninety-five percent of those interviewed reported that the work required by the peasant association on the collective plots and other projects caused a decrease in overall production as well as diminished productivity on the land allocated to them privately. The following explanation was typical:

> We have to work on the government's peasant association plot before we turn to our own. Both the peasant association's plot and ours require the same rain, but we have to give the primary time to them. Because of these reasons — and now also building houses for settlers — we cannot produce one quarter of what we produced before on the same land. The land and the rain are the same.

Work on the collective plots required an average of four to five days' labor per week during each critical plowing, planting, weeding and harvesting period. Peasant association members may not discuss or negotiate the amount of time they work on collective plots. The leadership dictates how much time they must work and the militia enforces these hours. Those who fail to comply are imprisoned.

The farmers deeply resent this system of production because they have no access to the communal produce. When asked what became of it, the most common replies were,

> It goes to the government.

> The trucks take it away to a place we do not know.

Or,

> They [government representatives] told us that it [peasant association grain grown on the communal plot] will bring us clinics, schools, shops and fertilizer but we never saw any of these.

> Sometimes we contribute to government campaigns by voting unanimously, by force, to send part of it [produce from the communal plots], but we must always replace what is sent from our own supply.

> If our personal supply of food is finished we can buy grain from the peasant association supply but the price is high. I had to sell an animal to buy what I myself had produced.

> What we produce for the peasant association is like a tax payment but we could not calculate its value. When we used to give to the landlord what was required, at least we measured the amount. It went from our hand to his. But not this one. We don't even smell the grain before it goes.

When the refugees were asked whether they thought the peasant association plots' and individual plots' produce, if added together, would equal or exceed the earlier amounts, the usual reply was,

> It cannot come near to the earlier product even when added together because the way we are forced to use our time does not fit with nature. The use of the oxen, the method of preparing and planting is poor — it doesn't bring the land

and the people and the oxen and the rain together well. Even the farm that was wide became narrow — grass has overtaken the area while we go hungry. If we complain, they imprison us.

These farmers said that deposited grain and coffee was originally supposed to bring them a host of benefits, which they never received. Shops, roads, clinics, fertilizer, schools and welfare services were all promised to the peasants from the sale of the communal plots' produce, but after 10 years the farmers had yet to see any of these promises realized although they continually saw this produce trucked away to unknown destinations. Resistance against participation in the joint labor on communal lands brought instant harsh reprisals; so peasants saw their options as limited.

Another major cause of decline in production was a large number of obligations due the peasant association from each peasant farmer. Forced peasant association labor involved not only plowing and general agricultural work on communal plots using their own oxen, but also building houses for militia and working for the wives and children of men who have been sent away to the military. The respondents generally agreed that the widows of military veterans should receive the produce from this work, and argued minimally over this obligation. However, peasant association members had to continually farm the large plots, which were designated for single militiamen or ones whose wives remarried. Peasants could not account for the disposition of the produce from these plots except to say that it went "to a place known by God and the peasant association officials."

In 1978, required fees for mass organization memberships were introduced for the peasant association, women's association and youth association. These payments varied only slightly from one area to the next. National membership in the All-Ethiopian Peasant Association cost each farmer E$5 per month. Women's association membership is E$3 per month per woman — no married woman or woman over 18 years old is exempt. Youth association membership fees are also E$3 per month per child up to age 18.

Work obligations imposed upon Oromo farmers of Wollega to support and supply settlers who had already been brought into regions as part of the Dergue's resettlement program fall into this category of labor forced through peasant association mechanisms. Many farmers taking refuge in the Sudan had participated in the receiving end of the resettlement program. Requirements to build houses and supply equipment, food and oxen for incoming settlers in 1984 and 1985 merely expanded earlier obligations that had begun in 1979 and 1980 to house and feed settlers. The more recent obligations were unprecedented in scope but, nevertheless, familiar. Good land was selected in well-watered sites near the borders of coffee regions and areas of increasing Oromo Liberation Front strength and popularity. The residents of these areas were pushed off their land and told to move in with friends or relatives. They were not allocated new land elsewhere. Then in a series of meetings political officers from the capital announced the obligation to build houses and accommodate the newcomers. These new work obligations were the last straw for tens of thousands of farmers who were close to the edge of hunger already. They resisted both actively and passively. Some openly objected that they could not meet the demands. Individual acts of resistance and rebellion such as this met with immediate reprisal. Obligations for unwanted settlers were imposed in addition to all other required taxes and contributions.

The state's resettlement program merely extends to greater extremes forced labor policies that had already been introduced in the Oromo countryside. To ensure implementation of the resettlement program the government's political concerns take priority; policies are implemented regardless of their economic and social costs to local populations. And a strong argument could be made that they are implemented in specific areas because of such costs, i.e., as punitive measures (see Chapter X). Aside from the ecological effects of simultaneously building 800 to 1,200 permanent houses for the unwanted settlers in these areas using local wood and materials, the labor that had to be diverted from agriculture had an immediate, negative impact on production. Those interviewed reported, however, that those who oppose the government's policies are labeled "resistant," "rebellious" or "subversive of the revolution," and dealt with accordingly, which means imprisonment at best.

Required attendance at peasant association meetings and literacy programs was cited by nearly three quarters of these refugees as a major cause of production decline. During the initial administration of the survey questionnaire, it seemed a non sequitur when the response to "How do you account for the difference in previous high production levels and recent ones?" was often "Because of the literacy program" or "Because of peasant association meetings." Yet the responses here are consistent; 73 percent of the farmers interviewed mentioned required meetings to account for food shortages. Strong, coercive measures were used to force the unwilling farmers to sit through long general membership association meetings in which they had no voice and no interest. The meetings were held even when weather conditions were favorable for farming. Farmers who had to work for the peasant association several days during periods of peak labor needs for plowing, planting, weeding or protecting the crop from wild beasts were especially bitter that they had to neglect their crops because of the mandatory meetings. One person explained their dilemma:

> During the meetings the weeds take over the crops and the wild pigs finish the rest later while by force we sit in the peasant association meetings, our wives sit in women's association meetings and the children sit in youth association meetings.

Peasants who defy the peasant association officials' order to spend the full day in a meeting are usually imprisoned immediately for 10 days, a severe punishment during the peak agricultural season.

Even the process of calling meetings, which is the responsibility of the peasant association chairman (although he often receives his instructions from higher levels), takes several people away from their farm work. One man reported that his father had been appointed to a small position in the peasant association (which he did not want but could not refuse for fear of being considered "anti-revolutionary") that required him to spread the word about an upcoming meeting to other farmers. "When he was starting to work to farm," the son explained,

> The peasant association representative would arrive and tell him to go out to inform the others within a certain period of time. He could not do it in that

time so others such as myself had to assist him to prevent him from being punished. As a result, none of us could work in the field.

Not including travel to and from the meeting place, these mandatory gatherings lasted from nine or ten in the morning until six in the evening. The fixed time was nine to noon but the meetings never adjourned on schedule. Farmers observed that the speakers seemed to measure the importance of a subject by how many hours they could speak on it. When asked about the subject of the meetings one respondent answered,

They tell you how to make this government strong. Also we get sermons about how one who is farming should not trade and traders should not farm. The seminar is a means of locking your head. They are trying to make the collective work strong. Sometimes we are called to a seminar for one full week.

When the respondent was asked when this week-long seminar took place, the reply was,

During the weeding time. It took the time when we are supposed to be farming. We don't know why it is held at that time. They [government officials] choose the time; we don't ask. If we ask we are put in prison and accused of sabotaging the government's plan or revolution. "Because of your own interest you are undermining the good of the whole," they say to us. If we go to prison even for such a small thing we will never come out.

Similar reactions occurred near harvest time when farmers were required to attend political education classes while baboons destroyed their corn crop. One farmer vehemently commented, "The Dergue is the best friend of the pigs and the monkeys. He allows them free access to the fields while we sit imprisoned in useless harangues about paying more tax out of the crop that at that time is mostly eaten by animals." In an informal discussion following another interview, one young farmer remarked, "They should put the baboons in the meetings and let us go to farm the field. Then we could eat and get fat like the animals do." Others agreed, adding wryly that the baboons should learn and understand Amharic, and that the Dergue's cadre would probably be happy with that arrangement because the attendance would be large.

Attendance at literacy training meetings held during prime farming periods was also required. Farmers' typical complaints about the meetings included,

If a person does not go the literacy training they will imprison you for seven days during which you cannot do any work.

They intensify the literacy program when we should be farming. At that time we should be plowing the fields, and harvesting coffee and trading.

As if to confirm the Yabuus farmers' claims, while we were conducting interviews in March 1985 and the farmers were anticipating the spring rains, *Radio Addis Ababa* announced that the literacy program would be stepped up during April when university students were on a spring break. Within a few days of the announcement we heard thunderclaps from the mountains near the farmlands. Many of the Oromo peasants, who had fled only weeks earlier, commented that for those living under Dergue control, the planting time would come and go while bitter Oromo farmers were forced to sit in Amharic classes at the behest of a government-supplied Amharic teacher.

These refugees predicted that if they resisted, they would suffer. Either way, they would go hungry.

Disruption of the agricultural work cycle was devastating. Farmers explained that before the Dergue came to power, they had to work up to 16 hours a day to complete the job of plowing at the precise time when the land was ready. Describing how they broke the ground to allow the rain to soak the soil, the refugees explained that they not only farmed smaller amounts of land due to lack of time and freedom to plow, but also had planted different crops. Teff, for example, requires many more passes with the oxen-drawn plow than sorghum or horsebeans, but it is a more desired crop and fetches a better price. As a consequence of having less time for their own crops the farmers are forced to plant less desirable crops in order to have any harvest. Even so, the seeds often do not sprout because the soil is poorly prepared or planting is delayed.

Weeds were also mentioned as a major factor in reduced yields, but always in relation to the programs that kept farmers from fields when they should have been weeding. Alemneh Djene, who recently produced an account of peasant associations – based on interviews with peasant association members in Arsi – reported that farmers listed "too many weeds" as the most serious farming problem (Alemneh 1985:3). While Alemneh interpreted this factor as a technical problem, we found that it was a consequence of political coercion in the management of farmers' labor.

The Wollega Oromo farmers reported that the most grievous problem reducing their productivity was the destruction of the mature crop by predators while they were attending required meetings. Several mentioned that the meetings were not emergencies but were concerned with peasant association organization, the workers' party organization and philosophy, and one long seminar that ironically addressed the subject of why wild animals should no longer be killed. When asked why they did not suggest different times for meeting, the farmers answered that those who did were imprisoned, tortured and if released, always suspected of being an "enemy of the revolution." These farmers' very presence in Sudan indicated that they had given up all hope of resolving their problems by appeals through the system to change it.

A large majority of the farmers from Yabuus, 63.6 percent, said that the Dergue's confiscation of arms was a serious factor in the decline of production. Without arms and ammunition, the peasants had no defense against wild animals and predators ravaging the crops. The farmers' obligation to attend peasant association meetings compounded their inability to defend their crops from predators. One farmer explained,

In the past we had guns – old guns, Flowbers – for shooting the wild animals. The ammunition cost E$1 for 12 bullets. If we shot or wounded one baboon, the others would not come back for 14 days. Now they [the Dergue] have taken even those old guns away from us and the ammunition as well. But now the farmers, our wives and children are all in meetings unable to guard the fields.

Another refugee described it this way:

We used to chase the animals away with bullets. One birr would buy 15 bullets then. Those who did not have guns used sticks and stones to drive the

animals away. Now there is neither—no time or chance to wait for the animals and they took the guns away. Bullets are expensive now, but even if you find the bullets, there is no gun to use. It is not easy to estimate how much of the crop they destroy, but they certainly destroy more than we eat ourselves. That means more than half.

Another farmer reported that at one time the government representatives and the farmers agreed that local militia would ward off the beasts, but that proved ineffective. "They told us at first that the militia could come to shoot the animals if we called them. But they would only shoot if they had an eyewitness that the wild boars were actually *in* the crop. Otherwise he [the militiaman] will be punished."

Farmers reported that they had contributed substantial sums of money to government representatives to purchase ammunition through official channels in order to deal with the problem. According to one refugee,

We were told to contribute money and 10 to 12 kg of grain each year in order to buy bullets, and we sent a representative with these things. He delayed one year and eventually did not bring us the guns or bullets after all. After one more year we were given one gun with 50 bullets for 100 farmers. The gun was old. If the bullet misses the target [the monkey], the one who shot [the bullet] is fined. The monkey has to be killed and the tail brought in to the officials for each bullet used; otherwise, the marksman is liable and has to pay a large amount of money.

We were also forced to contribute 20 to 24 kg of grain two or three times for the same purpose but without any result because the bullets and guns never came for the militia. Since we were forced to live without guns and bullets, we have no way of dealing with this problem. Whenever we try to discuss this problem—or any problem—they only tell us to contribute more money and then the issue is ignored. Nothing is ever done.

In an intensive interview, one Oromo farmer explained that they were told that the Cubans eat baboons and that the government was going to sell them to these Cubans for a profit so no Oromo could attack them and no militia would be allowed to shoot them.

Killing baboons and pigs is illegal now because the government told us they have a use. Those who try to kill them will be caught. This is because they need these animals in Cuba. I don't know what they are going to do with them. I never saw the Cubans come though, and our crops continue to be destroyed. This is the reason they gave us.

Another farmer said they were told not to harm the wild animals because

They told us these animals may be eaten as food if there is hunger or starvation. But we never ate these animals for food. Anyway there were people who were hungry and starving who went into the forest and killed ibex [kudus] to eat. They were arrested and put in the Awaraya prison for six months. So I don't believe that this is the reason.

Another refugee reported that in his village they were told in a special seminar held by the Dergue that no one could kill animals anymore because "White foreigners are going to come to our country and look at these baboons and pigs. We never saw the *farenjis* [foreigners] but the animals became more and more a problem for us."

Farmers were exasperated at being unable to ward off animals from their fields; mandatory meeting attendance prevented following even a strategy of round-the-clock vigilance with sticks and stones to compensate for the lack of arms. One man remarked, "The Dergue is inviting the baboons and wild boars to drive us out of our homes and we are defenseless."

This remark is significant in light of reports that in the settlements in Asosa and on producers' cooperative-style collective farms run by the government in the same general vicinity the government action is different. During harvest time on those farms, when the risk of animals destroying crops is the highest, all work and government meetings are suspended while workers are dispatched to the fields to guard the crop (Niggli 1985a). This discrepancy in policy suggests a deliberateness in the failure to protect Oromo farmers from crop destruction. Perhaps this is an example of the system of negative and positive incentives utilized to organize farmers into large state-run collectives.

Military conscription of able-bodied youths was reported by 15.6 percent of those surveyed as a direct factor in declining production. The absence of youth who were sent away to the war front, they explained, caused a reduction in food supply at home.

A vast majority of respondents said that recruitment of young people to the war front had been a major issue a few years earlier, especially when the young were told they were being sent to defend the local area but were sent somewhere else instead. On average those interviewed recalled that only two out of 10 persons sent for short-term military service returned. Those that did return brought back stories of fighting in wars in places their parents had never heard of for purposes that remained unclear to them all. After 1981, peasant resistance to send children into the military became so great that when the government continued to push this policy, it drove young people into Sudan or into the ranks of the Oromo Liberation Front operating near their areas. This reaction of the peasants along the border may account for the decrease in conscription in this area.

Appointment to local government positions also had a deleterious effect on agricultural production. The burden on the family to feed and house family members who were required to work full time for the peasant association, whether as militia, secretaries, chairmen or in some other position, was mentioned more often (27.2 percent) than military recruitment as a contributing factor to declining production. Sons who were appointed to carry out peasant association work in the militia did not receive any compensation and were not available to help farm even enough to cover their own subsistence. One man explained,

> In our peasant association there are 300 members and 20 are selected to serve as militia. I was selected but I did not want the job but was appointed anyway. I had to work every day and any hour when I received orders from above. I didn't have time to work or to farm. I had to get my food from my parents. Sometimes I tried to hide from the authorities and work one to two hours a day on our crops.

On occasion, those appointed to act as peasant association militia and to enforce the association's laws clash with the leadership over acts they deem particularly outrageous. For example, when a highly respected 80-year-old man was ordered imprisoned for failing to pay taxes, the militiaman given the order said it violated his sense of justice so deeply that he refused to carry out the act. Both the elder and the militiaman were eventually imprisoned. Another example involves one of the militia's assigned tasks – to comb the area for delinquent farmers during peasant association meetings. Tension often develops between locally assigned militia and their neighbors who beg to go unnoticed if caught skipping a meeting so that they can provide enough food for the family. Militia who do not account for absentees are punished. In one area an offender had to work additional days for the government before he could return to his own plot.

Most of the farmers interviewed in Yabuus mentioned imprisonment in two different contexts. For several, imprisonment or the immediate threat provided the final impetus for their flight to Sudan. In addition, a large proportion, 86.3 percent, mentioned imprisonment as a contributing factor to decreased agricultural yields. Using the militia to enforce its decisions, peasant association officials could imprison anyone at any time. Reasons cited for imprisonment varied:

- For speaking up in a meeting.
- For suspicion of helping the OLF.
- For suspicion of trading contraband.
- For "being an Oromo."
- "The strong and brave are in prison. The weak cannot farm. The government is trying to destroy us."
- For inability to pay taxes.
- For "farming on my field when a seminar was called."

When women were imprisoned, the children had to accompany them, because other women who were required to attend mandatory women's association meetings could not babysit.

When a person is imprisoned, his or her family is also restricted in their work in the fields. Food is not generally provided to prisoners; family members have to drop their work to prepare their relative's food, bring it to the prison and wait for the guards to take it.

Those interviewed reported that they constantly feared imprisonment. When asked why they had not opposed government policies, they always replied, "We would be imprisoned and then our families could not eat." Because imprisonment jeopardizes both a family's present condition and their future food supply, many families encourage their members to comply with government demands and to avoid antagonizing government officials.

A constant theme in response to questions concerning declining productivity was the issue of land confiscation and redistribution. Of those surveyed, 52.2 percent indicated land redistribution as a direct cause of production decline. This percentage does not include the farmers from Kissar (Berta) who had been displaced directly from their land in the Asosa region during earlier phases of resettlement. These farmers, who comprised 26.6 percent of the sample, responded on the basis of what had limited their production while they remained on their land. Analysis of land redistribution is thus separated here from that of direct land confiscation, though the two processes overlap significantly in many cases.

In discussing the issue of land, the farmers in Yabuus did not have any basic grievance with the concept of land redistribution per se. In fact, a sizeable proportion of them had initiated land reallocation among themselves and had begun to redistribute tools and produce prior to Haile

Selassie's demise (see above). Some initially understood the Dergue's land reform policy to be a legitimization of what they had already begun. They said, however, that the later different kind of reallocation introduced by the Dergue was a major factor in the overall decline in productivity. These farmers felt that there were two major differences between the local Oromos' distribution policy and the Dergue's: first, that people who were judged nonviable producers but who had an independent loyalty to the Dergue were incorporated by force in the midst of the farming community, and second, that the Dergue controlled the land and could take it away without warning. In many cases these "nonviable producers" were sons of local farmers who had not taken up farming; in others, they were people who had previously lived in towns with other sources of livelihood but who had now been incorporated into the local peasant association. Both situations were cited as contributors to production problems in the Wollega region. One farmer addressed the Dergue's land redistribution policy at length.

People who before did not like to farm were given land in very rich areas when the land was divided up. Also they [government officials] took pairs of oxen from good farmers and gave them to those who do not want to farm like the rest of us.

We were given three days of oxen plowing for the husband, three days for the wife and children. The fertile land [chooma] was given to others who did not like to farm and did not do a good job. After plowing the land only twice — usually we plowed three to four times — they planted the seeds and the tchokorsa *[vine] comes and chokes the crop. The oxen that were given to the inexperienced farmers died because they were not his own and he did not care for them properly. Also, it was affected by God — showing that it is not God's will for them to have someone else's oxen. The farm that was wide became narrow — the grass overtook the area.*

These people do not want to work — from the beginning they are not working. Even today the ones who strengthen and cooperate with the Dergue are these people.

What were they doing before? Before they used to clean themselves and their clothes to pretty themselves and run around to different places as thieves and cheaters. They farm with somebody today — daily . . . taking the oxen on loan and in return farming two to three days for that person. Then they turn around and ask the Dergue for those oxen.

For example, one man farmed as a tenant and divided the product equally. He went to the Dergue and said, "This man has too much for his family," and asked the Dergue for the land. When he got it, he did not care for it properly, as I said. The grass grows over it and the animals eat it.

There are people from that place whose fathers were farmers. They are the ones who refused their fathers' orders and went anyplace they liked before.

They are the ones who inform on the people. They do not like to work. When they get nothing from the farm to eat, they go back to the Dergue and become spies for him, exposing people who they did not like as being EDU, contrabandists, supporters of the Dergue's opponents. For this the Dergue gave them clothes and food and later made them militias for the village, but the government never took them to the war front; they were kept at home as spies.

The Dergue put some of them in production cadres, orienting the people from the district how to farm, how to organize their production. These are the "experts" preaching to the people, but the people know them and they have had no respect for them, even their own fathers don't respect them.

I don't know how many of these types there are in the country; there are a lot of them in the government.

In my peasant association there are five out of 220 who are primarily involved in this spying who were shiftless people before. But they are in every peasant association and play a primary role throughout the country. They are not alone, they are working closely with the government. They have their own office or center in the district governor's office.

We call them peasant association representatives. All? Well, the ones who are coming from different places accusing peasants of contraband, feeding shiftas, etc. The word of these people is worth more to the government than the words of others, and when they make their accusations, the government asks for no further proof or documentation except their word.

From the beginning they liked the Dergue. Immediately after the Dergue came to power, they began to receive rewards for their acts, and later the government organized them. From our peasant association two were killed on the false accusation of these people, and now 21 are in prison in Lekemste on their accusation.

Another farmer explained how the land of Dergue loyalists was allocated in such a way within the peasant association territory that it surrounded the land of producers who resisted Dergue agricultural programs. Later the rules of collectivization allowed farmers within a peasant association who lived on discontinuous plots to choose to change their plots into a collective farming model. Then producers who lived interspersed with them had the choice to join the collective farm or move out of the area. Those farmers we interviewed pointed out that once people joined collective farms, they had to give up their oxen and other animals, work from 8:00 a.m. until 2:00 p.m. on the collective farm and take only a small portion of the produce. They saw the collectivization moves as schemes to surround them with unproductive farmers who wanted only to coerce them into giving up their oxen and then live on the hard work of people who really know and like farming and who do it well. This land redistribution process reportedly decreased even the good farmers' desire to work hard.

Others who cited land redistribution as a reason for the deterioration of agricultural production described how much good farmland was not reallocated when the Dergue implemented its land reform. For reasons about which the peasants could only speculate at the time, the government kept the fertile land that had belonged to rich merchants and landlords who left the area. Some of this land was given to incoming settlers in 1981 and again in 1984.

People who were directly displaced from their land as a result of redistribution or resettlement often went to live and work with relatives or friends before finally fleeing to the Sudan. These individuals reported that their land was being "lived on but not properly farmed" by the settlers who came to replace them. Typical comments included, "They don't know this land. The way they were farming at their home destroyed their own area. Now they are going to destroy ours."

Dungula-speaking farmers who were displaced by the government in the Begi and Shengul regions around Asosa (lands that border the current Asosa settlement farms) reported that their land was being less productively used than when they had it. Refugees from Kissar who had heard how their land was being used following their expulsion said that part of their peasant association land had been given directly to settlers, while other plots were left vacant. One man reported, "Nobody is on my land now except some soldiers who come occasionally to pick the mangos."

Obligatory transfer of resources to the state emerged as a significant obstacle to productivity. Forty-one percent of those interviewed reported that high taxes and contributions were a key factor in decreased agricultural productivity. Taxes and other obligations were distinguished by peasants and government officials as those payments for which receipts are given — "taxes" — and those that are not receipted — "contributions." In actual practice, contributions are equally mandatory as taxes. Tax collection was strictly enforced. More than a third of the refugees, 36.3 percent, reported that they even had to pay the next year's (1985) seed grain in taxes. No exceptions or appeals were tolerated. Failure to pay either resulted in imprisonment (most commonly), direct confiscation of household resources by government militia or security forces, or additional fines or increases in future payments.

All obligatory payments the farmers in this sample recounted were drawn from their private household plots and animal stocks or through sale of personal property. The produce from the large, communally farmed plots — which officially belongs to the peasant association — is not included here as a "payment."

Determining the total amounts paid for taxes and contributions became such a time-consuming part of each interview in Yabuus that that part of the general survey questionnaire was abandoned in Yabuus and relegated to the intensive interviews. Consequently the manner in which such payments to the state affected hunger or economic hardship and, in turn, led the refugees to flee was assessed in each intensive interview. Thus while these data are suggestive, they do not reflect a statistical average.

All those interviewed pointed out that the new government had promised to eliminate taxes and payments to landlords. This promise, along with endorsement of peasants' initiative in expelling further Amhara landlords and their Oromo collaborators, accounted for the initial positive response by the local population to the Dergue and its policies. The breaking of these promises, however, accounted for the peasants' bitterness and sense of betrayal. Outrage was so strong that all respondents remembered with precision the exponential rise in baseline taxes. The first tax payment required was a E$7 land tax. This land use fee jumped to E$20 the next year in 1978. Following that, it rose from E$30 in 1980 to E$50 in 1984.

In addition to the land taxes, peasants itemized a wide range of other taxes. Farmers were given receipts when they made some of their payments, although few could remember the exact explanation for the tax. Some of the farmers could not read their receipts and none of them brought any of them to Sudan. Examples of the taxes reported follows:
• Land use fee, E$20
• All-Ethiopian Peasant Association, E$5*
• Building a house for the peasant association, E$5*
• District courthouse, E$5*

- Collective farm, E$10*
- Rehabilitation (for people who have been displaced or hit by *shiftas*—euphemism for national liberation front fighters) amount varied from appeal to appeal
- Women's association, E$3 per month per woman and E$1 required purchase of organization pamphlet*
- Youth association, E$3 per month per youth and E$1 required purchase of organization pamphlet*
- Photograph of oxen, E$5 (a farmers' association advertisement charge)*
- Chairman's fee, E$.50 per month (amount varies)*
- Roads, E$5*
- Schools, E$5*
- Siad Barre's death, E$1*
- Nekempte district committee, E$2*
- Woreda (district) committee*
- "Sleeping tax," E$.50*
- "Hair tax," E$.25*

(*Indicates those taxes for which the peasant had seen no return and/or did not even know the purpose.)

Those interviewed also reported being forced to make contributions, both in cash and in kind, for which they received no receipts. The most memorable of these were the 1978 "Call to Motherland" obligations for the war against Somalia, of which the peasants had no clear understanding. This contribution was reportedly the first major unreasonable, illogical, unexplained financial obligation, and it stayed in everyone's memory as the beginning of inexplicable yet unavoidable charges for which the government made no attempt to account for itself. Those interviewed said that they also learned at this time that the Dergue would retaliate harshly against any person or group who questioned its right to make exorbitant demands. People were first imprisoned during this period. "Even children were required to make payments of chickens at that time," remarked one farmer who had been forced to give livestock (an ox and two goats) plus wheat and barley without getting a receipt. It appears to have been the first of many efforts to extract "emergency" funds from the population. Later, Wollega Oromo were asked to give money and grain for starving brothers ("fellow Oromo") in Wollo, beginning in 1980 and for the resettlement of "famine victims" in 1984-85.

Among the 12 farmers who described in detail their payments of taxes and fees in the agricultural year of 1983-84, the average amount transferred was E$188. The totals ranged from E$102 to E$250 and were based on AMC prices—notoriously low—for grain and equivalent values for livestock and confiscated household goods.

Taxes over the previous five years had increased to such an extent that farmers were forced to sell livestock—even oxen—to pay them. Animals were sold to pay taxes and fees by two thirds of the refugees in the sample. Several farmers said that if they did not sell their assets, government forces entered their compounds and confiscated property in lieu of payment. The military's estimate of the property's value was far lower than the farmers could realize if they sold the assets themselves. Oxen were a prime target for this sort of action. In 1984-85, when the use of special security forces to extract delinquent payments from peasant association members was introduced, such raids increased. These troops were drawn from among settlers who had only shortly before been moved to Asosa. Using these troops, the government forced local residents to pay large sums for which they were given no receipts or explanation, or face forced confiscation by the troops, imprisonment or flight from the area (see Map 23).

Some 40 percent of the farmers reported that animals had been confiscated by the government for specific programs, of which the most common were resettlement and collectivization. During our intensive interviews, it became clear that the reduction in productive, agricultural assets — especially oxen — resulted in large part from transfer of property from the indigenous inhabitants living in regions selected for resettlement to

Map 23

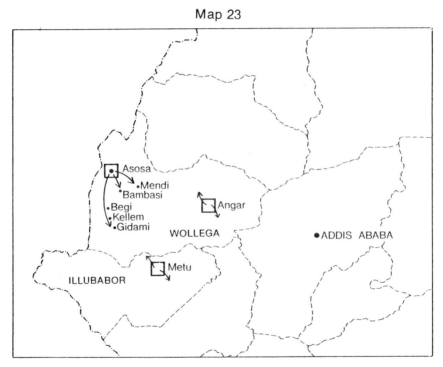

MOVEMENTS OF ARMED SETTLERS SENT AS SPECIAL SECURITY FORCES AGAINST LOCAL INDIGENOUS POPULATIONS

Squares indicate resettlement sites about which Cultural Survival obtained eyewitness accounts regarding the arming and dispatching of settlers by the Ethiopian government into the surrounding countryside. These settlers, initially provisioned by local Oromo and other inhabitants of the areas from 1980-83, have been designated as Special Security Forces and mandated to carry out "search and seizure" operations against suspected contraband traders in coffee, grains and other manufactured goods, and to arrest, punish or kill persons accused of supporting "counterrevolutionary bandits" (e.g., Oromo Liberation Front). Attacks are guided by information from local government cadre (see text). The behavior of these earlier settlers has greatly influenced the response of local residents to the recent 1984-85 influx of settlers.

the government. This was done in the name of supporting resettlement. Those who reported the loss of resources through this process considered it simply one of several guises under which the government dispossessed people and prevented them from being able to feed themselves.

Property was also confiscated by force under collectivization. Even though their own peasant associations had not yet been collectivized, 13.6 percent of the Yabuus refugees said that the collectivization program was a contributing cause of hunger and decline in agricultural production in their regions. Oxen and tools had either been appropriated "as a step toward" collective farming or had been made available "for the use of the peasant association." This was in addition to the requirements to build houses for incoming settlers as well as to supply them with oxen, tools and food, thus further decreasing farmers' productivity. One Tigrayan settler's account of the Oromo farmers' reaction to these settlement obligations sheds light on the issue.

> When we arrived we were taken to an open area where the local Oromo were called together and told to share half of everything they had. One Oromo elder said, "We have nothing to give. We ourselves are starving. If you put this on us, both of us will die. You cannot blame us." For this the man was beaten in front of the entire gathering of Tigrayans and Oromo and taken to prison. The other local Oromo said, "We are not keeping anything from them. Come and search our houses. Look at our property."

On one occasion settlers from Tigray who arrived where they were to be settled reported that they overheard all the Oromo residents of the area called together and given a speech in Amharic, in which a military commander said, "You must share everything you have with these people. If you have two glasses, you must give one to these new arrivals. If you have three, then you must give two of everything — clothes, furniture, household equipment."

Table No. 7
LIVESTOCK LOSS AS A RESULT OF PAYMENTS DUE THE STATE

Animals Sold to Pay Taxes and Fees	66.7%
Government Took Animals For Collectivization or Resettled People	40.0%

Increased taxes and obligations constitute a negative incentive in the drive toward collectivization. High taxes and fees in these regions also strengthen the government's enforcement apparatus, which ultimately assists in restructuring society. In short, Oromo peasant farmers are being coerced to finance the destruction of a way of life that they want to protect.

Economic hardships imposed on the Oromo caused them to seek income by smuggling coffee to Sudan. Increased contraband activity and the government's introduction of special security forces composed of old and new settlers to monitor this smuggling are signals of economic hardship. In the last year settlement and increased taxes and obligations have led people to search for this alternative and risky means to survive. Contraband sales then spurred a much more overt confrontation between increasingly burdened Oromo peasant farmers and the state. Peasants bearing the heaviest burden noted that they were being "punished" by this settlement program. One old man sighed, "Whatever we do to survive is wrong in the eyes of the Dergue." Another summed up the situation, "We cannot do what they require and live."

A few of the refugees in Yabuus provided details of government programs designed to improve crop production and water control and to prevent soil erosion in their areas. In the Wanga area of Begi, the entire peasant association was ordered to follow the instructions of a man sent from the district capital who directed the farmers in the construction of an earthen dam. The undertaking required several working days for all able-bodied men in the peasant association. However, the entire structure was washed out after the first rains, confirming the farmers' suspicions about the "expert" who "never farmed in his life." Aside from being a failure, the project also reduced agricultural production that season by taking laborers away from their agricultural activities.

Another example offered was a scheme to restrict the runoff of rainwater and topsoil. The association was told to build small terraces and plant certain new grasses on them to make them hold. The grasses overran the area and choked out the grain. The farmers received no compensation for their reduced food supply. The instructor's "expertise" had been acquired at a seminar on terracing in the capital, but, according to the farmer, he had no previous experience.

Reasons Respondents Left for Sudan (see Tables 8 and 9)

Respondents overwhelmingly reported that land takeovers by the government (56.8 percent) and fear of imprisonment (82 percent) for not complying with government programs and policies were the immediate causes for their flight to Sudan. In addition, some respondents (11.8 percent) reported that they wanted to go to Sudan to join others and fight the Dergue or to protect their sons from conscription (6.8 percent) into the Ethiopian army.

Table No. 8
REASON RESPONDENTS LEFT FOR SUDAN

Land Taken by Government	56.8%
Imprisonment or Threat of Imprisonment	82.0%
Decision to Fight Dergue	11.1%
To Protect Sons From Conscription	6.8%
Warfare	0.0%

Specific government actions had displaced 56.8 percent of the Yabuus respondents from their land. This includes 26.6 percent of those refugees from Kissar near Asosa who left during the massive expulsions of Beni Shengul (Berta), Dungula-speaking people from the regions where massive resettlement took place from 1978-80 and where resettlement has been stepped up as part of the 1984-85 resettlement of famine victims. The existing resettlement program has been undertaken on a grander scale since the creation of the Workers' Party of Ethiopia and the subsequent decision to invite the Western media to witness the extent of the famine crisis in selected regions of the country. More than a quarter of our respondents in Yabuus were among the people who have formerly occupied the regions of Asosa that are continually referred to in the Ethiopian and Western press as "uninhabited, virgin territory to be settled by famine victims." Others were displaced through various processes that in effect penalized them for resistance to programs that they thought were destroying their ability to survive. Their lands, too, were destined for settlement by others either in collective farms or settlements of populations more compliant or politically controllable by the government, or who had been moved long distances and made dependent upon government programs.

Table No. 9
YEAR RESPONDENT DEPARTED HOMELAND FOR SUDAN

1976	Gitaan	2.2%
1977	Gitaan	4.4%
1978	Gitaan	22.3%
1979	Berta	4.4%
1980	Berta	11.1%
1981	Berta	4.4%
1982	Oromo	8.9%
1983	Oromo	2.2%
1984	Oromo	22.2%
1985	Oromo	17.8%

Map 24

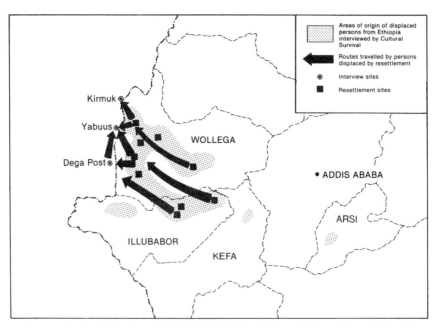

ROUTES TRAVELED TO SUDAN BY DISPLACED PERSONS FROM ETHIOPIA WHO WERE INTERVIEWED BY CULTURAL SURVIVAL IN SUDAN

Actual imprisonment or threat of immediate imprisonment accounted for the major factor causing refugees in Yabuus to leave their homeland for Sudan. The Dergue's coercive actions directly incited 82 percent of the refugees in the Yabuus sample to flee. (The figure includes individuals in the above category who were imprisoned for opposing the confiscation of their land.) An overwhelming proportion of the refugees cited imprisonment as the immediate cause of their flight to Sudan, but this explanation masks the specific activities that caused people to be imprisoned. People in this category reported the following reasons for being imprisoned:

- Actual or suspected trading in contraband such as smuggling coffee or trading outside the prescribed government channels
- Failure (refusal or inability) to pay taxes or meet required levels of contributions
- Resistance to government orders such as opposing the re-election of a specific officer or refusing to arrest a neighbor as part of a militia duty
- Opposition to a government policy such as recruitment of militia or resettlement
- Continuation of farming activities in defiance of government literacy or political education seminars
- Suspicion of helping the OLF
- Suspicion of having a family member who was a known or suspected opponent of the government or supporter of the resistance movement

One particular respondent explained that he left his homeland for "fear of imprisonment for failure to pay taxes."

In the place known as Gibba 1,200 settlers came and Oromo had to build houses for each of them. The land selected was actively farmed cropland that the residents had to leave and make way for the newcomers after providing them supplies.

The local peasant association was ordered to buy oxen and other supplies. In addition, the local inhabitants had to pay E$10 each for support of the resettlement program.

When land was taken from people they were forced to move wherever they could persuade someone to take them in. No new land was made available for the locals. Many of them were said to have escaped through Asosa and Kirmuk into Sudan.

The primary reason that they left was that their land was taken out from under them; no new land or any provision was made for them [to make a living] and they had to give all they had for the newcomers, which stripped them of all their belongings. Then, there was additional money required from them to buy oxen for settlers. The same requirements were made of women and boys and girls equally even though they had all produced as one household previously. They have nowhere to go. Isn't it enough to get out? When they have no more to give they were imprisoned. People in the same conditions as those who were imprisoned took notice and ran for safety.

I myself did not wait to be imprisoned. I left after they made the announcement. The reason they gave for doing all this is that "The Wollos have to be fed; there is nothing to eat in their country. Whatever you have, give them. Let them eat. Buy them oxen. Let them plow and eat." No one was allowed to complain or even ask questions about the process. Some who did were killed. Others were imprisoned and disappeared. Even a slight protest was punished *harshly so people kept quiet and swallowed their reaction. They value their souls; they don't throw them away when the outcome is certain. People remain quiet until they finish all the animals they have and then they leave.*

Many refugees who fled to Sudan for fear of imprisonment were, in fact, opposing settlement — farming rather than building houses for settlers, not providing equipment for settlers or showing sympathy to the OLF who they hoped would drive away the unwanted settlers.

Throughout the interviews the Oromo farmers often explained their fear of imprisonment by referring to the capricious, inexplicable executions of persons they personally knew to be innocent of the "crimes" of which they were accused when arrested.

There were repeated references to the belief that "If I go to prison for that, I may never come out," or "It doesn't matter whether I did it (sell contraband or support the OLF), Mr. X did neither of those things and they killed him."

Limitations of time prevented our following up on each of these kinds of statements, but occasionally we did. The following is an account of the public execution of eight men accused (falsely in several cases, according to our information) of supporting the Oromo Liberation Front. The man who recounted the executions was in the process of explaining why he had left the country following a false arrest for aiding Oromo guerrillas. His statement is quoted at length.

The Dergue appointed me as a chairman of the peasant association against my will. They later complained that I should be able to stop these people who go back and forth to Kurmuk and Sudan and who support the Oromo [OLF] by influencing people to leave the country. The government at the district level sent a paper to arrest me. Those who brought the paper took me secretly and held me five days in the meeting hall. One good militiaman who did not want to see my death informed me of the plans and persuaded me to escape to save my life.

I was imprisoned for something I absolutely did not know about. I had not seen these Oromo [OLF] for even one moment with my eyes at the time I was caught. It was a complete lie.

I saw the Oromo [OLF] when I arrived here [in Sudan]. It was a false accusation.

However, eight men were killed in front of me for the same reason. Among them Berama Gheeresa is a case I knew. He was shot dead, accused of ordering his wife to prepare food for those people whose hair is long [presumably OLF] and forcing her to feed them and give them shelter before allowing them to go. This account of his crime was given in a speech to people who were gathered by force to observe his killing. The officials asked the crowd to raise their hands and support Berama if we know he is innocent. We knew he was innocent, but no one would raise his hand, including me, because we were afraid for our lives too. There were people on that day who shit in their pants literally out of fear and frustration. Sbin Nureen Mohammed was another example. The authorities who delivered the speech in the town of Begi asked the crowd to raise their hands for the person. If anyone did, they said that he would be released and saved. Again nobody raised his hand, including me. All the people were afraid for their own lives.

The one who killed the eight people was Negussie Fanta [governor of Wollega administrative region and Politburo member]. He did so by standing and delivering the order to a soldier to shoot them. This soldier is from Wollo.

He was among the Wollo [to whom] we have contributed our grain crops — 36 kg per person the year he came.

More than 1,000 people witnessed this execution of the eight men in September 1984 on Saturday, Meskerem at 1:00 p.m. The place was Qochimo in Begi town at the place of the former Abderatim's house known as Latto Qochimo.

Everyone witnessed it unwillingly. It was market day, Saturday. We live in the rural areas so nobody informed us that there was to be a mass killing. Many people were on the road to market pulling many animals, especially goats. When the people arrived, they were told to leave their animals there and go to the place where this persecution took place. Nobody knows whether their animals were taken by the Wollo or not, but the animals disappeared. It was raining.

After we reached there, people were already so afraid, they wet their pants. Some started escaping.

The people to be killed were bound with iron chains and their eyes were covered with red cloths. They were killed by bullets not sticks. Berama was killed by nine bullets. Nobody received only one bullet; they shot each person at least four times — four to seven times. The people were buried in Qochimo right there. After a single hole was dug by us, the unwilling witnesses, we were also forced to cover the corpses with soil. After that, another speech was made where the official [Negussie Fanta] said to the crowd of people gathered there that the eight men had done something against Ethiopia, and declared for the others not to do such a thing against Ethiopia.

Following the speech, we were told to stand in three rows and were guarded by soldiers not to go out. Then a bomb was exploded and the bodies were blown up into small bits and scattered throughout the area like the seeds of a farmer who goes out to sow. The hole where they had been buried was left empty. The bomb also uprooted eucalyptus trees in the vicinity.

The exploded grave was located right in the same place where we were forcibly gathered and where the killing took place. It is where the officials train, educate and certify the militias. The officials then boasted to us that they, the government, have such weapons as these bombs which can disperse human flesh to the sky. Then they asked, "What do the people whom you support have, those who went to the bushes and the forests (the OLF)? Do they have this kind of bomb?"

The people who watched had no power, they have nothing in their hands because their own guns were taken away from them. We all wanted to release these eight men since we were many in number, but we could not. We were furious and we were terrified.

When I was arrested after that, I was innocent of any charge, but there is no justice, there is no hope for me to live. Berema [one of those who was shot] appealed to them to kill him on Sunday if they kill him and allow him at least to see the market on Meskerem, our holiday. They refused even that to an innocent man.

This account is quoted at length to reveal the logic and experience that lie behind the peasants' fear of imprisonment, fear of drawing attention to themselves, fear of attracting the disfavor of spies or of officials. Behind the statistics of actual or threatened imprisonment are case after case of increasingly well-orchestrated state terrorism strategically carried out to the maximum effect.

People in our sample were able to supply more detail of this sort than we were equipped to record. In fact, the account given above came from a man routinely slotted for an intensive interview from among those who responded to our random sample survey. He fell into the statistical columns of having escaped due to "fear of imprisonment" for "suspicion" of anti-Ethiopian activities. His elaboration paints a picture of direct and indirect coercion that enables us to shed light on the possible responses of others who operate in a similar context.

Fear of imprisonment was cited in response to the question "How do people pay their debts when you say they have nothing to pay?" One man said,

> Once the decision has been taken by the authorities of the peasant association, then people have to pay even their seed corn which was reserved for the coming year's planting or sowing season. It is mandatory. Whether they take it or not, they will pay. There is no alternative.

How do peasants react?

> In fact, the people have complained so many times. But there is no official who will take their complaints into consideration. The moment they tried to discuss the problems concerning contributions, debts, the Wollos and the Dergue soldiers, the authorities call them counter-revolutionary elements, a kind of criminal, and then beat them till the blood lets from their bodies and then burn them one after the other. For this reason they try to pay their debts by selling grain — or those who have anything give it automatically. The problem is that when they finish the grain and everything else they have, they are forced to leave for Sudan.
>
> I have seen many people imprisoned for three to four months and labeled as "counter-revolutionary" when they were unable to pay the required amount.
>
> There are almost 500 people in prison in Begi who are our peasant brothers. It is not possible to see them in prison; even money and provisions that were brought to them were left in the hands of soldiers. Two of these that I know personally were called "counter-revolutionary." They falsely accused them of saying that the reason that they were not able to pay their taxes was because they finished what they had to feed and to help the OLF fighters. This accusation comes to them simply because they are poor. These were shot dead on this accusation in Begi Wereda.

This account makes clear one of the linkages between the economic hardship which results from governmental policies and the political interpretation that is imposed on the economic disability.

The arbitrariness of the accusation as well as the arbitrariness of the execution were noted repeatedly. People felt extremely vulnerable and victimized. Individuals who had actively supported and aided OLF themselves were adamant about the false arrest and killing of others who had not. Such a climate is reported to have existed from 1977-78, when duly elected local officials were arrested for opposing government directives on behalf of their peasant association memberships. Several refugees expressed the sentiment, summarized by one, "The strong and the courageous are in prison or killed and the weak remain." The ability of the state to enforce many regulations about "counter-revolutionary activity" and to sniff out "anti-Ethiopian" sentiments has increased as the settlers who were brought to Asosa in the early 1980s have been armed and transformed into special security forces, then given blanket powers to interpret and enforce laws regarding both support to "bandits" (OLF) and the sale of contraband items, particularly coffee (see Chapter IX, section on settlers as security forces).

The ordinary farmer has come to conclude that he raises his head to his peril. The role of the state-sponsored coercion which has been brought in to back up even the most illogical and unjustifiable order from a state representative is a crucial factor in interpreting the behavior of the Oromo and Bartha farmers in this region.

Eleven percent of the refugees had left their homeland in order to find a way to oppose the government, to "get my land back," or to "liberate our land from that group [the Dergue and its supporters] so we can have our land back and return home to eat and live in peace."

Some of these individuals were aware that there were "anti-revolutionary" (anti-Dergue) forces in the forests and set out to find them and join them. The Oromo Liberation Front personnel who operated in liberated zones in their vicinity had mobilized others. One refugee explained,

> OLF forces came to our area and talked to the people. They are our children and our brothers. Their objective is to free us from the strangle hold that the government has around our throats. The people like it very much, although the regime is beating like bulls anyone who helps them (the OLF). This frustrates some people. The rest, like me, do not care about their life if they must live under the Dergue's kind of government, and they help those who are fighting for our liberation.
>
> Another 6.8 percent of the refugees left, as one put it, "To protect my sons from conscription from which they would never return."

None of the respondents mentioned warfare as a cause of flight, though individual stories often mentioned forced entry into their houses, burning of their homes and supplies, and public executions of suspected supporters of the OLF. They considered these acts an extension of enforcement of specific government policies and interpreted the events as such rather than as warfare.

Plans for the Future

In the Yabuus sample, 93.3 percent of the refugees indicated their plans "to return home when the Dergue is overthrown." This was stated in a myriad of ways.

> I want to raise my family in peace on my grandfather's land. The Dergue will never allow that. They have to go out.
>
> We have to remove this enemy sitting in our country before they destroy everything.
>
> We have to go home. We are here in this country [Sudan] by force. This land will not even grow the grass itself, though our souls are safe here. While we are sitting here, we are thinking of the trees in our country, the water in our country, the breezes of our country, the hills and mountains of our country. We can't sleep from thinking about our country. We have to get it back from these strangers.

Each refugee was asked, "If the Dergue gave you land, tools and supplies, would you go back? If the Liberation Front gave you land, tools and supplies, would you go back? If the international community gave you land, tools and supplies, would you go back?" These questions were asked routinely rather than inferred from the refugee's earlier statements. In response to the question about the Dergue's supplying incentives to return, the overwhelming response was, "How can you listen to all that I have told you about the condition created by the government and ask me that question? The Dergue is our problem. He cannot solve our problem. I can never go back until the Dergue and those who help him are out of our homeland."

In response to the question about international assistance, there were usually questions to clarify what or who the international community was.

> The one who solves my problem is the one who helps me get my land, who guarantees that I can work on it with my wife and family in peace with nature. Can the international community help me to do that? While the Dergue is there, none of these things can be guaranteed.

> Any proposal that people make which leaves the Dergue sitting in that place is not a solution. As long as the Dergue is in power, I won't go. I would rather die here.

> With this government still in power? No. I would not. How could I when I have just saved my soul then take it back to have it killed?

In response to the OLF providing assistance, people said,

> I would definitely go with the OLF. I would be able to live in my country in peace.

> The OLF is us, our children, our neighbors, trying to loosen the grip of the one who will choke us to death. Of course we will go with them. That is our hope for the future.

Only one person — besides the Komo from Sudan who was netted in the random survey — indicated that he wanted to stay in Sudan to find either a job or an education rather than go home to struggle with the difficult problems there. Another refugee said that he would work in Sudan to survive and help his family. If they decided to return, he would go.

The Dungula-speaking refugees offered detailed accounts of their attempts to survive in Sudan since their evictions from their homelands in Ethiopia in 1979 and 1980. They cut bamboo poles in areas around Yabuus and sold them to Sudanese merchants for SL1.5 per 1,000 or merely exchanged them for the food (primarily sorghum) they had received on advance at a high price. Caught in a downward spiral of indebtedness to merchants who sold the bamboo as building materials at a 700 percent markup elsewhere in Sudan, these refugees expressed a longing to return to a "normal" life of farming and tending mango trees and coffee. They mentioned that some of their group had gone to work in large commercial farms in eastern Sudan, but were not able to accumulate anything to bring back. None of the respondents nor their fathers had ever worked for wages in their home regions.

With regard to their immediate future in Sudan, most refugees, 86 percent, said that given the necessary equipment, they could farm around Yabuus. One farmer explained,

This [Sudan] is not a country, it is a burned place. I don't know if there is any ox or machine that can bring fruit from this land. I will try the best I can. The wood in this country is not like the wood in our country. I don't know what can be used to cut this wood. Our country is different, fertile. There you can take some wood and leave the rest and live with the remaining. Here you cannot. But we will try.

Another,

We do not have a single shilling to buy animals, but sheep and goats could survive here. Here we have no implements — no hoes, no plows, not even hand tools — to attempt to grow our own foods. We hate sitting. At home we were working. If we had the essential equipment, we could probably grow ... sorghum here. We could grow enough to sell and then buy other things.

Chapter VIII

POLICY-RELATED FOOD SHORTAGES, DISPLACEMENT AND COERCION: SUPPLEMENTARY DATA FROM REFUGEES IN THE SUDANESE BORDER TOWN OF KIRMUK

The data presented in this chapter were collected from refugees found in the trading town of Kirmuk located in Sudan on the Sudanese-Ethiopian border, some of whom were registered with the authorities as refugees and some of whom had reported themselves as labor migrants. These people were eking out an existence through a variety of extremely low-paying, petty, income-generating activities, agricultural and casual wage labor.

Refugees in the Kirmuk/Yabuus region of Sudan were receiving no assistance from the UNHCR or any of the larger humanitarian assistance agencies in March-April 1985. The Oromo Relief Association assisted many of them. Refugees in Kirmuk town care for themselves by a range of activities from casual wage labor to petty sales. Since these forms of income are rarely regular, they have built up networks for sharing with each other. Nearly half of the refugees interviewed in Kirmuk were met through an informal network in which Oromo speakers come together to exchange information over coffee, tea or even cool water. Others were located as we walked through town speaking with shopkeepers and their workers, observing people engaged in drawing and transporting water, and selling and reselling fruits, vegetables and contraband items coming in from the Ethiopian side of the border.

Since Bonnie Holcomb spoke the Oromo language, and her assistant spoke Arabic and Amharic, they were able to chat with many workers who were indiscriminately selected for conversation and identify them with regard to homeland area, language, religion and current condition. Our impressions and casual findings were that two thirds to three quarters of the laborers we encountered were Oromo refugees. Others were poor Sudanese. At first glance, these people, who were refugees from Oromo homelands, appeared to be Sudanese. Their language, their appearance, their names all fit the local Sudanese context. Some, who had arrived as recently as three months earlier, told how they had been thoroughly briefed by other Oromo about how to pass for Sudanese and had taken work in which they could pass undetected. This ploy was aimed not at local Sudanese — who could usually distinguish Oromo from transient Sudanese — but at Ethiopian authorities who crossed the border in search of refugees, contraband traders and defectors. Refugees tried to escape discovery in order to spare their families reprisals.

In Kirmuk, for example, refugees pointed out an Ethiopian district governor from Wollega who was sitting under a shop awning near the center of town and observing the proceedings, including our chats with refugees and Sudanese alike. Refugees explained that he came often and watched the contacts between traders and persons of all kinds on the Sudanese side of the border. They interpreted his visits and those of his associates as part of the recent crackdown on the transport and sale of contraband coffee. Our interviewing in Kirmuk was much easier outside his purview and after he left.

Personal History of Respondents (see Tables 1, 2, 3, 4 and 5)

We talked to and surveyed 23 people in Kirmuk town. Their average age was 33 years. Some 47 percent were married and 52.2 percent were single, compared with 77.8 percent married in the Yabuus survey. About 45 percent of those married had at least some of their children with them in Sudan; 27.3 percent were accompanied by all of their children.

Table No. 1
PERSONAL HISTORY OF REFUGEES
INTERVIEWED IN KIRMUK TOWN

Average Age of Respondent	33 years
Sex	
Male	73.9%
Female	26.1%
Marital Status	
Married	47.8%
Single	52.2%
Number Children per Married Respondent	6
Respondents With All Children in Sudan	27.3%
Respondents With Some Children in Sudan	45.5%
Number of Children in Sudan per Family With	
Children in Sudan	7.2

Nearly 74 percent of those we talked to were male. In Kirmuk, we could talk to women by adjusting our schedules to meet them when they were free to talk. Consequently, we talked to the women we encountered as freely as we did to the men. The low percentages here reflect the low percentage of women refugees in the area. (We later learned that some women we had interviewed in Kirmuk in March had, by April, moved to Yabuus camp or Damazine town to live in family settings or a larger community with more stable work opportunities and lower visibility.)

Several refugees reported that Oromo women refugees coming across the border were often captured by Sudanese who kept them as servants under the threat of handing them over to the Ethiopian officials if they did not cooperate. Oromo Relief Association representatives confirmed that they were aware of this problem and in fact had enlisted the assistance of Sudanese security personnel to retrieve Oromo refugees from houses where they were known to have been held against their will. Refugees in the area insist that a large number of women crossing the border are lost in this fashion. The same may well be true for children who come alone or with women. Each of the women we interviewed had come with a specific contact person in Sudan and a clear set of directions as to how to find that person on her own. Each had found her Sudanese destination on her own and was then taken by other refugees to the Sudanese authorities to be registered, and thereby avoided abduction in Sudan.

Over half of these refugees in Kirmuk claimed to have been Moslem in their home areas; 26.1 percent were Christian and nearly as many, 21.6 percent, stated that they had been Christian at home but had become Moslem in the Sudan. (In the Damazine camp, refugees also had told us that three days earlier they had been Christian but had decided to become Moslems since arriving. In Damazine problems of food and water distribution had led to this decision. The slaughtering of meat acceptable to a Coptic Christian must be done by another Christian; the same is true for Moslems in Ethiopia. These dietary practices deeply affect relations between those of different religions in Ethiopia.) Neither Christianity nor Islam is indigenous to the Oromo, however, and both practices contrast with traditional beliefs. Oromo refugees in Kirmuk explained that they had no qualms about shifting their religious identities in a new setting, since it had been a formality required by the authorities at home anyway. The reasons they offered for the change were as casual as "to fit the environment," "to have better relations with my new brothers [the Sudanese]," "because it is so simple to change my name to Mohammed," "the advantages are many for eating, dressing and registering," "the Sudanese cannot write the other name." Most of these refugees, interestingly enough, had been given Amharic names to use in Ethiopia in addition to their Oromo birth names. This is probably why they considered the other name and religion expendable.

Table No. 2
RESPONDENTS' RELIGION

Moslem	51.2%
Christian	26.1%
Moslem in Sudan, Formerly Christian	21.7%

An overwhelming majority of the refugees interviewed in Kirmuk were from Wollega, although one man was from Arsi and two women were from Illubabor. Nearly 22 percent of these refugees had lived in urban areas in Wollega (Asosa, Nekempte or Gimbi); the others were from rural areas.

Table No. 3
GEOGRAPHICAL ORIGIN OF THOSE INTERVIEWED

	Number	Percent
Wollega Province	20	86.9%
Tongo	1	
Begi	7	
Qellem	2	
Jimma Horro	2	
Asosa	2	
Nekempte	1	
Mendi	3	
Gimbi	1	
Buno Baddale	1	
Arsi Province	1	4.3%
Illubabor Province	2	8.6%

All refugees interviewed in Kirmuk spoke Oromo as a first language. In town we met one other person who spoke Amharic but did not interview him. Refugees informed us of a few non-Oromo refugees living in Kirmuk town, but we did not encounter them.

Of those surveyed, 34.7 percent spoke only Oromo. The same percentage spoke Oromo and Arabic; however, the refugees' knowledge of Arabic was often so limited that they had little contact with Sudanese. Thirteen percent spoke Oromo and Amharic, while another 13 percent spoke Oromo,

Amharic and Arabic. One woman from Asosa spoke Oromo and Berta fluently. Although we expected that the refugees trying to survive in Sudanese towns would be somewhat cosmopolitan, and speak more than one language, we found that 34.8 percent spoke only Oromo.

Table No. 4
LANGUAGES SPOKEN BY THE RESPONDENTS

First Language Spoken	
Oromo	100.0%
All Languages Spoken	
Oromo only	34.8%
Oromo-Arabic	34.8%
Oromo-Amharic	13.0%
Oromo-Amharic-Arabic	13.0%
Oromo-Berta	4.3%
Number of Languages	
One	34.8%
Two	52.2%
Three	13.0%

Only 26.1 percent of the refugees were literate — one person each was able to read and write Oromo and Arabic. Three people had learned Amharic in formal schools (government or foreign missions in Wollega), one person had been certified in Amharic in Asosa's literacy program. This person, though she had passed Asosa's literacy exams, said that she could read and write only her name. A special case to be noted under literacy is that of two sheiks who had departed Wollega when their source of livelihood had dried up following a Dergue decree against Koranic schools. These men, who had depended on income from their students, escaped to Sudan, citing religious persecution. They reported that although they could write Arabic and teach it, they could not read or understand the language. Therefore we made a special category for them.

Table No. 5
LITERACY OF RESPONDENTS

Literate	26.1%
In Oromo	4.3%
In Arabic	4.3%
In Amharic	17.8%
Can Write Arabic But Cannot Read It	8.6%

Economic Background of Respondents (see Table 6)

All reported that their fathers were farmers who kept animals, and all declared in no uncertain terms that their fathers had been far better off than they. Most interviewed had taken up some sort of income-generating trade or wage labor in Ethiopia and certainly since moving to Sudan. The only exceptions were recent arrivals.

Many of those interviewed had sought ways other than farming or herding to bring money and food into their households prior to escaping into Sudan. These efforts included coffee smuggling, and in one case, even signing up for military duty. Some had defied government requirements to work peasant association land while their own land stood idle. Others had skipped peasant association meetings to do other work for farmers who would pay them for taking the risk of being caught but who would not take the risk themselves.

Table No. 6
ECONOMIC BACKGROUND OF RESPONDENTS

Respondent's Occupation	
Farmer	34.8%
Farmer/Trader	13.0%
Farmer/Wage Earner	.7%
Farmer/Trader/Wage Earner	4.3%
Wage Earner	13.0%
Trader	8.7%
Farmer/Student	4.3%
Sheik	8.7%
Farmer/Student/Trader	4.3%
Father's Occupation	
Farmer With Animals	100.0%
Who Is Better Off?	
Father	100.0%
Respondent	0.0%

Battle for the Coffee Crop

These refugees reported their problems and dilemmas initially in economic terms, but in almost every case they explained how their economic activity had been initiated in response to political policies of the government that made it impossible for them to farm for a living as their fathers did. Through these interviews the link between increased illegal activities such as coffee smuggling and the Dergue's agricultural and marketing policies became quite clear. These refugees described themselves as victims of programs that prevented them from farming properly. They sold coffee to make up the difference. The government, however, sent representatives to estimate the coffee harvest of the region while it was still on the trees. Once the crop was harvested, peasants were required to bring all their coffee to the government inspector for measurement and sale. Peasants were not even legally allowed to drink a brew made from coffee husks without first registering them and having them weighed by the government. If the amount of coffee registered did not match the earlier projected yields, special contraband forces composed of former settlers in the Asosa settlement project would be directed to search the houses in the area to find the missing coffee. These troops would arrive unannounced, at any time of day or night, ransack houses and supplies and seize coffee and other items. People who were holding any coffee for consumption or sale were arrested and declared to be "anti-revolutionaries."

Refugees in Kirmuk explained that they had indeed held coffee to sell later in order to pay taxes and contributions. Because farmers were allowed to work only a few days on their own grain crops, they had small yields and few surpluses. One man pointed out that they were to undertake their subsistence farming during the left-over useless times of the year, just like they were supposed to drink and be satisfied with "coffee" made from the hulls and scraps of the crop; "the government took the best time, best land and coffee kernels, everything that is valuable."

According to those interviewed, government policies forced them to save coffee and to sell it to pay their required taxes and contributions. This is what led to harsh government actions. Thus, a battle for the coffee crop has begun that is similar to that for food crops, except that the government has not yet secured a hold over coffee planting, tending and harvesting to match its control over the cultivation of grain in communal plots. Many of those displaced by resettlement as well as some of those recently resettled see the present push for resettlement as an intensification of the battle over who controls the coffee crop. Efforts to remain financially solvent led many local inhabitants in the southwest to be branded "anti-government" and subject to imprisonment and worse. These conditions led to their flight as refugees. However, most reported that they left for Sudan only after repeated imprisonment and threats to their family led them to fear for their lives. They lamented that the government would rejoice at their departure and take over their coffee trees. Some of the refugees speculated that strangers would be brought to pick and tend the coffee and that the local people would lose their coffee altogether. Talk often turned to armed resistance during these conversations.

Causes of Famine (see Table 7)

Refugees who came to Kirmuk often addressed the causes of famine and their present hardships as they spoke about their economic activities in their homelands. They attributed the hardships to government policies that either kept them from working or allowed the government to confiscate legally what they produced. All respondents cited high taxes and "voluntary" contributions as a major contributing factor in causing hunger in their areas. Equal numbers (91.5 percent) reported government obligations to work on communal plots, to prepare the ground and houses for settlers brought into their areas, to clear and build public works projects of various sorts and to attend long meetings at the command of "higher authorities." Some 65 percent cited the military conscription of young men as a factor in declining agricultural production. Another factor was the repeated imprisonment of workers, which prevented 78 percent of those interviewed from farming their land.

Declining soil fertility, lack of rainfall or insects, so-called natural factors, had not affected these people's homelands. Whenever such "natural" factors as wild animals eating the crops or weeds taking over the crops were given as a cause of declining yields, they were cited as a consequence of one of the specific government policies listed above. One man even insisted that a hail storm had ruined his teff because he had not been able to bring it in when it was ready for harvest. While his crop was lost, he noted, the crop of the peasant association plot was not. He went on to explain that teff is a fragile grain that cannot be salvaged if a storm knocks it to the ground. Since all farmers know this and harvest their crops as quickly as possible, he said, the government, not the weather, was responsible for his ruined crop. The same logic was applied to weeds overtaking crops and wild animals plundering the ripened grain while farmers were forced to sit in meetings required by the peasant association authorities.

Table No. 7
CAUSES OF FAMINE-LEVEL FOOD SHORTAGES
(Factors Often Cited in Combination)

Taxes	100.0%
Peasant Association Meetings	91.3%
Peasant Association Labor Obligations	91.3%
Imprisonment of Work Force	78.2%
Military Conscription	65.2%

Reasons for Leaving for Sudan (see Table 8)

A majority of refugees in Kirmuk (56.5 percent) told us that the final decision to leave home was made in the face of imprisonment or reimprisonment.

When I left school due to the fact that I could not afford the school uniform, they forced me to write [become the secretary] for the peasant association. I had to spend long hours keeping records for no pay. They said it was my revolutionary responsibility. I could not refuse the job of secretary or they would imprison me. I was afraid of the government. I could be called at any time from my house. I could not help my father on the farm, but they had to feed me. I brought nothing to the household but was taking food so that my family was starving.

In order to leave the peasant association position this man had to leave his home since he would be imprisoned for resisting conscription to peasant association work.

Another man was arrested for refusing to imprison his neighbors who were too poor to pay taxes and contributions. He had been assigned to bring them to jail, but chose to defy the authorities out of concern for the old couple. He said it went against his belief to do such a thing. Others, who had seen friends and relatives taken to the military never to return, escaped when they and their families could no longer protect themselves from being taken by force to what they considered certain death.

Also among those who had escaped prison and reached Sudan were those who had resisted forced labor for the peasant association, those who had been arrested for the performance of an Oromo dance at a youth association meeting and two people who had been unable to pay taxes. One woman in this latter position was sent to prison in Asosa town when she was unable to pay for a magazine distributed at her women's association meeting that cost E$1. Since the purchase was obligatory she was sent to prison with her child, who was 10 months old. The woman had no idea what the magazine was about since she could not read, even though she had a certificate for passing the literacy course. Passing the course, she said, required only reading and writing her name. In prison she was required to perform hard labor as are all prisoners. Upon release she left for Sudan with her baby.

Other reasons for leaving for Sudan included the confiscation of good farm land by the government to be given, in turn, to those being resettled. One man told us that many people were removed from their land and their houses in order that settlers could take over both the houses and farms. Several people reportedly planned to ask the OLF for help, while others moved in with relatives. Still others were "waiting by the border or in the forests until the program falls apart and they can return." This man reported that many people were directly displaced by the resettlement program, but few came directly to Sudan because they had not given up hopes of retrieving their property. This man expressed a desire to earn money in Sudan and then return to fight for his land.

A sizeable proportion of Oromo refugees from Wollega who were in Kirmuk (21.7 percent) left for Sudan because of religious persecution. These people were either sheiks who had taught Koranic school or students who wanted to pursue Koranic studies. They explained that despite the official policy stating that religious freedom is protected by the Dergue, Moslems were, in fact, not allowed to practice their religion. One person related that he had been searching for a teacher of Kitaab (the second stage of Koranic learning) and was staying with a devoutly religious man who had opened his house to Koranic students and housed and fed them in keeping with his strong religious beliefs. At one point everyone in the house was arrested and held for two months by peasant association officials who said, "This religion is not good for the revolution." Following imprisonment — "without committing any crime except practicing my religion" — the person interviewed had left for Sudan with traders as soon as he could. The same man commented that during his search for a religious teacher, he had journeyed to Arsi and found "the condition in Arsi is much worse than it is in Wollega." Another refugee who also went to Arsi to find refuge from religious persecution in Wollega discovered more restrictive conditions for the practice of Islam than those he had experienced at home. Another refugee reported that his Koranic school in Kefa was forced to close in 1984.

Some refugees in Kirmuk reported that they had left their homes in search of money to help their families make ends meet. They explained that declining agricultural production had forced family members to look for ways of supporting themselves and those at home by leaving and going as far away as Sudan. High taxes and new means of enforcing payment — many of the earlier settlers were organized to collect payments — had placed many in Wollega in a destitute situation. Some families decided to send their younger members to Sudan in hopes of their finding sources of income to assist their families.

Another cause for flight was recounted by a group of Oromo women who had married Sudanese traders and merchants and settled in the women's homelands to raise their families. Their husbands had prospered and bought land in their wives' regions during Haile Selassie's reign. After the land reform policy was implemented, this prosperity continued as markets expanded for items from Sudan. The families' moves to Sudan were made to protect their children from conscription into the army. The move was also made in order to establish a firm economic base in Sudan. These Oromo women referred to themselves as refugees and emphasized their plans to return to their homeland as soon as a change in government made peace possible. Although their position would seem secure in contrast to that of others, these women refused to take Sudanese citizenship, taught their children Oromo in the home and declared their intent to return as soon as possible.

A final category of interviewees included a defector from the Ethiopian military who had served on the Eritrean front. He had originally joined the army when his family could no longer pay to fight his recruitment. He reported low morale in the military, discrimination along ethnic/nationality lines and lack of confidence among the fighting forces. This man left to seek ways to oppose the government and stated that he had come to Sudan to find ways to join the Oromo Liberation Front.

Table No. 8
REASONS FOR LEAVING FOR SUDAN
(Factors Often Cited in Combination)

Fear of Imprisonment or Reimprisonment	56.5%
Religious Oppression	21.7%
Resisting Conscription For Military or Militia	21.7%
Search For Money to Help Family Inside	8.7%
Objections to Forced Labor	8.7%
Sale of Contraband Coffee	8.7%
Inability to Pay Tax or Fees	8.7%
Marriage	4.3%
Land Confiscation	4.3%
Sought Medical Care Not Available at Home	4.3%
Defection From Ethiopian Army	4.3%
Fear of Imprisonment For Performing Cultural Dance	4.3%

Plans for the Future

Most (74 percent) of the refugees interviewed in Kirmuk stated that they wanted to return home and would do so when the current government was overthrown and replaced. Twenty-six percent of the refugees expressed a desire either to pursue religious objectives (i.e., Koranic studies) or to get work or education in whichever place they could do so in peace. These refugees said that they would return home if the government changes, but they were passive about their role in bringing that about. Seventy-four percent, however, expressed an active interest and determination to do whatever they could do to bring about the necessary changes so that they could return home.

Chapter IX

THE IMPACT OF RESETTLEMENT:
FURTHER TESTIMONY FROM PEOPLES INDIGENOUS TO
AREAS TARGETED FOR RESETTLEMENT

This chapter focuses on the information concerning resettlement that was available from peoples indigenous to the affected areas found both in Yabuus and Kirmuk. Ironically, these data come from the inhabitants of the so-called "uninhabited lands" receiving settlers.

The development of the Dergue's resettlement apparatus is discussed in its historical context in Chapter II. What is revealed through discussions with residents of the targeted areas is the actions taken locally to implement the Grand Plans of the newly established Workers' Party of Ethiopia, beginning with the identification of lands to be resettled.

Resettlement Site Locations

Information concerning the location of all resettlement sites targeted for the 1984-85 program is not available to us as we write this report and may not be compiled anywhere until a cumulative building of the record is carried out. The most recent and complete map of settlement sites, however, was made available by Eshetu and Teshome in November of 1984 (see Map 6). According to the authors these 87 sites reflected "regular" and "special" resettlement schemes that had been established through mid-1984. We have added to the map those resettlement sites about which we obtained firsthand information in the course of our research. In three cases, the Asosa, Bombasi and Angar River projects, settlers or local residents who were present in Sudan had information about preexisting sites.

According to the government, WPE officials were involved in the site selection and their visits to oversee the progress of the resettlement programs in late 1984 were accompanied by a great deal of local public fanfare (see Appendix G).

Former RRC officials interviewed by our team in Sudan on March 15, 1985, reported the heavy hand of the party in the orchestration of the resettlement program, especially in its initial design. Those interviewed pointed out that site locations were selected despite considerations such as soil fertility, drainage, deforestation, lack of water supplies for projected irrigation, etc. They reported that following the formal establishment in September 1984 of the WPE there were purges within the RRC that were designed to ensure more efficient party control over the agency. (They explained that the earlier shift from Shemelis Adguna to Dawit Wolde Georgis as commissioner of RRC presaged this direction.) They further pointed out that a Special Party Committee under the direction (at that time) of Berhane Bayeh had taken over responsibility for drought and famine from the RRC. One consequence of this has been that although humanitarian agencies work with the RRC to plan implementation of various projects, the authorities that finally approve agreements are the Party Committees. It seemed obvious to these former RRC officials, who had been involved in resettlement at Asosa, that resettlement was 1) a gambit in the colonization of Oromo lands, 2) an attempt to destroy the TPLF infrastructure, and 3) a move to destroy private farming in the move toward the collectivization of agriculture.

In the government's resettlement program, in both the early phases and the present one, there is a significant overlap between coffee-producing lands and the sites selected for resettlement. In some cases the sites selected for resettlement are in the middle of the coffee-producing areas and potential coffee-producing areas; in other cases the sites border the coffee regions. In both cases, the use of settlers for special security forces to carry out, among other things, searches and seizures of the coffee harvest appears to be a key component of resettlement. From 60 to 80 percent of Ethiopia's foreign exchange is earned from the coffee produced in the country. That foreign exchange is absolutely essential if the government is to pay its debts for arms. In fact, in order to arm even the local security forces in the southwest, the government needs to confiscate a larger portion of the coffee crop. This is part of the vicious cycle that resettlement reinforces.

The Selection and Acquisition of Land for Resettlement Sites

In November 1984, *Addis Zemen* reported that, "Comrade Legase Asfaw, the Member and Secretary of the Politburo went to the three regions [Wollega, Illubabor and Kefa] to see the most efficient way of finding settlement areas in these three [administrative] regions" (see Appendix G). Although little more is publicly known about the site selection process, the experience of local residents confirms top-down decision making.

The place where settlers are coming to . . . was being farmed by Oromos. The woreda (subdistrict) governor made the place selection.

The land [for resettlement] was selected by the government.

The land they take is fertile land belonging to the sympathizers of the Oromo Liberation Front.

The land selected by the government was not necessarily land of those who have a bigger problem with the authorities than others. There is not a single person who gets along with the authorities in the entire area.

The actual lands used for resettlement were made available through a variety of mechanisms. Our findings shed light on a few of these.

One source of land for resettlement sites was fertile, previously farmed land that had been withdrawn from production during the land distribution that began in 1975. After the creation of artificial land scarcities in some areas, the good land was offered as an incentive to peasants so that they could be enticed to volunteer for collective farming in producer cooperatives. Local farmers reported that much of this land had belonged to large landlords or merchants who had left the area, but some had belonged to current peasant association members.

Some people [settlers] were moved to Gulanza near Giba to land that was owned by Al Kadir, a merchant, who produced a lot in the time of Haile Selassie.

During the land allocation of 1975 such areas were "held for government use." When the local response to forming producers' cooperatives was extremely poor, these lands were allocated to "famine victims" from Wollo. Imported to the area by the government, these people were forced to work at the direction of government officials where local people had refused. While the settlement of some of these lands began in 1979, other land originally designated for local producers' cooperatives stood idle at central government discretion until 1984 with the latest wave of resettlement. These "confiscated" plots usually bordered existing peasant associations. Farmers facing food shortages deeply resented the fact that they were denied access to lands to which they had historical claim. This dynamic has contributed to the fierce resentment of local Oromo to northern settlers being moved onto those lands.

A second category of lands designated for resettlement was those that had been cultivated until recently by Oromo farmers who were members of the local peasant associations. These were lands that had been made inaccessible to the local farmers gradually as the labor requirements of the peasant association had increased and forced the local farmers to abandon the plots. Through this process lands actively tilled by peasants had been reduced to less than a quarter of what they had cultivated from 1974-75. The loss of oxen and equipment to various government programs and the mandatory attendance at government meetings had prevented the farmers from working their lands. One farmer put it this way:

> The land the settlers are on was our land; we farmed it in the past. But how can people farm without time and without tools and without what is necessary to farm with — oxen? What is the use of land alone? You cannot eat dirt. We had the land, but we had no time to farm it, no tools to farm it with, so the government took it.

Plowing, sowing, weeding and harvesting on communal plots is mandatory for all members of the peasant association, though none of the produce from such activity goes to those who work the plot. Produce from these lands is kept in separate granaries and "withheld for absent militiamen" or "held to be taken or sold to the government" to raise money for shops, clinics, schools or roads that are never built. As the farmers lost hope — never benefiting from the grain, pulses, oil seeds or sometimes coffee produced in those long hours given at peak farming seasons — their work began to slacken. The amount of land they could or would farm was reduced and large areas, though still designated "peasant association land," remained uncultivated. As one man said,

> These lands have also been taken by the government to use for resettlement. We had to leave our own land for the settlers. We have grazed animals on that land and farmed that land and lived on that land and done all kinds of work and activity that people are capable of doing on it. Now because of government programs, we were not able to farm on it the way we did in the past, though we wanted to. We are tired from doing the government's work and from not eating. Some of the lands that had been highly productive in the past are in disuse by force.

Map 25

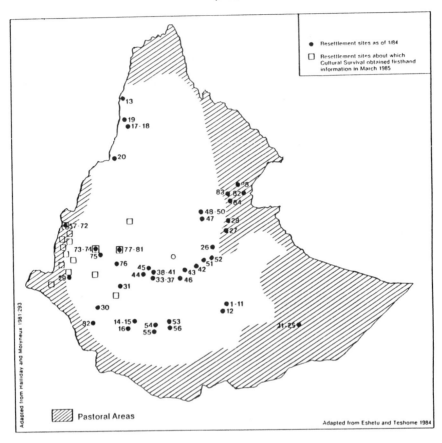

PASTORAL AREAS IN ETHIOPIA AND THE RESETTLEMENT SITES

Nomads in Ethiopia constitute 10 percent of the country's population and include pastoral groups throughout the lowland areas that border on the agricultural zones as well as nomadic hunters/cultivators in the southwestern border regions. In 1983, nomads accounted for 21 percent of all people settled by the Relief and Rehabilitation Commission — more than twice their representation in the overall population (note the relationship of resettlement sites to areas occupied by nomads). Resettlement appears to be a deliberate policy to dispossess nomads of their traditional lands even though similar policies in other countries appear to be socially and environmentally disastrous. (For a brief account of the settlement process of the Anuak, a pastoral/hunter/cultivator group, see Appendix H.)

A third category of land made available for resettlement was that from which people indigenous to the area had been forcibly evicted. The primary examples of this type of land we found were near Asosa, where both Berta and Oromo had been subjected to wholesale purges. The most common method of eviction appears to have been imprisonment and torture of key community leaders on different pretexts — "corruption," "selling contraband produce to Sudan," "supporting the anti-government forces." In two cases, about which we took direct testimony, entire peasant association memberships took the decision to flee to Sudan with their leaders, leaving lands dotted with cultivated mango trees and crisscrossed by rivers. Others were evicted by armed military personnel and simply ordered to go "elsewhere," either to clear forests if they wanted to continue farming or to move in with relatives farther from the road or away from the border. Such evictions of Berta and Oromo occurred primarily in 1979 and the early 1980s.

The first groups of settlers who arrived in 1980 in Asosa were from Wollo. They moved onto lands from which the occupants had been pushed out only recently. These were lands that had been described by the government as "unutilized," "virgin" or "uninhabited." Some of these lands were left vacant until the 1984 resettlement program began. Other lands from which the local inhabitants had been evicted in 1979 still stand idle. In both cases the land had been productively farmed and grazed by people pushed into Sudan or into more remote areas of Ethiopia. Consequently, settlers and visitors from the international community, for that matter, see no residents when they disembark in Asosa or Bombasi and often assume that the lands have always been empty.

A fourth category of land on which settlers in our survey had been placed in 1984-85 are fertile plots near the rivers from which peasants were recently displaced. These were actively farmed or planted by Oromos up until at least mid-1984. These lands were selected for resettlement in mid-1984 by officials — Politburo members and regional peasant association authorities — who traveled through the region identifying specific plots of land that would be taken by the government for the use of "famine victims from drought-afflicted areas." The residents were told to "vacate" the property, to live with relatives or neighbors or to obtain permission from another peasant association to clear new land to farm. There was no appeal.

> The place where settlers are coming to is Gibba. Before these settlers came, the land was being farmed by Oromos. The sub-district governor made the place selection. Those whose land was taken were moved to a place that has to be cleared and plowed several times before it can be farmed. They were required to build new houses for themselves and begin again with everything. The settlers live in their former homes.

> The land given to the settlers was good land close to the water. It produced large quantities of corn and millet last year.

> The government official gave a speech and told us that if the settlement site included someone's land or house, he will be forced to move from the area. This happened to many people.

Occasionally, though not always, residents in this category were informed that they could remain on their land if they chose to join newcomers in a collective farm to be established there. These farmers had not elected to join collective farms even with their close friends and relatives; they left the area.

People whose land was taken this year have left for Kirmuk and Sudan; haven't you seen them [in Kirmuk]? They are going every day.

The Settler Population

Our findings regarding the nature of the settler populations are reported in previous chapters (Chapters V and VI). To the preceding material we add one brief note here. Occasionally during interviews refugees revealed that there had been a selection process of sorts during recruitment. Virtually all settlers we interviewed were from either Tigray or Wollo regions. One person each from Gondar and northern Shoa proved the exception in our own random sample. Eritreans netted in the course of urban sweeps were reportedly released during the months of October and November 1984. Settlers captured in Addis Ababa from the bus station reported, "There were many Gondarites taken with us, but they all managed to escape. I don't know how." One man from Wollo reported to us that he was rounded up with an Oromo man from Arsi, who had not yet managed to escape from Asosa. A few individuals stated that one or two of the militia guarding them were able to speak Oromo; the rest spoke Amharic. No other nationalities or ethnic groups were mentioned by the settlers we interviewed.

A social profile of the randomly sampled camp population of escaped settlers (i.e., age, gender, family composition, occupation, religious affiliation, homeland region, languages learned and formal education) is presented in Chapter V and supplemented with data in Chapter VI. Refugees consistently reported the presence of the very old, the pregnant and the disabled who had been taken for resettlement. The ages of settlers ranged from 78 to infancy. Three different escapees volunteered the information that blind people had been taken and were present in the camps.

Relations Between Settlers and Indigenous Peoples

Oromo indigenous to Wollega had been willing to give money to impoverished famine victims in previous years. Contributions had been collected in the name of their fellow countrymen (with the announcement that they were helping Oromo). Peasant association officials explained that they were helping their "brothers" and "victims of nature." The following observations and comments indicate the major attitude shift that we found, however:

> In previous years we were asked to contribute to those in Wollo who are suffering famine and we contributed willingly. The government promised that we will be helped in the same way if we face problems. After some time we stopped cooperating and were no longer willing to give so much; after that they forced us.

> They told us that those in Wollo are our brothers [fellow Oromo]. But when they came here, they speak [sic] only Amharic; we cannot talk to each other.

Referring to an event in which several local men were publicly executed by settlers in Begi, one man observed, "The one who killed them [Oromo prisoners] was a Wollo who was transferred to Dejazmach Abdrahim's camp to guard the camp. He was among the Wollo we contributed crops for. We gave 36 kg of grain per person." Another said, "The Wollos themselves are the ones who now strengthen the regime against us. They came with empty hands but now they are armed and we are empty handed."

The irony of the situation in which the indigenous peoples found themselves did not escape the notice of a single person interviewed. As if the fact that they had fed and equipped — through contributions of supplies and land — the very people who now had been turned against them was not outrageous enough, they now pointed out that the government was forcing them at gunpoint to supply yet another group of settlers.

When the settlers came the first time, all were from Wollo. The "militia farm" was transformed into a "Wollo" farm. The Oromo came together and farmed it for them. The settlers were fed from that and the Oromo had to feed themselves from their private plots. We know this system. The ones who came before to Asosa were armed and sent to Begi. They spilled and splashed onto the surrounding area from there.

Another Oromo farmer pointed out that earlier settlers had been transformed from one status to another by the government.

The earlier settlers — those from Wollo who came in 1981 — they farmed collectively. At first they were fed by the Dergue and they later began farming together while still being fed by the Dergue. Now they received guns to do different work — and they go into the areas and eat from the people [the Oromo] as well as from the hand of the government. In their camps the government feeds them. In the countryside, the Oromo feed them.

Apparently some of the government representatives who first explained the resettlement program to the Oromo suggested that the new arrivals were "the brothers" (fellow Oromo) of the local people. When they came, however, and Oromo from Wollega saw that the two could not communicate because they did not share the same language and because the government kept the two groups apart, they felt betrayed. Large numbers of the arrivals were able-bodied young men who had been transferred without their families; it was not long before several incidents of attack, abduction and raping of local women occurred. This led to hostilities between settlers and local people and rounds of revenge killings until the settlers withdrew to their camps. Each group appealed to authorities to support and/or assist them.

Not surprisingly, local Oromo farmers anticipated that the same process would repeat itself with these new groups. Official statements made internally and to the international press reveal that the government is quite willing to encourage conjugal unions between settlers and local people in the creation of a new breed of Ethiopians. Comments such as the following disclose official sanction of such liasons:

... at Sambo settlement in Illubabor, one of several places where the government has built 40,000 such huts to house the settlers.

Do the settlers, who speak the languages of their home provinces, have problems integrating with local people? No, said an official of the Kefa settlement scheme. "Since the exercise started in November, there have been 40 marriages between the settlers and the local people."

The Weekly Review (Nairobi), 25 January 1985

At the time of our interviewing, however, neither settlers nor local people were aware of any cases of unions between persons of these groups. Individuals interviewed from both groups acknowledged that the situation was frustrating and unnatural. In short, there were not enough women for all the settlers. Prostitution was officially outlawed in the sites, and desperate settlers renewed attacks on local Berta and Oromo women while the government did nothing.

In the wake of hostilities over the raping of local women, the settlers from Wollo reported that the government renewed former unkept promises to bring their wives and families from home. When the government finally brought women to the sites, so much time had elapsed that they had to force many of them to come. Many women who had been married to settlers had often remarried in the unexplained absence of their former husbands. They were captured and taken to Asosa anyway. Some brought children, fathered by other men, with them to the resettlement sites. In some cases such children were killed by the former husbands.

Local Oromo reported that government officials ignored their appeals to protect Oromo women. The officials told them that the settlers were doing important work for the new Ethiopia and that local Oromos had to respect them and to keep their wives and daughters out of their way. As one man reported, "The officials told us, 'Don't send your wives to the river or to market.' But human beings must go to market to get things essential for life." The government announced that it would not intervene. A delegation of Oromo journeyed to the district capital to protest what they saw to be "state-sponsored muggings" in 1983. All who went were imprisoned, where they remained at the time of our research in 1985. The government appears to be engaged in a cruel social experiment and merely standing by to await the outcome.

In spite of such events, local residents in Wollega placed remarkably little blame for their problems directly on the settlers themselves. As the following remark by a displaced Oromo indicates, they saw that their major grievance was with the government.

He [the government] tries to take better care of the settlers and keep them loyal by helping them to survive better than we do. He wants to remove the Oromo from that place and bring these settlers to our location. The government feels that the Oromo can never work for this government with a clean heart [will never openly and honestly support this government].

Throughout the interviews the following sentiment, which is in effect an acknowledgment of the predicament of the newcomers, was expressed by the displaced Oromo farmers:

The Wollo do not care for their lives because they were taken away from their home country and villages. They simply do this or that without concern: they do not want to live in the area and probably think that the government may send them back. It looks like the government knowingly imposed them on our people.

We are treating these new people as guests for the time being and acting politely to them.

Obligations of Indigenous Peoples to Support Settlers

As pointed out in the discussion of tax obligations in Chapter VII, the burden of supporting the settlers who were brought into the Wollega and Illubabor regions was originally seen as an intensification of the contributions required for "famine victims." One man, examining the government's explanation in light of his recent experience asked, rhetorically, "Why did the government bring them here? Why did it not feed them in their own country? This is what we would like to know."

It appears that in many, though not all regions, the initial costs incurred for the resettlement program were covered from the peasant association granaries that hold the produce of collectively farmed plots. The decisions to dip into these were made from above. Local farmers were then required to replenish the supply. "We contributed money and crops for the settlers. They took from the peasant association granary freely and then forced us to replace it from our own supply."

As we have pointed out previously, the failure of the regime to budget food from sources controlled directly by the state for the massive 1984-85 program and the absence of international funding sources resulted in the local residents of targeted areas bearing the greatest burden of the following exorbitant – and still uncalculated – costs:

- The land itself was alienated from indigenous peoples.
- They were required to build and then stock houses for the settlers. The ratios varied greatly but the average proportion was three new houses to be built and provisioned by 12 households. Each new house had to have a latrine dug for it.
- The settlers were to be supplied with oxen.
- Equipment and tools for farming as well as household equipment for settlers was contributed by people (usually Oromo) in the locality of the settlement. This included plows, hoes, pots, pans, beds, chairs and bedclothes. In several cases local people were required to supply clothes for the new arrivals.
- All initial food supplies were contributed to the settlers from the local residents. In many cases, cooked food was delivered to new arrivals for at least three days. When the settlers' dependence shifted to grain donated from international sources, the local people were required to carry it to the settlers from town (see the descriptions given by Tigrayans resettled in Illubabor, Chapter VI).
- Labor services required were substantial, though as yet largely un-calculated. Building houses and delivering government supplies to the settlers were the most often mentioned.
- Plowing, planting, cultivating and in some cases harvesting and threshing was performed by Oromo residents in the settlement vicinity.

The following statements concerning contributions are representative of those we received from Oromo indigenous to the areas resettled.

The appropriation of land from the indigenous peoples has been discussed above, and constitutes the dispossession of the people in the wake of settlers (see previous comments).

A massive construction of houses for settlers was carried out by all local peasant association members. The following is a typical comment:

We were ordered to build 900 houses. I do not know how many people are in each house. The type of house was a permanent finished house. The materials were bought by the local people. We had to search the area thoroughly, cut wood for poles, hidda [vines] for tying them, etc., then build the houses and dig the holes for latrines. The entire peasant association worked on this.

In addition oxen were demanded of the indigenous Oromos, many of whom had already lost much of their own lands to collectivization.

We had to buy or bring oxen for the people who were coming to live in the houses we built.

All the residents, including boys and girls who have never plowed with oxen themselves, pay for oxen for the settlers.

There was a man in my peasant association who asked a question and was imprisoned. His question was this: "Why do we buy oxen for these people when we ourselves do not have oxen to plow and have to use gesso [hoes]. Why don't the settlers use hoes like we do?" He asked this in a public meeting and was taken away in front of everyone.

Our separate interviews with settlers reveal that oxen were not made available to them. This raises the obvious question as to the whereabouts of contributed livestock. Required contribution of equipment varied greatly as is reflected in these remarks.

We spent E$5 per person to purchase for settlers what we did not have in our houses.

We had to bring all household equipment including skillets, pots, pans and beds. We brought bedclothes and the government told us that we have to provide them with clothes to wear—enough for all the settlers who live in those houses—but they haven't been given the clothes yet.

For the time they are eating entirely from our peasant association. The government has not given them anything yet. We have given them everything essential for life.

The settlers have started to arrive and they are still coming. I do not know where they are coming from, only that they speak only Amharic—no other language. I have seen them only in the market, though they are using my furniture and cooking in my pans.

Labor obligations that fell on the indigenous Oromos to plow and cultivate for settlers were cited by settlers and the Oromos, as the following indicate:

This year Oromos who live near the settlers have to plow all the land for them—after that I don't know. I do not know why they can't plow for themselves. How would I even know? I cannot ask.

The settlers themselves reported the policy that indigenous Oromo were to plow for them in Illubabor; they also found it inexplicable:

They told us that the Oromo will farm for us next season. Why don't we farm for ourselves? I don't know of any reason except that this is their plan. Of course the Oromo hate it.

Adding insult to injury in the perception of the indigenous peoples was the order to cook and carry food to settlers in addition to donating it:

The leader of the peasant association forces us to give food for the settlers, but we do not have enough for ourselves. They ordered us to give for the newcomers. If we do not, the militia enter our houses and take something of value, saying they will sell it for our contribution.

The government told us that the people came because there is great hardship in their country—no rain at all. But when we talked to the people, they said that they were brought here by force and that they do not have any problem in their country. When we gave them our food, they do not want to eat it. They turned their noses up at it. They said they have much better food, wheat and teff, at home.

An example of additional kinds of labor services required of indigenous peoples on behalf of newly arrived settlers was provided by Tigray escapees cited previously.

The Oromo faced several problems because of us. Since September 1984 they have been building houses for the settlers. And they are ordered to feed us. They had to feed us from their own land and prepare all the food for the first three days. Then when we began to receive international wheat [at this point they showed the sacks this wheat had come in [from Canada, the West German Red Cross and the EEC], these Oromo had to carry the wheat to us, but they could not eat it. They were ordered to bring the grain to us on their own donkeys. If they did not have donkeys, they had to carry the wheat on their backs. Because of all this work for us, they could not watch their own crops. The wild animals finished all their crops this year.

Government policy, announced in November 1984, was quite clear on the broad nature of the services to be demanded from the indigenous peoples (see Appendix G for full text).

. . . like when a child is moving out, all parents try to settle their children with the essential household items. Thus the residents of this area today — because of the drought, and for those people who have lost everything and have been uprooted . . . — are preparing what is necessary for the new settlers to live. Even the plow and the yoke have been remembered, the people have provided everything for them. Even in some of the areas in this region everything has been provided for our brothers so that they can be self-sufficient as quickly as possible. Their brothers [local residents] have begun farming for them. This example should be the cornerstone, the main centerpiece or model, for others to follow in settling famine victims.

Peasants commented, after detailing the obligations required of them and their families,

There is not a single human being who is not complaining bitterly and murmuring about this obligation. It is too much for us to bear. They had to force us by every means.

These obligations, in combination with the direct displacement, further undermine productivity and drive indigenous peoples, both Oromo and others, from land that they have proved themselves capable of farming efficiently. The long-term effects on production are clear to them if not to observers. The Dergue's failure to budget for resettlement indicates that the obligations will continue into the foreseeable future.

The Role of Settlers as Special Security Forces

The reaction of farmers from the Wollega region to the arrival of settlers from Wollo, Tigray and northern Shoa in 1984-85 has been very much affected by their experience with the settlers who arrived as "famine victims" in the Asosa area in the early 1980s. Large numbers of settlers who were transferred to Wollega in the 1979-83 period had been armed and subsequently turned into special security forces that operated throughout the border areas, but primarily in the coffee regions and in the vicinity of the Oromo Liberation Front zones.

Those forces who were directed specifically to "protect" the coffee crop for the government against indigenous "contrabandists" and "hoarders" were described as the most rapacious. The settlers received arms as early as 1981 and were granted virtually unlimited powers of search and seizure in pursuit of contraband coffee and other trade items. They have become well known and dreaded for unpredictable and ruthless, almost vengeful, ransacking of the homes and granaries of local Oromo who live in coffee-producing regions.

The armed former settlers come into our houses without warning. If there is milk, they drink it; if there is alcohol, they drink it all or pee in it! Whatever they need, they take from us and there is nothing for us to do. They search; if they see anything that came from outside the country (a shirt or radio), they take it.

They [the former settlers] come at night when people are sleeping in their houses. There is no warning, no protection.

The settlers destroy food by taking it from the granary and pouring it on the ground, saying that they are "looking for contraband." Then it is spoiled and cannot be eaten by humans — all is finished by animals. They take men to prison, leaving women and children.

They butcher a cow or any kind of livestock and eat it. They can take whatever is in the house and eat it or ruin it.

By robbing people they brought oppression to the area. They dump everything the family owns into the dirt and take all the family to prison. If no one remains behind, the entire household's possessions are destroyed and animals overrun the place.

Those from Wollo can come at any time — summer or spring. They are employees of the military government. They go from place to place in the area. They have been doing this for one and a half years at least. They came to my area last summer and the year before that.

There are 300 to 500 at a time when they come. They speak only Amharic; they never speak Oromo. They beat people. They grab and rape the women. I know they have raped women. I have personal knowledge. By doing this they have been creating trouble in the country. I am an eyewitness to this.

The Battle for the Coffee Crop

From the accounts given by refugees, it appears that each year government representatives travel from region to region to assess the coffee crop while it is still on the trees. If the coffee harvest finally sold to the government does not equal or surpass the estimates made before it is picked, security forces are directed to the appropriate areas to find the "missing" coffee. Local people are not allowed to drink their own coffee although they can make a brew from the husks. Even the husks, however, have to be weighed by government officials before they can be used. Discovery of any amount of coffee in a house is sufficient crime for imprisonment and further punishment.

Refugees both from Wollo (settlers) and Wollega (indigenous people) confirmed that the government informed the settlers that their payment, food, salary and supplies are to come from the local farmers, but that these farmers had refused to give the required sums of money to the government for the settlers' care. Instead, they are accused by the officials of having hoarded coffee, and thus of having been responsible for the shortages of all supplies and compensation due the settlers. Therefore, settlers are instructed to find the hidden coffee, using any means possible, and to punish

Map 26

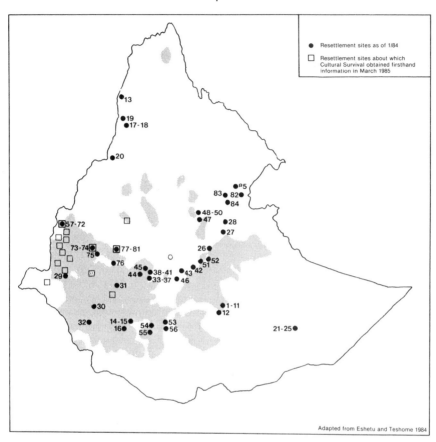

Resettlement sites as of 1/84

Resettlement sites about which Cultural Survival obtained firsthand information in March 1985

Adapted from Eshetu and Teshome 1984

ACTUAL AND POTENTIAL COFFEE-PRODUCING REGIONS IN ETHIOPIA AND THE RESETTLEMENT PROGRAM

The relationship of Ethiopian resettlement sites to actual or potential coffee-producing areas is striking. This map, a composite of coffee regions depicted in two maps in the *Atlas of Ethiopia* (1981) and in one map from Hance (1978), indicates that the vast majority of resettlement sites are located in or near areas of actual or potential coffee production. Coffee, which accounts for 60 percent or more of Ethiopia's exports (most of which is sold to the Netherlands and the US), earns the foreign exchange that is necessary to arm the current government. As interviews with refugees from the areas of previous resettlement sites indicate, settlers are not usually expected to cultivate coffee. Instead, they are armed and used as special security forces to confiscate it from coffee producers indigenous to the area.

the people for their "stubborn refusal to cooperate with the revolution." In effect, these settlers/security forces are given license to take whatever they find of value in the houses they ransack. Farmers claimed that local riff-raff would note when a farmer had sold an animal to pay taxes or for some other purpose, then lead the "security forces" to that house to raid for contraband on the "suspicion" that this farmer was hiding coffee. While coffee would not be found the money would invariably be taken. Settlers who are sent by the Dergue to "enforce the law" (reportedly armed with BMTOVs, DMT-4s and Kalishnikovs) force their way into people's houses and take what they want. One man describing the situation said,

> Whenever the coffee harvest comes, they enter houses without permission and search and grab anything of value. They call us "counter-revolutionaries" and take whatever we have. One day after my father sold two cows in order to pay his taxes and meet other expenses, the Wollo "security" entered the house and searched everywhere, destroying many things and terrifying us. They would not stop, even though they found no coffee. They found the money from my father's sale and took it. They must have been told about those two cows. We could do nothing. They think everything we have should be theirs.

In interviews with former Ethiopian teachers and civil servants, we learned that this pattern of investing civilians with the power and responsibility to secure their compensation directly from taxpayers is not new to this government. Teachers and other workers were often told by their superiors to demand from local farmers or urban residents directly the payments and benefits that were delayed by lack of government funds. Predictably, this led to conflict and frustration on both sides.

Another task formally assigned to armed settlers is to locate and imprison or directly punish local farmers suspected of sympathizing with or supporting the Oromo Liberation Front, who are referred to as "the *shiftas*," "the counter-revolutionaries," "the bourgeoisie" or "the outlaws."

Mandated to arrest persons suspected of assisting resistance fighters in the area, the settlers/soldiers rely on networks of informers in each peasant association to identify "suspects" throughout the region. Oromo peasants reported outrage against the devastating reprisals taken against the population by these armed settlers (whom they refer to with a word best translated as "henchmen"), based on what they say is the false or jealous word of a handful of government "spies." Reportedly, hard evidence against suspects is not required. From 1981-84 farmers' homes have regularly been broken into at any hour of the day or night, property destroyed, items of value taken and those accused (often falsely accused, the farmers insist) beaten, imprisoned or killed. The truck and bus convoys now bringing tens of thousands of additional settlers are seen in this context by the indigenous Oromo population. Their response has ranged from smoldering silence on the assumption that many settlers will die or leave, to outrage and armed resistance.

> These former settlers come and say, "You sell contraband." "You feed shiftas." They say this to people and on this ground they grab people and put them in prison and take them to the office and burn them with iron bars that have been put into the fire.

Refugees interviewed by Cultural Survival in Yabuus and Kirmuk fell fairly evenly into two categories: 1) those who had actually supported the OLF by providing food or information and 2) those who had not assisted the OLF but had been falsely accused and punished. People reported that they had been terrified of taking the chance of openly helping the liberation fighters. But this did not seem to protect them from the government (see Chapter VII). Armed settlers swooped down on them as a result of false accusations and tortured, and even killed, innocent suspects. Several refugees reported that such experiences caused them to turn in desperation to the Oromo Liberation Front operating in their vicinity and to ask for protection or retaliation, despite the risks such a move posed to family and friends.

OLF officials interviewed in Khartoum (26 March 1985) indeed stated that one of the most urgent demands made upon them by peasants in the area is to stop the resettlement of new *neftanya* on their lands and to protect them from the capricious attacks of the settlers from earlier periods who have become armed security forces. Oromo Liberation Front military communiques issued between April and July 1985 report the dismantling of three resettlement camps in the Begi vicinity.

Relation of the Government to the Settlers and Indigenous Peoples

While the peasants confirmed that this resettlement program is one of their biggest problems, they insisted that it is not different from numerous other problems created by the Dergue. Their difficulties were usually described as an intensification of an ongoing battle they had with the government over land, animals, children, produce and even women. They described the government as their adversary, rather than the settlers themselves in most, though not all, cases. In their view, resettlement was a case in point. One man, who summed up the situation, said, "The government wants to destroy the Oromo and make them vanish from the land." Another noted, "Their plan is to get rid of the Oromos from their own land and distribute it to people from Wollo." Another Oromo made a similar assessment when asked about the future of the settlement.

> The settlers [the Wollo and Tigrayans] and the local Oromo can never live together in the long run because the government put them there and the Oromo are running away from them, leaving their country in front of these settlers and going to Sudan. This makes the government happy. He [the Dergue] is even willing to carry your agilgili [picnic baskets] out for you in order to make way for the settlers.

This individual went on to raise the question,

> Are we going to disappear or what are we supposed to do? Even the settlers believe as they have been told, that we are simply following our "bourgeoisie." What does that mean? What is the "bourgeoisie" except Oromo fighting? Since the Oromo are zari tokitcha [one seed] they will behave in the same way. The "outlaws" are simply the local farmers. There is no difference among us.

Others commented:

> We [the Oromo] have understood the program of the Dergue and have seen that there is nothing for us if we remain in our homes. They are trying to exterminate us. The government sees the Oromo as a contamination — like the kind of contamination that can never be thoroughly cleaned from the intestines no matter how hard one seems to try.

With a red eye [as the eyes of someone who is furious at you] they [the government] look at the Oromo. With a calm and peaceful expression they look at the settlers as if they will stay forever. They are making them strong enough to hold onto the area where they are settled.

The government favors them [the settlers] over us.

Opposition against the resettlement obligations, against the alienation of land and against the arrival and behavior of settlers is as old as the program itself. In fact, Oromo residents compare their situation with the situation of their grandfathers and fathers who had labor and payment obligations to settlers who came under Menelik's and Haile Selassie's periods of rule. Protest songs composed by their grandfathers against the settlers of their day apply with remarkable accuracy to the situation of the current Oromo farmers of Wollega today.

Open challenge to the policy through public channels is extremely risky, however.

If anyone protests, let alone refuses, he or she is put in prison immediately and the others keep quiet. Even if anyone asks a question about it, they put that person in prison.

No one can protest. He will be killed. He must finish [sell] all his animals [to pay taxes and contributions] and keep quiet though he is left with nothing.

He [the Dergue] is killing those who shout and can be heard.

If we even ask a question we are put in prison and accused of sabotaging the government's revolution. They say, "Because of your own interest you are undermining the good of the whole." If we go to prison we will never come out.

The ultimate testimony to the government's calloused approach to the plight of local Oromo, according to one refugee, was reflected in the visits of government officials. "Even when the officials come to deliver speeches about settlement and what we should give and do, we have to contribute for a feast for them also."

Increased Militarization of the Border Region

Our data indicate that by the hardships placed both on the settlers transferred into Wollega, Illubabor and Kaffa and on the Oromo and other peoples indigenous to those regions, the Dergue is creating a political and economic tinderbox.

Settlers are offered no way out of a life of forced labor and deprivation except to take up arms as militiamen for the government. Intent upon returning home and frustrated by the extremely uncomfortable and regimented conditions in the settlements, young and old alike are offered upward mobility from ordinary laborer to gun-carrier as the only available ticket out of their situation. Individuals motivated by an intense desire to return home are virtually forced into an ever-growing military machine.

Once armed, they turn against a highly frustrated peasant population that is faced with the loss of their very means of production as well as the destruction of their families, culture and way of life.

The government has not shown any concern to minimize the highly combustible situation that its own policies have created. On the contrary it has prepared to move into the region with the full force of military attack at the slightest provocation.

In fact, the conflict has already ignited. Refugees reported that settlers who are sent by the Dergue to enforce the law are now armed. They recounted the landing of planeloads of soldiers on the Begi airfield in early 1985. The Oromo Liberation Front has issued a series of military communiques that report armed conflict in the vicinity of resettlement sites in Begi and Anfillo districts around Begi and Gidami towns and also in Qellem and Asosa districts. If the inaccessibility of these general regions to observers to date is any indication, the government is prepared and equipped to continue the policy of keeping events there, even those of a dramatic nature, hidden from the public eye until long after they reach irreversible crisis proportions.

The tranformation of resettlement sites into armed garrisons is not a remote possibility and not without precedent within the empire. Once the infrastructure for an armed camp has been laid the retention rate of settlers and the humanitarian assistance of the international community will be of less importance than now appears to be the case. The political and military agenda, not far beneath the surface, may well be the most important one and must receive serious attention in any consideration of events in this region.

Internal Displacement

A large majority of the Oromo refugees interviewed in Kirmuk and Yabuus had remained at various sites inside the borders of Ethiopia after having been forced to leave their homes before crossing the border to seek refuge in Sudan.

They had remained close to their homelands for a variety of reasons, the primary one being that they simply preferred to remain within a familiar ecological niche and among people who share their cultural and linguistic background and nationality. However, they cited the economic burden that their presence creates on their friends and relatives struggling to survive, the absence of tools and equipment with which to produce for themselves and the long arm of the Dergue's surveillance and settler security forces as causes for them to enter Sudan.

Many, many people have left for Sudan because their land was taken and the requirements [contributions in cash, kind and labor] are too great. People simply leave the area—many go to other places within the borders of Ethiopia—Foofoor, Buuduur, Shiirgoolee—near Begi on the border with Sudan. They sit with relatives waiting for the settlement obligation to be withdrawn and for settlers to leave. Then they will return home.

Refugees told us that there is a "very large number" of displaced people who prefer to be nearer home. Many have sought the protection of the OLF while they attempt to farm or trade in areas beyond the control of the government. According to those who talked to us, the OLF has established farming and trading communities within the territories that it controls—areas comprised in large part by peoples displaced directly or indirectly by the Dergue's agricultural and settlement policies.

ORA officials interviewed in Khartoum (26 March 1985) stated that the number of internally displaced persons of which they are aware in the country has reached the hundreds of thousands. While the internal social, economic and political implications of such a large population alienated from their traditional lands are staggering, it should not come as a complete surprise to a public who has been told that 1.5 million people are to be moved in a country of 35 million. The populations of Wollega, Kefa and Illubabor have been required to absorb the impact of one of the most massive population relocations in history. The creation of famine here, among an indigenous people whose production (of grain crops and coffee and livestock) historically has virtually sustained the empire economically, is a remarkable occurrence. Agencies would do well to note that assistance to this population of internally displaced people in the receiving areas of resettlement has the potential of preserving the viability of a productive people and preventing the type of exodus that resulted when evacuation in Tigray became inevitable in 1984-85.

Deforestation

Though our research design did not equip us to deal with deforestation adequately, the refugees themselves constantly raised the issue of the destruction that resettlement has brought on the environment. They pointed to the impact of earlier settlements, e.g., Angar River, where forests were destroyed by the activities around the site. Refugees highlighted the effects of building 900 or 1,200 houses at a time when all materials were locally derived. The government had not delivered any building materials to Asosa, where tens of thousands of people were to be accommodated within a few months.

Regarding the impact of resettlement on his area, an Oromo commented, "The land in Tigray and Wollo is dry. If those people come here our land will also be dry. We loved it and saved it, but in the Angar River area settlement they cleared the forest and the rains stopped."

We have adapted available maps of Ethiopia's forested regions and indicated the locations of settlement sites (see Map 27). Former RRC officials speaking freely in Sudan expressed the concern of Ethiopian government forestry specialists in Asosa who said that massive reforestation efforts should begin immediately. They feared that the dramatic destruction to the environment in that region might rapidly change the climate and influence the water balance. The party has overruled them.

The consequences of massive deforestation are inescapable. Such an outcome would be ironic. The government would be creating the very problems it ostensibly set out to solve.

Specific Resettlement Sites About Which Cultural Survival Obtained Information

• Asosa

The most well known of the resettlement sites in the Wollega region is that of Asosa, established in 1979 and constructed on a large scale. This site is described in detail in Chapter V.

• Angar River Project

Another Wollega settlement built on the same large-scale model as that of Asosa was established along the Angar River. Some of our respondents

Map 27

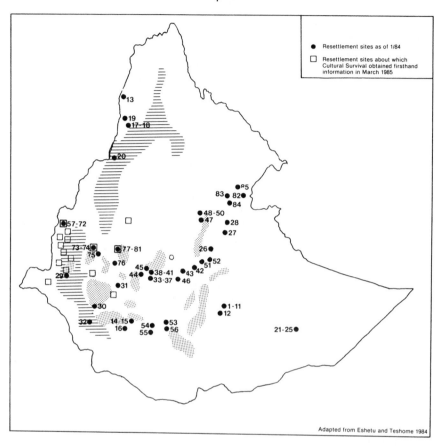

Adapted from Eshetu and Teshome 1984

FORESTS IN ETHIOPIA AND THE RESETTLEMENT SITES

Approximately four percent of Ethiopia is covered with forests. Deforestation and soil erosion in the northern highlands are frequently cited as two of the primary reasons international support should be given to the resettlement program. Resettlement sites, however, appear to be targeted for some of Ethiopia's remaining forested lands. Deforestation, which results from the need for building materials as well as from clearing agricultural land (these cleared areas may total as much as 250,000 hectares), appears to cause the same environmental problems it is intended to solve. In the Asosa area of Wollega, local forestry officials began to call for reforestation in the areas of resettlement as early as December 1984.

were familiar with this site. In 1978, 7,000 settlers from Wollo went to the Angar River site in Wollega. Observers — refugees with whom we spoke — reported that "they cut down all the trees in the area and the rain stopped." One commented, "They ruined the land. All the forest is cut down because of them."

Thus Horo Gudru site is a well-known disaster among local people. They reported that the settlers were forced to settle against their will and that they had little or no equipment.

The government ordered local Oromo to provide the settlers with everything they needed. Then, according to Oromo formerly resident there, the government told the Wollo people of this arrangement, and armed them to "enforce the law" by forcing their way into people's houses and taking what they saw to be "rightfully theirs." They were reportedly armed with BMTOVs, DMT-4s and Kalishnikovs.

One refugee indigenous to the area commented, "The government encouraged them to be thieves against us." A delegation of Oromo who journeyed to the district capital to appeal to the authorities was imprisoned.

The original 7,000 settlers from Wollo reportedly tried to farm but did not find it fruitful. As a result, they dispersed, either selling their arms locally or taking them and going home.

Our findings, however, indicate that the Asosa and Angar River sites are quite different from the bulk of resettlement sites established in Kefa, Illubabor and other parts of Wollega.

• Jimma, Kefa

The resettlement pattern in the area around Jimma, for example, was unlike that of Asosa. Transplanted settlers were placed into several smaller sites that were interspersed among preexisting communities of indigenous Oromo farmers. One of our respondents estimated 1,000 settlers had been placed at one time in late 1984 in a site near Alga past Jimma town. The settlers were moved into houses that had been constructed by resident Oromo under orders from the government. Settlers were fed by local Oromo who cooked the food and carried it to them for the first three days after their arrival. A Tigrayan settler to this area reported that they were not allowed to visit with or exchange information with Oromo farmers. Of these local people he said, "They did not complain, but their faces showed everything."

After this initial period, the political cadre arrived from Alga town to tell the settlers, "You will have oxen, clothes and better food." Each cadre carried a pistol, the symbol of party membership, and lived in the town. After the initial announcement, they did not return during the following three weeks, the period of time that our informants stayed before escaping. In those three weeks none of the programs the cadres had outlined had been fulfilled. The militia had taken the settlers to town where they received unground wheat, but the settlers had no means of grinding it, no containers for soaking it, and no pans for cooking it. In Alga town they had to gather soda cans and other scrap metal to make a pan for cooking. After these had been smashed by cars and trucks, they were thick enough to use over a fire.

The settlers had no organized work to do in this area. One told us, "The militia who had to guard our camp never showed us their faces inside the camp." Regarding the organization of work activities, he said,

The entire settlement did not make an organized impression on me. We were left alone. We didn't have to work. Nobody ordered us to do anything. We finally ventured out and found work on a non-government coffee plantation for two days for E$.50 per day plus food.

Another commented, "Most of us did not have friends or relatives in that place. When somebody died, his body was left in an open field. The bodies decomposed and the whole area stank."

Although the information from this area is quite sketchy, it does indicate that the settlers sent there were captured and sent in the same fashion as people who were taken to other regions. It was a coffee-growing area and one thickly inhabited by Oromo who provided initial supplies to the settlers including houses and cooked food. Groups of settlers were interspersed with indigenous communities. In contrast to other areas, no tools or equipment had been delivered more than three weeks after the settlers had arrived, and the usual regimes of meetings and work programs had not been established. One interviewee, appalled at the death toll and forcibly transported in the first place, slipped past armed guards with his young daughter without waiting to learn how events would unfold.

• Metu, Illubabor

The 14 Tigray settlers who had escaped from the resettlement program in Illubabor and crossed the border into Sudan while we were in Yabuus camp surveying the camp population there were interviewed the same day that they arrived in Sudan. They painted a vivid picture of the resettlement area to which they had been sent in Illubabor. We quote their account at length in Chapter VI. Their model of resettlement appears to be consistent with that of Jimma and one that will absorb a large number of the settlers taken during the 1984-85 program. It differs from the Asosa type, as does that of Jimma, in that settlers are destined to become geographically interspersed directly with the local population, though organized into separate peasant associations from the outset.

These Tigrayans had been part of a group of 350 settlers forcibly captured (see Chapter VI) and taken in buses to a site beyond Metu, Illubabor. Local Oromo built houses for all the settlers, complete with latrines and space reserved for garden plots behind the houses. The land had been lived on, but not recently. The area was described as mountainous and "as far as the eyes could see in every direction the area was full of coffee."

When we reached Illubabor, the district peasant association brought us bread they had made from corn and sorghum. The local Oromo were ordered by the government not to speak to settlers or interact with us in any way, but we could see from their faces that they did not like us.

The group of 350 was one cluster of settlers among thousands. One man, when pushed to estimate the number who received food from the town where their rations were distributed, calculated 10,000. Three refugees who were present at the interview agreed. They estimated that the number of local people was even higher, revealing a pattern of government-supplied settlers interspersed with previously homogeneous populations of indigenous Oromo farmers. That the Oromo had built houses, supplied tools and carried grain for the settlers and were slated to farm for them indicates differential treatment of these groups by the government. Also the fact that Oromo purchased internationally supplied grain from the settlers shows that they are short of food, that the prices of the peasant association stocks are high and that there is a discrepancy in food availability to these groups.

The shortage of personnel to organize the activities of the settlers — except for a hastily called speech delivered by the district administrator — and the lack of roles for the militia who were milling around the settlement suggests that the resettlement program here has far outstripped the administrative capacity of the government to implement the scheme. Responsibility for the care of these inactive newcomers has fallen on the residents of the area who have been told to abandon their own work to serve the settlers' needs. According to the Tigrayans, the local residents (Oromo) of a region that was described as "full of coffee" are starving and unable to cope with influx, angry and feeling trapped by the government.

It was through the clandestine relationships that these Tigrayans established with the local people to sell wheat that they learned of the attitude and obligations Oromo had toward them.

While the circumstances had already produced a killing and heated exchanges, other kinds of exchanges had also begun, including trade and information concerning conditions and organization in Tigray as well as Illubabor. Settlers from here, nevertheless, shared the same pessimistic view of the future of settlement in this region, as in other areas. "There will be no peace," they said.

• Ya-a

This settlement site is located in a border area. The entire site is situated on land previously farmed by Oromo indigenous to the area. The land was selected by district officers without involvement of any local residents. Then the people were ordered (the precise translation is "commanded and threatened") to build 1,200 houses. The ones whose land was taken also had to build houses for the settlers.

• Begi

Begi is more secure. Some of the settlers who try to escape from Bombasi were caught by the Dergue and sent to Begi.

• Bombasi

The settlers came to Bombasi last year and they had problems with the local people, and those problems continue unresolved.

We gave them land, oxen, meat and spices, household furniture on the government's order. We built their houses by ourselves. We cut our forest for their benefit. Now the government orders them to kill us.

The government watches both groups and arms neither.

The land selected by the government was not necessarily land taken from those who have bigger problems with the authorities than others. There is not a single person in the entire area who gets along with the authorities.

• Gibba

In the place known as Gibba, 1,200 settlers came and Oromo had to build houses for each of them. The land selected was actively farmed land from which the residents had to leave to make way for newcomers after providing supplies.

The area is a region where the OLF is active and has the sympathy of the local population. The selection of the site was made in 1984 by the authorities—specifically the district governor.

The peasant association was ordered to buy oxen and other supplies. In addition, the local inhabitants had to pay E$10 each for support of the program.

When land was taken from individuals they had to move wherever they could persuade someone to take them in. No new land was made available for the locals. Many of them were reputed to have escaped through Asosa to Kirmuk, Sudan (see statement in Chapter VII).

• Qashmando

The area's residents are providing even more for the settlers there. Their burden is greater than ours at Gibba if anything because there are more settlers there and they have been there longer.

All the settlers live together in one place. There are no guards around them. They are mostly men but a few women, children and old people are among them.

The Future of Resettlement

Settlers and indigenous peoples alike were asked to comment on the future of resettlement. Their responses are self-explanatory.

The people can never live and farm according to the government's plan. They are there by force. They are sick and dying every day. The only ones who won't try to get out are the ones too weak to walk out.

Those who stay behind in the settlement will die. There are so many diseases that I myself saw more than 73 people die in only one day. Nobody can survive there. If you go there a year from today you will not find one person [who is there now] alive and remaining there.

The ones who have been put into the settlement [Asosa] are being turned back to another place—sent to another settlement site [Bombasi] that is further away from the border—back toward Addis Ababa so that they cannot escape.

There will be no peace.

Chapter X

CONCLUSIONS

The bulk of this report consists of the findings of our research conducted among refugees in Sudan. As necessary, preliminary interpretation has been interspersed throughout the report, and to an extent has shaped the discussion of the findings. This chapter presents in summary the conclusions drawn from the results of our investigation. These conclusions are organized according to the major research questions that guided the study and to the topics that logically fell within the scope of those questions.

Dimensions of the Famine

Since 1977 there has been an overall decline in the standard of living of peasants in government-held areas in the three regions where we conducted our research: Tigray; Wollo; and Wollega, Illubabor and Kefa. This decline has been a direct consequence of specific government programs that adversely affected food production, which has decreased by as much as one-half to two-thirds since the Dergue implemented its agrarian reform program and other policies. The effects of these policies began to be felt in rural areas as early as 1977 and 1978. Producers from many areas insist that in addition to the decline in total production, the amount of produce the government takes is equivalent to or greater than what the landlords took during the previous government. In short, producers report having less food after harvests than they or their fathers had before the current government came to power.

By the 1984 agricultural year, extreme food shortages existed in the home regions of all refugees interviewed for this study, i.e., in the administrative regions of Tigray, Wollo, Shoa, Wollega, Illubabor and Kefa.

Causes of Hunger and Famine

The crisis of 1984-85 was the result of a combination of long- and short-term factors that affected both food production and food availability. Both sets of factors must be taken into account in assessing the famine.

Long-Term Causes of Famine

Long-term causes of food shortages (indicated by comparison with the condition of the previous generation at the same period in the life cycle) were due to the deterioration in the productive capacity of the peasant populations and to the elimination of traditional methods of coping with predictable fluctuations in climatic and environmental factors. Foremost among these factors were government programs, redistribution of land, confiscation of grain and livestock through excessive taxes and obligation, and coercive labor programs and a decline in available labor force.

Government Programs That Affected Food Production

Specific government programs and policies designed to organize the peasantry and to centralize state institutions and power have had a negative impact on peasant agriculture and have resulted in dramatic food shortages throughout the country.

Land Redistribution

In Tigray, where land degradation is most often cited as a major cause of food production declines, the imposition of government controls through peasant associations was reported to be a more significant factor contributing to declining yields. In fact, farmers from Tigray reported that their highest yields in the past 10 years occurred in 1982-83, a period in which most of those interviewed (97.5 percent) no longer lived under government control or belonged to government-controlled peasant associations. During this period, peasants abandoned the Dergue's land policy and reallocated land along more productive lines — that is, land to the tiller. As a result, they harvested significantly higher yields in spite of the fact that reduced rainfall affected production in many of the areas in question at that time.

In Wollo, land redistribution, confiscation of agricultural "surpluses" (often including seed grain) through taxes and "voluntary" contributions, and coercive government labor programs that interfered with production all crippled the ability of the people of Wollo to cope with the regular, cyclical lack of rainfall experienced in the area.

Throughout the government-held regions, fertile lands reportedly have been allocated systematically to peasant associations for communal cultivation or to peasant association officers and a few privileged individuals with connections to the officers. While these land allocation practices have reduced significantly overall production, they have dramatically reduced private, individual production.

In Wollega, Illubabor and Kefa, government programs introduced through peasant associations (to which all peasant farmers must belong) led to absolute declines in food production and availability. Artificial land scarcities were created when lands previously used privately were confiscated by the state. Some of these lands were designated for collective farming. Others remain idle. When local peasants could not be persuaded to farm collectively, some of these lands were designated as resettlement sites. Choice regions have already been set aside for communal farming; peasant labor is now controlled to the extent that private production is severely limited. This, in turn, has allowed the government to take control of even larger areas under the pretext that the lands are not being used productively.

Confiscation of Grain Stockpiles and Livestock Through Excessive Taxes and Obligations

In Wollo, previous forms of averting famine due to frequent poor harvests — for example, stockpiling surplus grain from years with high yields for consumption during periods of low yields and maintaining sufficient herds of livestock to rely substantially on animal products during periods of poor agricultural yields — have become impossible as a result of high taxes levied according to visible stockpiles of grain and herds peasant producers possessed. These high taxes were paid through divestiture of farmers' productive assets — oxen, seed, tools, valuables.

In Wollega, Illubabor and Kefa, taxes, "voluntary" contributions and the forced sale of grain at artificially low prices to the AMC have crippled the production of Oromo and other farmers in the region and have depleted their herds and rendered local investment in agriculture impossible. In this region where agricultural production previously was among the highest in the country, the effects of the government's policies on production and food availability have been devastating.

Coercive Labor Programs and Decline in Available Labor Force

Appropriation by the state of all grain produced by forced collective labor on peasant association communal plots has been a major obstacle to maintaining adequate levels of local food supplies and a major disincentive to retaining previous production levels on communal lands. Those who work on the communal lands receive neither cash nor produce for their "contribution"; nor do they receive compensation in the form of services, education, health care, store goods or transportation. As a result, farmers have slackened their pace in the forced labor programs. Meanwhile the contraband sale of coffee and other supplies across the border to Sudan has gained momentum, further reducing food availability inside Ethiopia.

Conscription to the military or militia service, appointment to peasant association positions, imprisonment and killings have led to a reduction in the size of the local labor force of able-bodied young people to adequately manage agricultural, herding or other economic activities.

In Wollo, obligations to contribute labor on demand for government activities—primarily farming communal plots, lands designated "militia lands" and the lands of peasant association officials—have had a deleterious effect on peasant food production and supply, and have impoverished and marginalized large portions of the peasantry. Government policies have created famine, and are setting the stage to "relieve" future food crisis conditions with forced collective farming.

In Wollega, Illubabor and Kefa, mandatory communal farming and clearing of house sites, even fields, for those being resettled amounts to systematic forced labor programs in these regions. These programs do not allow peasants to farm their own fields according to the agricultural cycle; they cause plowing, planting and weeding delays, and prevent farmers from defending their crops from predators and pests. Declines in production from these factors are reported to amount to one-half to two-thirds of production levels achieved prior to the current government's rule.

Obligatory general meetings of the peasant association for political education, Amharic literacy campaigns, announcement of new taxes, explanation of government policy, and numerous other pretexts prevent agricultural work and directly undermine food self-sufficiency throughout all regions from which people were surveyed, but especially in Wollega, Illubabor and Kefa. Once peasant association representatives observe overall production declines, they announce mandatory steps farmers must take toward collectivization. Such circumstances create negative and positive incentives for moving the population into collective farming despite the severe famine conditions produced by the collectivization process.

In the southwestern administrative regions imprisonment of large numbers of working people (particularly farmers who resist the programs that affect agriculture), appointment to perform local peasant association functions, withdrawal of officers and militiamen from active farming and the requirement that their peasant associations cultivate plots for them, conscription to the Ethiopian military, and political killings and displacement of people from entire regions so that the lands can be reallocated for resettlement have resulted, collectively, in a marked decline in the labor force and in production.

Causes of Hunger in 1984-1985

The food shortages that brought on widespread conditions of hunger were triggered by different factors in Tigray, in Wollo, and in Wollega, Illubabor and Kefa.

In Tigray
- Planting delays due to military actions made crops especially susceptible to insect (armyworm) and weed infestation.
- Rainfall shortages contributed to decreased overall production. However, military activities, which delayed planting, caused reduced rainfall to have a greater impact on yields than it would otherwise have had.
- Extensive military actions by the Ethiopian army, including the destruction of standing crops, stored food, animal herds (especially oxen) and fodder for oxen contributed significantly to famine conditions in contested areas. Army attacks were accompanied by people who collected back taxes and contributions, further depleting the productive assets of local farmers as well as their ability to remain self-sufficient food producers.

In Wollo
- Oxen shortages delayed planting and made many areas susceptible to the devastation of armyworms.
- Lack of rainfall in an area where all surpluses had been appropriated and animals sold to pay for taxes or food left many people in Wollo destitute.

In Wollega, Illubabor and Kefa
- The intensification of resettlement, which required indigenous people to supply land, houses, food, equipment and services to arriving settlers, introduced famine where it had not been known recently, and displaced families within Ethiopia as well as across the border into Sudan.

Famine has resulted primarily from government policies that have been implemented in order to accomplish massive collectivization of agricultural production and to secure central government control over productive regions of the country where indigenous peoples have developed strong antigovernment resistance. The lack of compensatory measures prevents economic alternatives and portends an imminent crisis of greater proportions in areas now virtually closed to public access.

Assistance in the Ethiopian Context

Governments as well as humanitarian assistance agencies have not attempted to systematically understand the causes of the present famine.

While their assistance, they claim, feeds the hungry, they fail to address the issue of whether their assistance will eradicate or exacerbate the conditions that led to the present famine. If the West is willing to feed starving Ethiopians without asking how they came to be in that condition or evaluate whether Western assistance programs alleviate those conditions, then they will face a monumental task in the future. The government of Ethiopia is establishing a social and economic system that will produce starving people for generations to come.

Assistance to the government, unless scrupulously monitored:

- Facilitates the uprooting of distinct peoples in one region of the country and the displacement of self-sufficient food producers in another, primarily through the resettlement program.
- Gives hostile Ethiopian government forces access to areas that had successfully withdrawn from the reach of the state and reestablished efficient, autonomous agricultural production systems.
- Reinforces transport and communication lines of obvious strategic military importance in areas that the government has not been able to control militarily.
- Supports programs designed by a tiny minority of the region's inhabitants while simultaneously undermining programs that have broad popular support.
- Allows the government to reinforce the programs that lead to the famine as well as intensify programs, such as resettlement and villagization, that will spread the famine to previously productive and fertile regions.

According to our own research and the efforts of numerous other individuals and organizations, Ethiopian government policies have become the major cause of death in the country. The provision of "humanitarian" assistance, with no questions asked, helps the Ethiopian government get away with murder.

Chapter XI

RECOMMENDATIONS

Our findings and the conclusions we have drawn from them lead us to recommend a number of specific and general alterations in current relief and developmental assistance programs being implemented in Ethiopia. Our findings also suggest a number of areas of research that should be undertaken in Ethiopia. We list these recommendations briefly here. They arise directly from our findings. Cultural Survival would be happy to discuss them further with governmental or humanitarian agencies that currently have or are considering starting humanitarian assistance or developmental programs in Ethiopia, Sudan or cross-border into contested areas of Ethiopia.

Humanitarian Assistance to Victims of Food Shortages in Ethiopia

We recommended that:

An umbrella organization, either one in existence or a newly created one, be given the mandate of receiving, investigating and commenting on reports of human rights abuses and/or abuses of assistance in either government-held or contested areas of Ethiopia or with regard to refugees from Ethiopia in Sudan. Such an organization could more easily determine whether reported events are verifiable, and if so, whether they are isolated or systematic problems that should receive further investigation and/or exposure.

Relief and developmental assistance programs be extended to all areas affected by famine. At this time, such programs would require cross-border delivery at least into Eritrea, Tigray, Wollo, Gondar and the southwestern administrative units where displaced persons require assistance to remain productive. Assistance should also be made available to those who have fled to the Sudan as a result of resettlement — those who escaped from resettlement sites and those displaced from their homes by the resettlement program.

Agencies or governments delivering assistance through the government-held areas as well as cross-border into contested areas require direct access to the affected peoples through independent translators and long-term monitoring that would ensure that assistance is provided only on humanitarian grounds.

Agencies working in Sudan assess the needs of refugees from Ethiopia who live in eastern and southeastern Sudan. This includes the provision of seeds and supplies to get these people back to their homelands to plant crops and/or to install "semipermanent" facilities to protect those refugees who are unable to return at this time. It also includes working to unite refugees with family members who are presently in Sudan and informing family members in Ethiopia of the condition of their relatives. Finally, it includes the development of programs for men working on Sudanese commercial farms and for women and children in southern Blue Nile Province, where there are no international agencies to protect them from abuse.

Governments and agencies act together to assess independently government claims of food needs, numbers and locations of famine victims and causes of the present famine. Such information should be the cornerstone of the design and evaluation of their own programs.

Governments and agencies undertake jointly their own assessment of programs the government wants them to finance that will alleviate the famine. Such independent assessments should evaluate the nature of the official claims of the problems being addressed as well as the appropriateness of the proposed government solutions. Are there more appropriate alternatives than those proposed by the government?

Governments and agencies insist on the necessary freedom to monitor their own programs and to assess the stated goals of their programs as well as their broader regional impacts.

Agencies be accurate in their statements to the public about the causes of the problems they intend to address as well as the overall goals of their fund-raising attempts.

Criteria for Support to Assistance Agencies Working among Famine Victims in or from Ethiopia

We recommend that only those humanitarian agencies that either employ or contract people qualified to assess the scope and cause(s) of the problems they claim to be addressing, as well as the impact of their own assistance programs, receive funds for humanitarian assistance. Other agencies will be unable to make reasonable assurances to their donors that their help will not exacerbate rather than alleviate the famine conditions.

Types of Additional Information/Research Necessary for Assessment of Causes and Appropriateness of Solutions

We recommend that the following topics be investigated:

Extent and Causes of Famine
- The extent of the famine in 1986.
- The affected districts.
- The number of people per district affected.
- The nationalities that live in the affected districts.
- The short and long-term causes of famine in each of the affected districts (e.g., insects, drought, warfare, lack of seeds or oxen, erosion, conscription, confiscation of assets, government policies).

Humanitarian Assistance and Causes of Famine
- The capacity of Western governments and relief agencies to assess the causes of famine.
- The degree to which Western governments or relief agencies attempt to address the causes of famine through their assistance efforts.
- The degree to which Western governments or relief agencies attempt to assess the impact of their programs in terms of either stated goals or unstated effects.

Ethiopian Policies and Famine
- The degree to which Ethiopian policies created, maintained or extended the current famine.
- The present government policies that cause declines in agricultural production.
- The degree to which government programs that cause production declines are uniformly implemented throughout the empire.
- The relationship of peasant associations and producers' cooperatives to agricultural production; variations by administrative and national regions.
- The relationship of resettlement or villagization programs to agricultural production. Their impact on pastoralists as well as agriculturalists.
- An assessment of the overall cost and benefit of resettlement. Comparison of costs of resettlement to other rehabilitative programs for the northern highlands.
- An assessment of the political, economic and military objectives of the resettlement program.
- An assessment of the situation of the property of those displaced by famine or by the government's resettlement or villagization programs.
- An assessment of the use of Western assistance in the resettlement program, villagization program or development of new peasant associations.
- An assessment of the condition of the children who have been orphaned by the famine or separated from their parents.

A Moratorium on the Resettlement Program

Western governments and agencies unite to call upon Ethiopia to suspend the resettlement program until an international commission of experts has been able to go to Ethiopia and Sudan to interview affected people. The commission should assess:
- The economic feasibility of resettlement compared with alternative programs that would keep people in their own regions.
- The impact of resettlement on the people who previously used the designated regions where settlement sites have been established.
- Whether or not participation in the resettlement program is voluntary.
- The percentage of people resettled without their families.
- The mortality rates in holding camps, in transit to the sites and in the resettlement sites.
- The health and work conditions in all the sites.
- The condition of previous settlers and their relationship to the local populations.

BIBLIOGRAPHY

We have prepared these listings to reflect the fact that for most people of northeast Africa, the primary name for identification is the first name. Therefore, for example, Bereket Habte Selassie is designated and alphabetized accordingly, i.e., Bereket Habte Selassie rather than Selassie, Bereket H.

Abir, M.
    1968   *Ethiopia, the Era of the Princes*. London.

Agricultural Outlook
    1985   The Year After the Drought: How Much Recovery for Ethiopia and Sudan? Economic Research Service, United States Department of Agriculture.

Ahmed, H. M. M.
    1984   Oromo Analytic Study: Oromo Refugees in Sudan. December 29. Mimeograph.

Alemneh Dejene
    1985   Smallholder Perceptions of Rural Development and Emerging Institutions in Arssi Region Since the Ethiopian Revolution. Development Discussion Paper 192, Harvard Institute for International Development.

The Anti-Slavery Society
    1979   Forced Labor in Ethiopia — Slavery in the Sesame Fields. Report to the UN Working Group of Experts on Slavery.

Baxter, P. T. W.
    1978   Ethiopia's Unacknowledged Problem: The Oromo. *African Affairs* 77(308):212.

Bereket Habte Selassie
    1980   *Conflict and Intervention in the Horn of Africa*. New York: Monthly Review Press.

Blackhurst, H.
    n.d.   Ethnicity in Southern Ethiopia: The General and the Particular. *Africa* 50:55-66.

Bondestrom, L.
    1974   People and Capitalism in the North-Eastern Lowlands of Ethiopia. *Journal of Modern African Studies* 12 (1974):425-439.

Clay, J. W.
    1985   Food and Famine in Ethiopia — Weapons Against Cultural Diversity. *Cultural Survival Quarterly* 9(4):47-50. Prepared statement delivered to U.S. Subcommittees on Africa and Human Rights and International Organizations of the Committee on Foreign Affairs, U.S. House of Representatives, Washington, DC, 16 October 1985.

Cohen, J. M.
1975   Effect of Green Revolution Strategies on Tenants and Small-Scale Landowners in the Chilalo Region of Ethiopia. *The Journal of Developing Areas* 9(1975):335-358.

de Salviac, M.
1901   *Les Galla: Grande Nation Africaine, un peuple antique au pays de Menelik.* Paris.

Dessalegn Rahmato
1985a   *Agrarian Reform in Ethiopia.* Trenton: Red Sea Press.

1985b   The Ethiopian Experience in Agrarian Reform. In *Challenging Rural Poverty: Experiences in Institution Building and Popular Participation in Eastern Africa.* F. Kiros, ed. Trenton: Africa World Press. pp. 197-224.

Dines, M.
1982   Work Camps in Wollega. Unpublished manuscript.

Dolot, M.
1985   *Execution by Hunger: The Hidden Holocaust.* New York: W. W. Norton and Company.

Eshetu Chole and Teshome Mulat
1984   Land Settlement in Ethiopia: A Review of Developments. December. 63 pp.

Franke, R. W., and B. H. Chasin
1980   *Seeds of Famine: Ecological Destruction and the Development Dilemma in the West African Sahel.* New York: Universe Books.

Getahun Dilebo
1974   Emperor Menelik's Ethiopia—National Unification or Amhara Communal Domination? Ph.D. thesis. Howard University.

Gilkes, P.
1975   *The Dying Lion: Feudalism and Modernization in Ethiopia.* London: Julian Friedman.

Halliday, F., and M. Molyneux
1981   *The Ethiopian Revolution.* London: Verso Editions of New Left Books.

Hance, W.
1975   *The Geography of Modern Ethiopia.* New York: Columbia University Press.

Henock Kifle
1983   State Farms and the Socialist Transformation of Agriculture: A Comparative Analysis. Paper prepared for FAO Workshop on the Transformation of Agrarian Systems in Centrally Planned Economies of Africa. Arusha, Tanzania.

Hoben, A.
1973   *Land Tenure Among the Amhara of Ethiopia.* Chicago: University of Chicago Press.

Huntingford, G. W. B.
1955   *The Galla of Ethiopia: The Kingdoms of Kafa and Janjero.* Northeastern Africa, Part II, *Ethnographic Survey of Africa,* D. Forte, ed. London.

Keller, E. J.
1985   Ethiopian Socialism and Agricultural Development: The Pitfalls of Policy Making and Administration in a "Soft" State. Unpublished manuscript.

Ketel, J.
1985   Assessment of the Situation in the Damazine/Kurmuk/Yabus Areas of the Sudan. February 15.

Knutson, K. E.
1969   Dichotomization and Integration: Aspects of Inter-Ethnic Relations in Southern-Ethiopia. F. Barth, ed. *Ethnic Groups and Boundaries.* London. pp. 86-100.

Lipsky, G.
1962   *Ethiopia, Its People, Its Society, Its Culture.* New Haven: Human Area Relations Files.

Marcus, H. G.
1975   *The Life and Times of Menelik II.* Oxford: Oxford University Press.

Markakis, J.
1974   *Ethiopia: Anatomy of a Traditional Polity.* Oxford: Oxford University Press.

McClellan, C.
1979   Reactions to Ethiopian Expansionism: The Case of Darasa, 1895-1935. Unpublished Ph.D. dissertation. Michigan State University.

1980   Land, Labor and Coffee: The South's Role in Ethiopian Self-Reliance, 1889-1935. *African Economic History* 9:69-83.

Mekuria Bulcha
1983   Some Notes on the Conditions of Oromo, Berta and Other Refugees in the Kirmuk District of Blue Nile Province—Republic of Sudan. Unpublished manuscript.

Niggli, P.
1985   *Athiopien: Deportationen und Zwabgsarbeitslager.* Frankfort, May, 80 pp.

1985a   Ethiopia: Deportation and Forced Labor Camps. Translation by Cultural Survival.

1985b   *Ethiopia: Deportations and Enforced-Labour Camps, Doubtful Methods in the Struggle Against Famine.* Berliner Missionswerk.

Pankhurst, R.
1966   *State and Land in Ethiopian History.* Addis Ababa.

1967   *An Introduction to the History of the Ethiopian Army.* Addis Ababa.

Perham, M.
1969   *The Government of Ethiopia*. Evanston: Northwestern University Press.

RRC and UNICEF
1984   Joint RRC-UNICEF Workshop on Technical and Institutional Improvements in the Early Warning System.

Salale, G.
1979   Who Are the Shoans? *Horn of Africa* 2(3):20-29.

Shawcross, W.
1985   *The Quality of Mercy: Cambodia, Holocaust and Modern Conscience with a Report from Ethiopia*. New York: Simon and Schuster.

Shepherd, J.
1975   *The Politics of Starvation*. Carnegie Endowment for International Peace.

Smith, G.
1985   Report on New Refugee Arrivals to Blue Nile Province Sudan. January 13-14. Damazine, Sudan.

Stahl, M.
1974   *Ethiopia: Political Contradictions in Agricultural Development*. Stockholm.

1977   *New Seeds in Old Soil*. Research Report 40. Uppsala.

Terfa Dibaba
1982   The Refugee Camps in the Blue Nile Province of Sudan: Travel Report. Unpublished manuscript.

TPLF/OLF
1984   The Ethiopian Ruling Junta Is to Blame for the Famine. Joint Statement.

Trevaskis, G. K. W.
1960   *Eritrea: A Colony in Transition — 1941-1952*. London.

Trimingham, J. S.
1952   *Islam in Ethiopia*. London.

Triulzi, A.
1980   Social Protest and Rebellion in Some Gabbar Songs from Quellam, Wallagga. Unpublished paper.

Watts, M.
1984   Silent Violence: Food, Famine and Peasantry in Northern Nigeria. Berkeley: University of California Press.

Wood, A. P.
1978   *Resettlement in Illubabor*. University of Liverpool.

1983   Rural Development and National Integration in Ethiopia. *African Affairs* (Journal of the Royal African Society) 82(329):509-539.

Appendix A

GENERAL SURVEY
Sudan, 1985

Identification #
Date of Interview
Place of Interview

I. MALE/FEMALE

II. AGE

III. GEOGRAPHIC ORIGIN
Where were you born?
How long did you live there?
Did your father live there? Grandfather?
Did they move? If so, why? [Were they pushed? If so, by whom?]

IV. RELIGION
What is your religion? [Are you Moslem, Christian (Orthodox, Catholic, Protestant) or other religion (for example, do you visit the Qallu)?]

V. LANGUAGE
What language did you first learn to speak as a child?
What other languages do you speak?
How/where did you learn to speak each one?
Which language do you use most often? Which do you speak at home?

VI. FAMILY COMPOSITION
Do you have a husband/wife? More than one?
When did you marry?
Where is your husband/wife?
Is s/he with you? If not, why not?
How many children do you have?
Are they with you? Where are they?
How many brothers and sisters do you have?
Are some with you?
Where are they?
Do you know where they are now?
If they are not with you now, when was the last time you received word or news about them?

VII. EDUCATION
Can you read or write in any language? Which?
Where did you learn? When?
How long were you in school?
Were you in the literacy program?
Can your husband/wife read or write?
Can your children read or write?

VIII. FACTORS AND PATTERNS OF MOVEMENT

Where were you when you finally decided to leave your home?

How did you get to Sudan? [What route did you take?]

Did you face any dangers on the way?

Who did you travel with? Why with them?

Did you have a guide? From home or found later?

Did you have a ride or any other assistance? If so, did the people who helped you or gave you a ride offer to assist you or did you ask them for help?

How long did it take you to reach your original stopping point?

How did you know you had reached Sudan?

What is the name of the first place you arrived/settled in in Sudan?

What had you heard about Sudan? Who told you?

Did you find what you expected?

How do you spend your day here in this camp?

INDICATORS FOR SELECTION FOR INTENSIVE INTERVIEW

IX. RE: LONG-TERM CAUSES OF FAMINE; SOCIOECONOMIC HISTORY AND DYNAMICS

A. Change in Productive Activity in the Homeland Region

How did your situation before you left your homeland compare with the situation of your parents at your age? Was it better or worse?

What was the reason for the difference?

B. Livelihood

What was the major activity/work taking most of your parents' time and providing most of their food and supplies when they were your age/while you were growing up? What was *your* major activity/work taking most of *your* time and providing most of your food and supplies before you left your homeland?

Did they FARM? Did you?

Did they RAISE ANIMALS? Did you?

BOTH? How about you?

Did they TRADE or have a BUSINESS? What kind? Did you? What kind?

Were they WAGE EARNERS? Where? Doing what? Did you? Where? Doing what?

Did you work some OTHER way (student/office worker/other)?

What other activity helped you to get food at home?

Did your grandparents do the same things?

What was your best year for farming/herding/trading/wage earning?

How much did you produce then?

And this year, how much did you produce?

Which is more, before or this year?

What has changed that accounts for this difference?

Did the rain fail? Is that the only thing? Did you stop farming/working?

X. RE: IMMEDIATE FLIGHT/DISPLACEMENT FACTORS

A. Why did you finally leave your homeland to come here?

Drought/Ecological situation?

Warfare?

Conscription into the Ethiopian military service?

Collectivization?

Increased taxes/contributions?

Mandatory literacy and political education programs?

Resettlement programs?
Persecution/Discrimination?
Liberation front activity?
Increased opportunity in Sudan?
Other?

B. Tell me about the day you finally took the decision to leave your homeland. What happened?

XI.   RE: REPATRIATION ASSISTANCE AND SOLUTION-BUILDING

A. Knowledge of Events in Homeland

When you came here, did all your family/neighbors come with you or did some remain behind?

If some remained, why did they stay and you come? What was different about their situation? Do you know what is going on at your home now? Please tell me about it. [For example, who is on your land now? Who has your tools/animals/house? How did they get them?]

How do you know? Do you have a communication with any who remained behind? How did you hear from them or about them? What other information can you get about your homeland?

Has the trouble or the condition that caused you to leave been eliminated or changed?

B. Knowledge of Assistance Programs

When you were at home, were there people who tried to help you? From the government? From the liberation fronts? From other countries? Where did they come from?

What questions did they ask you? What did they give you? Did they give to everybody?

C. Plans for Return

Do you ever plan to go home? When?

How can you get the things you need to start producing again?

D. Solution Endorsed

What will be the best solution for these problems that you are facing? How will that happen?

Appendix B

INTENSIVE INTERVIEW #1
Re: Long-Term Causes of Famine — Socioeconomic History

CHANGE IN PRODUCTIVE ACTIVITY IN THE HOMELAND REGION
How did your situation before you left your homeland compare with the situation of
   your parents with regard to the following:

LIVELIHOOD
What was the major activity/work taking most of your parents' time and providing
   most of their food and supplies when they were your age/while you were grow-
   ing up? What was *your* major activity/work taking most of *your* time and pro-
   viding most of your food and supplies before you left your homeland?
Did they farm? Did you?
Did they raise animals? Did you?
Both? How about you?
Did they trade or have a business? What kind? Did you? What kind?
Did they work for wages? Where? Doing what? Did you? Doing what?
Did your grandfather do the same thing(s)?

PRODUCTION SYSTEM
Questions for Farmers
Did you/your father/grandfather farm the same land? What size was the land your
   parents/you farmed?
What was their source of water? What was yours?
Who used that water?
How was that decided?
Was their land rain-fed or irrigated? How about yours?
What was their source of firewood/fuel? What were your sources?
How did they clear the land and prepare it? How did you do it?
How was it planted? Watered? Weeded? Harvested? And in your case?
Were there baboons and wild pigs that ravaged crops in your area? How did you
   cope with them? Did you have locusts or other pests? What did you do to cope
   with them?
Do you still have land in your homeland?
Who works the land? What is their relation to you?

A. Tools, Plow Oxen, Other
What tools did your parents use to farm? Did you use the same kind of tools?
   Tractor? Draft animals?
Where did they get them? Where did you?
   Inherited? Obtained from the government? Purchased on the market?
Who made your father's plows? Who made yours?
Where did the materials come from? The forest? Elsewhere?
How did they acquire the materials? Where? How did you? Where?
How did they get seeds, fertilizers? How did you get seeds, fertilizers?

B. Labor Force
Who worked with your parents to farm? Who worked with you?
   Family members? How related? People from the neighborhood/area/peasant
   association? Hired laborers? Where were they from? How recruited? How compensated? How much per day?

206   Politics and the Ethiopian Famine 1984-1985

How many people were needed?

C. Nature and Distribution of Product

What kind of crops did your parents produce? And you, what do you grow?
How were these crops decided? Did your father teach you to work with those crops?
Was what they produced sufficient to feed the family? Was what you produced sufficient?
Was all their produce consumed? Was yours?
How many were in your parents' household to be fed? How many in your house?
How much of your crop did they keep for the household? What percentage of your crop?
What did they do with the remainder? What did you do?
What did they do to supplement the needed amount? What did you do?
Did they exchange with others some of their produce? Did you?
Who did they exchange with? And you, who did you exchange with?
How far were they from town/market? How far were you?
Where did they sell/buy? Where did you?
Did they sell any goods? What? Did you sell/buy any? What?
Who did they buy from? Who [did you buy] from?

D. Productive Capacity

When was the largest harvest you personally saw reaped from your land? Were you producing that amount recently? If not, what prevented you from producing to the maximum? Was it the weather?

Questions for Merchants

What kind of business did you have? Did you have a shop?
Did your father have a business, too? The same kind? Same one? How was it started?
Did you produce the goods or buy them to sell?
Do you own the land? Shop? Vehicle(s)? If not, who is your landlord?
Did you farm/herd animals in addition to running your business?

Questions for Herders or Mixed Herder/Farmers

What kind of animals did they have? What kind did you have?
How many animals did they have? And you? Who herded them?
Where/on what land?
How did they acquire the animals? How did you acquire yours?
Was what they produced sufficient to live on? Was what you produced sufficient to live on?
How did they supplement when that was not enough? How did you supplement?
Did they have grain? If so, how did they obtain it? Did you? How did you obtain it?
Do you have any animals left in your homeland? What kind? Where? Who herds them? What happened to the rest? Did you bring any animals with you (when you left the country)? Are they still with you? If not, what happened to them?
Could the animals you had at home survive here? Do other refugees have animals here? If so, where? Who herds them? How many?

Questions for Wage Laborers

Did you ever work for a daily wage? How were you compensated? By the day/week/month?
What kind of work did you do? How much did you earn?
Why was it necessary for you to work for a wage?
How did you choose to do that work?
Did you continue farming/herding or business?
If you did, did you have to leave your house to earn wages?

When you were away working for a wage, how did you obtain your housing and food? Was it provided for you or did you buy it?

How much of your earnings were spent on necessities? Were you able to save or send any of your earnings home?

How often did you work for a wage? For how long?

IMPACT OF THE DERGUE'S GOVERNMENT ON THE HOMELAND OF AFFECTED PEOPLE

What changed for you when the Dergue government came to power?

Did you live on the same land as before?

Did you grow the same crops as before?

How did the land reform program affect you?

Did you farm/herd/keep shop the same way as before? If not, what changed?

How did you decide what crops to grow? Which animals to sell? What to sell in business? Who decided these things?

Did you work with the same people to produce on the land? If not, where did the new people come from?

Was there a peasant association in your area?

   How did it get organized? Were/are you a member? What was your position?

   Did you take this position willingly or were you forced to take it? What would happen to a person who refused to take a position in the peasant association?

When you were in the peasant association, what was your opinion of it? What is your opinion now?

   Do the people in your peasant association know where you are? Would they accept you back?

TAXES/CONTRIBUTIONS

Did your parents pay taxes? Did you?

Contributions?

What kind, for what? On animals? Land use fees? And you?

   Who collected? How much? How often? Were the taxes and contributions the same amount under Haile Selassie and the Dergue? More? Less?

Did you pay contributions to the government for other purposes? What?

KNOWLEDGE OF CURRENT EVENTS IN HOMELAND

Who is on your land now?

Who has your animals?

How did they get it/them?

Can you have it/them again if/when you go home? (If yes, how will you get them? If no, why don't you think you can get them?)

Who has your house? What happened to your tools—farming, household equipment, etc.?

How do you know what happened to all this? Did you hear it from the people who are in your house?

If you heard from friends/family there, why did they stay behind when you left? Where did they stay?

Where are the people you used to farm with? Herd with?

Did they have the same problems you did?

Did all of you leave the area at one time or did you take different actions one at a time? Did people go to one place or different places?

Were the people who stayed behind prevented from coming out? Do you hear from them?

Are the ones you came with to Sudan your neighbors?

Appendix C

INTENSIVE INTERVIEW #2
Re: Immediate Flight/Displacement Factors

Checklist for a line of inquiry to be followed (together with suggested questions) when interviewing five categories of affected people: 1) refugees in camps, 2) refugees outside of camps, 3) displaced people, 4) participants in settlements, 5) people at feeding centers.

Why did you leave your homeland to come here? What finally made you decide to leave?

DROUGHT – ECOLOGICAL SITUATION
How did the rains this year compare to the year before? How can you measure the difference?
When was the last harvest before you left home?
Did you leave because there was no rain and the land was becoming unproductive? For some other reason?
Did you leave because there was no grass for your animals (cattle)?
If not because of dryness, why did you come here?

WARFARE
Has there been a war in your area?
  Who is fighting whom?
  Why are they fighting? Do you know?
What effect did this have on your local area? Has the war affected your ability to grow food? (Were there incidents of crop-burning, looting, civilian deaths? When, what month and year did these things happen? Where, in what locality? Did you see the place, event?)

FLEEING SPECIFIC GOVERNMENT PROGRAMS
A. Conscription to Ethiopian Military Service
Has anyone of your family/neighborhood gone to serve in the Ethiopian Army?
  How did they go?
  How many in your family are in the Ethiopian Army? Have any left the army? How many?
  Do you know how many of them are dead or alive?
How did you see the recruitment of young people in your area?
  Is it continuing?
How did the recruitment affect your area?

B. Collectivization
Did you participate in the collectivization of farms under the Dergue? Describe the process. How did it affect you? Did it increase or decrease the amount you were able to produce? How do you measure?

C. Increased Taxes/Contributions
Were you able to pay the taxes the year that you left home? What happens when you do not pay?

D. Mandatory Literacy and Political Education Programs

Did you attend literacy programs before you left home? What language did you learn to read and write?

How often did you attend political meetings? Did you have to go? Did these classes and meetings affect your work schedule? How?

PERSECUTION/DISCRIMINATION
Have you ever been put in prison or persecuted for any reason in your homeland? What was the reason? Was your experience common or unusual?

RESETTLEMENT PROGRAMS
Are people from other areas being brought to your land? Who are they? Where do they come from? How do they get to your area? What is your relation to them? Where are they being resettled? In what kind of place?

What is the name of the place?

How do they learn about the area? Do they live in a big state farm or settlement? How does that settlement operate, do you know? How do you know?

Did you have the choice of settling there?

How did you decide?

Do you think those new settlers are your enemy?

If you go back, do you think you could live together?

LIBERATION FRONT ACTIVITY
We have heard there is an Oromo Liberation Front, Tigrayan People's Liberation Front and/or Eritrean Peoples' Liberation Front in your regions. Were they present when you were there?

Do you have any knowledge of them?

What do they want to do?

What is your opinion of them?

What is the government policy toward them?

How much did this policy affect conditions in your area?

What is your opinion of that?

Did you help them? If so, in what form?

Who supports them?

If they are successful, would you go back home?

INCREASED OPPORTUNITY IN SUDAN
How do you compare the condition you are in now with the condition you faced at home (with regard to school, health care, opportunity for work, etc.)?

Did you know about these conditions here before you came?

Do you plan to help your people at home?

Appendix D

INTENSIVE INTERVIEW #3
Re: Repatriation

To be administered to five categories of affected people: 1) refugees in camps, 2) refugees outside of camps, 3) displaced people, 4) participants in settlements, 5) people at feeding centers.

CAUSES OF DISPLACEMENT
Why did you leave your land?
Do you have relatives or neighbors still at home?
  What are they doing? Why did they stay when you left (what was the difference between their situation and yours)?

KNOWLEDGE OF EVENTS IN HOMELAND
What happened to your land when you left?
Who has it now? Who uses it?
  How do you know—how did you hear about it?
  Do they use it the same way you did?
  Produce the same crops? Graze the same animals?
What happened to your animals? Killed? Confiscated? Given to relatives? Neighbors? Don't know? Did you bring them with you?
What kind did you have?
What happened to your house?
  What kind of house did you have? Who built it?
  Where did the materials come from? Who helped you?
What happened to your tools?

CONDITIONS FOR RETURN
Do you think you will ever go back?
Under what condition?
What changes have to occur before you will go back?
If you go back to the place you came from, would you be safe? How would you be sure?
Do you know anybody who has gone home?
  What plans did they have? What were they planning to do?
Would you all go home or some of your family first?

PERCEIVED NEEDS
What would you need in order to go home?
How would you obtain tools, livestock, land, household supplies?

AWARENESS/ASSESSMENT OF ASSISTANCE PROGRAMS
If the ETHIOPIAN GOVERNMENT gave you land, tools or tractor for farming or animals for herding, would you be willing/able to go back?
If the LIBERATION FRONT gave you land, tools or tractor for farming or animals for herding, would you be willing/able to go back?

If the INTERNATIONAL COMMUNITY gave you land, tools or tractor for farming or animals for herding, would you be willing/able to go back?

Do you think you could get your land back if you return?

Could you raise animals, farm or work in the same way as before you left if you went home?

CONDITION IN CAMP/SETTLEMENT
How do you compare the situation here now with the situation that you left?

How long do you think you will remain like this?

How do you view being settled here?

RELATION WITH LOCAL RESIDENTS
What is your relation with the people who lived here before you arrived?
   With other refugees?

Where would you prefer to be settled?

PLANS/PERCEPTIONS/ENDORSEMENT RE: ASSISTANCE AND SOLUTION-BUILDING
What do you think will happen in the future for your children?

What would you like to see happen?
   How will that come to be?

What will be the solution for these problems that you are facing?
   How will that occur?
   What are you doing to bring that about?

How can others help you?
   Do your friends agree with you?
   Does your family agree with you?

Appendix E

INTENSIVE INTERVIEW #4
Re: The Mechanism of Resettlement

How were you recruited for the resettlement program in Ethiopia?
Lorry — voluntary or forced?
Plane — voluntary or forced?
From which town were you taken?
Did you stop on the way?
Did you go by plane all the way?
If by plane, where did you disembark?
When you stopped, where did you sleep?
What were you given to eat?
If by lorry, how many people to a truck?
How did you sleep? Eat? Toilet?
Were the women safe?
Were you guarded by the military?
Were you in the militia in Tigray? Or at your home?
When you reached Asosa/resettlement site, were there any militia there already?
If so, who were they (were they Tigrayans)?
Did you volunteer to join the militia or were you forced?
What were your duties?
Were you armed? (Did they give you arms?)
Please describe the resettlement sites.
Who built the houses?
What did you eat?
What work did you do?
How did you get water? Wood?
What did you do all day?
How did you manage to escape?

Appendix F

COVERAGE OF THE FAMINE IN ETHIOPIA

Numbers of People Believed to Be Affected by Famine

. . . 6 million Ethiopians were threatened with starvation and as many as 100 were dying each day.

The New York Times, 28 October 1984

Several weeks ago, the Ethiopian Relief and Rehabilitation Commission said that 6.4 million people had registered for emergency food. Relief officials here say the figure was too low because it did not include secessionist guerrillas in the provinces of Eritrea and Tigre.

The Christian Science Monitor, 29 October 1984

They say that 8 million was a better estimate, but based on new figures from Tigre, 10 million is even more accurate. If true, this would represent about one Ethiopian in every four, based on a population of 35 million.

The Christian Science Monitor, 29 October 1984

Imagine 10 million people — almost one third of Ethiopia's population — facing starvation or death by the end of the year.

The New York Times, 8 November 1984

The number of famine victims in this East African nation is now officially estimated at 7.7 million — one out of every six Ethiopians, the head of United Nations relief effort said yesterday . . . .

. . . the new figure replaces the previous government estimate of 6.5 million to 8 million, which was considered too vague.

The Boston Globe, 4 December 1984

Officials of the Marxist military government said that 7.75 million Ethiopians now are threatened by famine — a figure 1.3 million higher than was estimated two months ago . . . .

The Washington Post, 12 December 1984

At Korem, the largest center, 225 miles north of the capital Addis Ababa, some 60,000 refugees were encamped; 50 were dying every day . . . .

At Bati, 2,500 people a day were arriving and 130 a day were dying, most of them children and old people.

The New York Times, 18 December 1984

Relief officials here say the U.S. food has helped save tens of thousands of the estimated 7.7 million Ethiopians threatened by the famine.

The Washington Post, 14 April 1985

AID and State Department officials estimate that roughly 2.3 million people are "in need" of assistance in northern Ethiopia.

The Washington Post, 14 April 1985

. . . 7.9 million people threatened by the worst famine in Ethiopia's history.

The Washington Post, 2 May 1985

Timely rain, however, does not help the more than 200,000 persons in Ethiopia's 152 feeding centers.

The Washington Post, 5 May 1985

... 10.8 million famine victims. . . .

The Washington Post, 8 May 1985

The World Food Program is less optimistic, said Mr. Taylor . . . "we think 3.5 million people are being reached."

The New York Times, 17 May 1985

Ethiopia's Relief and Rehabilitation Commission says 5.7 percent of the 7.9 million people estimated to be "at risk" as a result of famine are now receiving help. The United Nations' more conservative figure is 4.1 million, recently raised from an earlier estimate of 3.5 million.

Both the Government and the United Nations assert that up to 75 percent of the "target population" in the north is being reached.

Mr. de Reidmatten responded by saying, "The figures compiled in Addis Ababa are hardly reconcilable with what we in the field actually see every day."

The New York Times, 16 June 1985

Ethiopian officials say that 206,000 hungry people have registered for a monthly distribution of rations in Korem and the surrounding district. Yet fewer than 40,000 are being fed today. "Who knows where the rest are," says one official. "People come in and they go out and we don't know what's happening." . . .

The government has just escalated two estimates: It says Ethiopia's population has jumped to 42 million and that the number of people registering for emergency food has gone from 6.4 million to 7.3 million. This eclipses in scale previous famines in Biafra and in the Sahel region.

Western relief agencies say even the 7.3 million figure omits guerrillas in Eritrea and Tigre provinces and everyone else too weak to leave their villages where land has turned to dust after having been plowed four times this year in desperate efforts to survive. Livestock is dying or being slaughtered for food.

More and more relief workers here, including government officials, now accept an estimate that between January and December of this year 900,000 will have died because of the famine.

In the main Korem camp, the death toll has jumped from 15 per month last January to 1,549 in September and an estimated 1,800 in October, according to a local government official.

The Christian Science Monitor, n.d.

About 1 million people will have died in the 12 months to Dec. 31 in Ethiopia alone, according to the latest accepted estimates in Addis Ababa.

The Christian Science Monitor, n.d.

Causes of Famine: Nature-made vs. Man-made

The 10-year guideline points out the indispensibility of raising the agricultural sector to this high level of social productivity through the expansion of state farms and the organization of the peasantry into agricultural producer cooperatives under the objective conditions prevailing in our country.

Radio Addis Ababa, 9 September 1984

M. Peter McPherson, head of the agency that manages United States overseas food donations, said the Marxist Ethiopian Government had at times closed off its ports to shipments of emergency aid, giving priority to cargos of fertilizer and concrete from the Soviet Union.

The New York Times, 20 September 1984

A 10-year development plan issued by the Government recently forecast that Ethiopia would not be self-sufficient in food until 1994 at the earliest.

The New York Times, 8 October 1984

One of the strongest charges came from the Rev. Charles Elliott, the former director of Christian Aid in Great Britain. He said that the United States and Britain had deliberately withheld aid to Ethiopia in the hope that the famine would bring down the Communist regime....

American officials, in turn, charge that Ethiopia itself played down the famine until after it observed the 10th anniversary of its Communist regime in September, a celebration on which, according to Mrs. Fenwick, the Ethiopians spent more than $100 million....

The New York Times, 11 November 1984

Ethiopian head of state Mengistu Haile Mariam has denied allegations that his government wasted millions of dollars on celebrations marking the tenth anniversary of the country's revolution at a time when thousands of its citizens were dying of famine.

Radio Addis Ababa, 17 November 1984

... four Soviet helicopters arrived in Kembolcha on Nov. 7 and two days later began flying food to parts of the highlands so remote they are difficult to reach by truck.

The Boston Globe, 19 November 1984

The four transport helicopters at Kembolcha are part of 24 sent by Moscow, with 300 trucks and a dozen Antonov-12 transport planes to carry food and relief supplies to the 6.4 million people said by the Ethiopian Government to be suffering from prolonged drought and famine.

The New York Times, 19 November 1984

Relief workers returning from Korem, the largest famine refugee camp, say no new shipments have arrived there for more than two weeks and "it is a question of days" before reserve stocks are exhausted. Should that happen, they say, the death rate, now 30 a day, would rise....

The diplomats said that last week three British transports delivered 64 tons of grain to Alamata, an airstrip serving Korem. They say their records also showed that eight Ethiopian relief flights recently landed in Alamata.

It was not clear why none of that food has reached Korem, which accommodates 40,000 refugees. Food trucks have also been seen recently along the road from Addis Ababa to Korem.

The New York Times, 9 December 1984

In a meeting with donor nations, the government also used harshly recriminating language to scold the noncommunist world for what it said were apathy and neglect that had caused the country's "current tragedy."

The Washington Post, 12 December 1984

Dark hints about motives abound in the press: The Government is attempting to starve the guerrillas to put an end to secessionist movements in the northern provinces of Eritrea and Tigre; relocation is being pursued to channel the hungry into the large collective farms that are "favored by the Ethiopian Marxist-Leninist" government. Agriculture is being exploited through imposition of onerous taxes.

Most of the criticism is unjustified and stems from the anticommunist inclination of the Western media, combined possibly with the desire to file dramatic reports....

Droughts, which have always plagued the Sahel for periods of 5 to 10 years at a stretch, have been particularly severe since the late 1960s. But that affects harvests only in limited areas, and it takes more than poor local harvests to impose starvation. That "something else" is civil wars in the north, disrupting supply lines of food from the south....

The Christian Science Monitor, 14 January 1985

From 1975 to 1984, we were making available comprehensive, daily relief aid for an average of 3 million compatriots every year.

... we have been rehabilitating the majority of them in their former areas by providing daily food, seed, farm equipment and household goods and by helping them build houses.

.... our action was presented in detail in the 10-year perspective plan and in the central report to the founding congress of our party ... What we have to realize is that even if all these plans are realized, we cannot even satisfy our food needs.

... while they have freedom of producing without any restriction or domination since we removed those robbers and oppressors who were exploiting them by forcing them to pay a one-third tithe for the soil, for the chief, for the priest, and so on.

Produce from our regions where we say there are potential farmers could not even satisfy less than 14 percent of our population living in towns. The problem of unemployment could not be solved as we wished because there was no income from the peasant and government farms as had been expected.... At our stage of development, there is no reliable source other than the agricultural sector for income or capital which is needed for our economic progress.

Radio Addis Ababa, 9 February 1985

An official sat in his office at the Government's Relief and Rehabilitation Commission recently, answering questions about why, in this time of severe drought and famine, Ethiopia is still selling livestock and other food products to customers abroad.

The New York Times, 7 April 1985

"The Ethiopian Government's response has been totally inadequate," said Robert J. McCloskey, senior vice president of Catholic Relief Services, the chief American relief organization in Ethiopia, in a telephone interview today. "Only recently has Ethiopia declared the famine a priority and begun to buy some food itself." ...

The Washington Post, 26 April 1985

Dr. Charles Elliott, formerly of Christian Aid, would like us to believe that the West is responsible for the Ethiopian famine.

The facts tell a different story.... Between 1978 and 1982, the Ethiopian regime received one billion dollars of Western aid. What happened to the money....

The Times, n.d.

When Terry Page, a senior UN World Food Program official, visited Assab in late September, he found no grain vessels unloading. Port authorities were using a first-come-first-served rule rather than giving priority to grain ships.

The Christian Science Monitor, n.d.

The helicopters are to be based at the northern Ethiopian towns of Aksum, Mekelle, Kembolcha and Gondar and used for short shuttle flights, Ethiopian officials said.

The New York Times, n.d.

Resettlement: Famine Assistance vs. Ideological Motives

McPherson [US AID director] ... said that there are no assurances that Ethiopians who are resettled in the south would be better fed than they are now in the northern region, noting that no preparations have been made for their arrival in the new locations. *The Boston Globe,* 13 December 1984

Over the course of a year, the Ethiopian Government plans to relocate 1.5 million farmers at a cost of $35 million, according to Birhanu Deressa, deputy commissioner of the Government's Relief and Rehabilitation Commission. If the plan is successful, many more will be moved the following year....

The New York Times, 14 December 1984

The authorities will not only have to provide proper agricultural facilities and training, the officials say, but also deal with integrating outsiders into areas with different customs, climate and language. Furthermore, unless the program receives sufficient financial and technical aid, its chances of success are limited....

The Christian Science Monitor, 26 December 1984

Packed in Soviet cargo planes, battered blue buses and aging dump trucks, Ethiopian peasants by the hundreds of thousands are leaving the barren and overcrowded northern highlands and are being delivered to verdant southwestern lowlands where the grass is often taller than they are.

"It is quite staggering," said an Australian diplomat who has been ushered through the resettlement areas, "to stand there and look out at thousands upon thousands of kilometers of virgin agricultural land in a country that has been farmed for 3,000 years." ...

The United States, by far the largest food donor, is the most outspoken critic of the mass movement of peasants to the south. "Resettlement is a diversion of resources that could be better spent if used for people directly," M. Peter McPherson, director of the U.S. Agency for International Development, said in Washington last week....

Further, at least half of the 1.5 million peasants scheduled to be relocated live not in northern Tigray Province, where the Tigray People's Liberation Front claims control of 85 percent of the province, but rather in Welo and Gondar provinces, where rebels are not a significant threat to the government....

The Ethiopian government has proclaimed resettlement as its most important priority, and, with the help of 12 Soviet-built Antonov cargo aircraft and more than 300 Soviet-built trucks, about 20,000 peasants are moving south each week....

Ethiopia wants donation of machinery to clear land, oxen and hand tools for the destitute settlers, seeds, pesticides, fertilizers, fuel, well-drilling machinery, 300,000 sets of kitchen utensils and clothing....

The annual cost for Ethiopia of a similar program is estimated at about $1.5 billion — about double the government's annual budget....

Any assessment of how the resettlement is going is likely to take several months.

Thus far, the government has restricted outside access to the newly settled areas, allowing brief guided tours by outside delegations ... that it apparently believes are predisposed to support the program....

Farmers in the new areas will be allowed to grow what they want on their parcels of land and will be able to keep all of their profits, according to Tamrat Kebede, a chief planner. But, Kebede said, they will not own the land and, in time, all the resettlement farms will join in "producers' cooperatives" with shared production and shared profits....

Kebede would not say how quickly the resettlement farms would be collectivized. "We will leave it to its own historical process," he said....

It [the government] desperately needs outside help to make the resettlement work, but its plans to collectivize the new farms, turning them into proven money-losers, seem likely to keep out western money and technical help.

The Washington Post, 3 January 1985

... a resettlement district at Asosa, 300 miles west of Addis Ababa, where 14,000 families — more than 50,000 people — arrived from northern famine camps in three weeks. It is planned to settle 20,000 families there.

Ninety percent of the families were from the famine relief centers at Bati, Korem, and Komabolcha, and only the healthiest had been selected for resettlement, the Australians were told.

The newcomers were each being given two hectares (nearly five acres) of land, and a large number of Ethiopian Government surveyors were at work dividing up plots.

... Ethiopian authorities emphasized to the Australians that the settlers would each be given two hectares and would not be brought into the nearby collective farm.

Daily Telegraph, 4 January 1985

Mother Teresa, founder of the Missionaries of Charity, praised the Ethiopian Government today for making "a very good beginning" in its effort to resettle victims of the famine.

At the same time, Mother Teresa . . . called on donor nations to support the plan by "adopting" resettlement sites. . . .

So far, no Western donor nation or organization has been willing to support or assist the undertaking, and critics have raised numerous questions about the program. Some argue that the money being devoted to resettlement could be better spent on relief and rehabilitation work in the north.

Some say they fear that the people to be resettled, many of whom have been weakened by long periods of malnutrition, will be vulnerable to tropical diseases in the sharply different climate of the south. And some charge that the Government is using resettlement as a way to depopulate areas of the north, where rebel movements are active, and also recruit labor for collective farms in the south.

The New York Times, 8 January 1985

Some aid officials say the program has been formulated and put into effect hastily and that, as a result, those being resettled have little chance to become self-sufficient soon.

Other relief workers argue that moving hungry people from one part of the country to another only spreads the famine, complicates the logistics of feeding the hungry and causes more transportation snarls and delays.

The New York Times, 21 January 1985

"We are still a long way from having the situation under control in the famine areas," said a senior relief official. "By dividing the population at risk you only spread the famine, double the logistical problems and increase costs. For example, there are only so many trucks in this country. Divert them to carry settlers and you reduce your capacity to transport food to those who need it."

The Ethiopian authorities assert that those who are moved south will be producing their own food within a year. Most Western experts dispute that, saying that food aid will have to be supplied to the resettled population for a minimum of five to seven years. . . .

At most sites, wells for drinking water have yet to be dug — rivers are being used in the meantime — and medical facilities are not yet close at hand.

Several diplomats noted that in each resettlement site on the Government-sponsored trip, from Metu in Ilubabor to Kishe, it was an official of the Workers Party of Ethiopia, a Communist party established last September, who gave the briefings. . . .

"It looks like it's the party bureaucrats and not the technocrats who are running this show and I'm not at all convinced they know what they're doing," the embassy official said. . . .

Another experienced aid worker saw the situation differently, saying that "right now this Government's priorities are wiping out the rebels, moving population south and maintaining a relief effort — in that order."

The New York Times, 21 January 1985

. . . The cost this year of the immediate urgent campaign to save lives is very near to the budget set aside by the country for its general development.

Radio Addis Ababa, 13 February 1985

Another part of the solution, in the Ethiopian Government's view, is to move up to half the population in this area — roughly 100,000 — to virgin lands in the south and southwest of the country. . . .

Some critics of the plan argue that moving hungry people without adequate preparation and installations in place for them is only going to spread the famine while robbing areas such as this of the able-bodied people needed to make a land rehabilitation program work. Although the peasants in and around Alibar do not debate policy, they do appear dubious about the prospect of relocating.

The New York Times, 26 March 1985

With its decision to remove people from the northeast and resettle them in so-called underpopulated and land-rich regions of southern Ethiopia, the government is abandoning any effort to "control nature."

The impending arrival of Tigres and Wellos makes credible the Oromo Liberation Front's propaganda stressing the north's continued domination of the south.

Worldview, March 1985

They did not pinpoint reasons for the slowdown at Assab but agreed that much of the grain that has been unloaded has been diverted to feed northerners being resettled in the south. . . .

The US says families are separated, with the old and the young being left behind. Ethiopian Foreign Minister Goshu Wolde denied the charges in Geneva March 12. . . .

The Christian Science Monitor, 3 April 1985

Leaders of the farmers' association in one of the resettlement areas in the west of Ethiopia have told the Government that they can accept no more of the starving peasants who are being transported into the district every day in the thousands.

. . . Many find that their friends or members of their family have died on the long journey. The rate is high, for these people are very badly malnourished.

They see the place is not the land of milk and honey they had been promised and say things like: "If we must die, let us at least die in our own home, not here."

Often they rethatch the houses which the local farmers' associations have built for them. . . .

The Times, 2 May 1985

[U.S. AID Director M. Peter McPherson] criticized the Ethiopian government for diverting 600 trucks to resettle hundreds of thousands of famine victims from the north to the south, while there was a backup of 100,000 tons of food in the Red Sea port of Assab and another 80,000 tons waiting to be moved out of warehouses.

The Washington Post, 2 May 1985

Between 2,500 and 3,000 are being flown daily from Makalle airfield. . . . The evacuees travel in groups of 250 or 280, sitting on the aircraft floor.

The camp on open moorland was heavily guarded by soldiers against attack by rebel guerrillas of the Tigre People's Liberation Front.

Western Governments have declined to support the resettlement programme until they know more about it.

The programme is backed by the United Nations Food and Agriculture Organization, which is to seek international support for it.

Daily Telegraph, 12 May 1985

At least 50,000 and possibly as many as 100,000 Ethiopian peasants have died this year as a direct result of their government's resettlement programme, according to the secret evidence of international relief agencies and Western government sources in Addis Ababa. The relief agencies, however, have refused to publish this evidence because they fear that Ethiopia's marxist government will expel them and that such horrific news may dry up donations from the West.

A secret report by the League of the Red Cross shows that conditions in the resettlement areas of southern Ethiopia have been appalling. The peasants have lacked food, housing, tools, seed and medical facilities. The sanitation of their villages has, in many cases, been non-existent. Those resettled from the Ethiopian highlands have died in the tens of thousands from malaria, in the mosquito-infested swamps of the lowlands.

Many people died in transit because they were sick and malnourished when they set out. They had hopelessly inadequate medical facilities and travelled in over-crowded conditions. There is also evidence that thousands of people were forced to move by Ethiopian militiamen.

The Sunday Times, 3 November 1985

Resettlement: Voluntary vs. Forced

The first settlers from six provinces in the Welo region were given a warm send-off when they left Kembolcha for destinations arranged for them.

Radio Addis Ababa, 17 November 1984

. . . western donor nations question whether the resettlement is indeed "voluntary," as the government here insists. They also suggest the plan may be moving too fast to adequately provide food, housing and medical care to the destitute highlanders, who are arriving at a rate of more than 2,000 a day to begin new lives on previously uninhabited land. . . .

The government dismisses arguments against the move, saying that it is only organizing an existing "spontaneous reaction" by famine-emaciated people who want to move to better land. . . .

The Washington Post, 12 December 1984

At Aduwa in the far north of Tigre, ragged, impoverished peasants are loaded on-to trucks and ferried southward to ancient Aksum. . . .

There, at a dusty, unpaved runway, they are loaded onto Soviet helicopters, which whisk them farther south to Makale, the capital of Tigre Province. Then they joined local refugees and were herded onto giant Soviet Antonov transports, which take them on to Addis Ababa, the merging point for the mass evacuation. . . .

And Louis Christ, who heads the International Red Cross relief operation, said he believed that thousands of famine victims had fled back to their villages, at least tem-porarily, in fear that they might have to relocate.

The New York Times, 14 December 1984

But apart from the disruptive effects on communities, opponents of the regime of Mengistu Haile-Mariam allege that it is using the drought for ulterior political pur-poses to evict people from the politically dissident regions.

These allegations have been made by the relief associations of the resistance movements in Eritrea, Tigray, and Oromo. Evidence submitted to the British parliamentary Select Committee on Famine Relief and Food Aid by the Oromo Relief Assn. alleges that people are being forced into the resettlement areas against their will, that their selection is often arbitrary, and that in many cases they are dumped in new areas with no proper facilities to sustain them. . . .

Evidence collected from these Oromo refugees indicates that most have fled from a work camp called Angolit near Nakmate in Walaga Province, where there are said to be no reception facilities or even shelter, virtually no medical supplies, and a scarcity of food, although work rations were distributed. Conditions in the labor camp were described by refugees as draconian. . . .

—In some cases, whole villages in Tigray Province were surrounded by troops at night and their inhabitants were forced onto trucks to be carted away to new places of settlement.

—In other cases, agricultural workers, shepherds, and other villagers were simply taken away from where they were found and carried away without any attempt to ensure that whole families were kept intact.

—Because of the haphazard policy of forcible removals, the new agricultural set-tlements lack balanced populations; many consist of aged and very young people, and many don't have the family's male head.

The settlements in Walaga are intended to be converted into state farms producing teff, the local staple crop for bread, as well as wheat. Peasant villagers were cleared from these areas to create large land holdings suitable for large-scale operations on state farms. This has produced local antagonism toward the newcomers.

Thousands of hectares of forest and bush were also reported to have been cleared to provide additional land, thus opening up the prospect of further soil deterioration.

This policy of large-scale population removals first began under the Haile Selassie regime during the last great drought in 1973. But the removals have since been continued and intensified by the Mengistu regime.

According to one unsubstantiated report, over 2400 settlers in Angolit had already died from starvation, disease and neglect between 1981-82.

A further serious allegation is that many of the Tigrayans who were moved to the south came from areas that were not even afflicted by drought, and that many of them had some land of their own as well as cattle. They have been moved from the province where the armed opposition, the Tigray People's Liberation Front, claims to be in control of an estimated 80 percent of the area.

Christian Science Monitor, 19 December 1984

Others claim that they do not want to resettle, but that "soldiers are forcing people into the buses." . . .

The Christian Science Monitor, 26 December 1984

Government resettlement plans have thus prompted the EPLF, the TPLF, and other rebel groups to accuse the Mengistu regime of trying to drain guerrilla areas of popular support. They also claim that emergency food supplies are being deliberately withheld from the interior to force people into accepting resettlement in order to survive.

The Christian Science Monitor, 26 December 1984

The government claims it is moving only those peasants who volunteer, that it is keeping families together, and that it is giving each family about five acres of land. Reports from diplomats in Addis Ababa who have seen the resettlement areas support these claims.

The Washington Post, 3 January 1985

Initially, Western diplomats and relief officials were concerned that refugees were being forced to sign up for resettlement and that families were being separated. In addition, there have been persistent reports from the Sudan that hundreds of Ethiopian famine victims have arrived in that country, having fled from resettlement camps in and around Asosa. . . . "I think we want to be very, very sure," said one Western diplomat, "that we are not financing the eventual enslavement of these people."

Ethiopian authorities have responded by saying that none of the migrants are to be collectivized, at least not at this stage. Instead, they say, each family will be allocated about five acres of land as well as a home garden plot of about one-quarter acre. The peasants will not own the land they work, however, leaving the door open for collectivization at a later date. . . .

One senior Western diplomat said: "Certainly in a year or so we're likely to be informed that the people have unanimously expressed their desire to be collectivized. But we're not going to prevent that by refusing to dirty our hands with resettlement. On the contrary, the more we're involved the more influence we're likely to have."

The New York Times, 21 January 1985

Mengistu said that through the use of "subtle propaganda," the enemies of Ethiopia "denigrate" the government's resettlement program, which since November has moved more than 330,000 people from the drought-stricken central highlands to the country's southwest.

Western donor governments, particularly the United States, have criticized the resettlement program for moving too fast and have questioned whether it is voluntary, as the government here insists.

The Washington Post, 2 May 1985

Still other donors question whether those being resettled are accepting the change voluntarily, whether they will be forced to live and work on collective farms and whether the Government is concealing a political motive to depopulate northern areas of the country, where rebel movements are active.

The New York Times, 2 June 1985

... Korem is a feeding center in the Wollo highlands.... People who live in the mountains and valleys up to 30 km away come there once a month for dry rations.... About 23,000 people still live in the camp....

Ten days ago, at night trucks and buses arrived at Korem and more than 600 people were herded into them by militiamen armed with sticks and whips. It is during such enforced removals that families are split up.

Word quickly spread through the camp and by next day more than 10,000 people had fled, fearing that the militiamen would return and cart them away.

Medecins Sans Frontieres and other agencies say privately that this was not an isolated incident. Such forced resettlement still occurs in feeding centers in Wollo and Tigre.

The government's other method of forcing people to move is more subtle but hardly less brutal. Medecins Sans Frontieres [Doctors without Borders] says that a week ago the government banned the distribution of dry rations to 12,000 people who live near Korem camp. No reason was given. The agency has been prevented from giving intensive feeding to 5,000 children at the Kelala feeding camp in Wollo. Two thousand of these children are in desperate need, the agency says, and hundreds are dying.

Medecins Sans Frontieres can see only one reason why the government does not allow it to give humanitarian aid: the aim is to persuade people to resettle by depriving them of proper care in the areas in which they live.

The Sunday Times, 3 November 1985

Warfare vs. Famine Assistance

Modern Ethiopia is many times larger than its historic "Abyssinian" or "Amhara" core, and despite the so-called revolution of 1974 it remains an empire, not a nation....

The Oromo and Sidama, the Western Somalis, the Eritreans and the Tigreans likewise want the Amhara minority's all-pervasive colonial authority off their backs so they can manage their own affairs. Therefore they, too, fight. But it is misleading to refer to their struggles as "banditry" or "secessionist."

The New York Times, 23 October 1984

Guerrillas in Ethiopia's troubled northern province of Eritrea are prepared to observe a ceasefire with the government in order to allow emergency food aid to reach an estimated one-and-a-quarter million people threatened by starvation in the region, a guerrilla spokesman said here today.

Agence France Presse Radio, 6 November 1984

American officials said that Ethiopia had deployed far fewer trucks for food distribution than required and said that the food needs of Ethiopians in areas of civil conflict were being ignored.

The Boston Globe, 8 November 1984

... Makele and elsewhere, where allocations to adults have dropped to as low as five kilos per month, airlifted food gets only to those who have made it to feeding centers near the main cities. Little or no food is getting into the interior or areas controlled by secessionist guerrillas in Eritrea and Tigre.

The Christian Science Monitor, 8 November 1984

A regime that ignores its starving populace and spends billions of dollars to buy armaments is likely to misuse the relief aid to accomplish what its sophisticated weapons could not: it wants to crush the Eritrean struggle for liberation.

The Boston Globe, 13 November 1984

At a press conference, he [Ethiopian head of state Mengistu Haile Mariam] also asserted that there was a conspiracy to use international famine relief as a lever to force his Marxist government to negotiate with separatist rebels.

Radio Addis Ababa, 17 November 1984

Along the Addis-Asmara road, food is a principal weapon in the struggle for the support of the Ethiopian peasant.

The Washington Post, 18 November 1984

Molki is a small town "liberated" by the Eritrean Popular Liberation Front. It is Tuesday — market day — and about 500 people push and shove to buy the last available handfuls of dura, a sort of millet. So anxious are they in their quest that they do not bother to look up as two Soviet-built MG 21s tear across the sky, followed soon afterwards by three helicopter gunships.

Cluster bombs, napalm and machine-gun fire are showered on the seething human anthill below. One of the survivors tells us: "Parts of bodies were flying everywhere. A head landed in a sack of peppers." An estimate of the toll that day is 42 killed and 92 wounded.

The Sunday Times, 25 November 1984

"The case that Colonel Mengistu (the Ethiopian leader) is using British taxpayers' money to starve out rebel areas, indirectly to bomb innocent civilian targets in pursuit of his war aims and directly to oil the wheels of his bankrupt economy by selling food aid is overwhelming," Mr. Galloway [War on Want] said yesterday.

"The 'ruthless military Government' of Ethiopia is deliberately starving out whole areas of its country, paying its militia 120 kilos of Western grain a month and stepping up its bombing raids against civilians at a cost of 30,000 (pounds) a sortie — enough to feed 3,000 people for a year," he said.

"More and more people are coming back from Ethiopia with eye-witness accounts of what is going wrong, but it is odd that no criticism is coming forth from the West."

The Times, 3 December 1984

Recent reports confirming that Ethiopian fighter jets bombed and strafed famine victims fleeing to the Sudan ... bolster the credibility of rebel claims that the Ethiopian government is using the famine to serve ideological ends.

The Boston Globe, 17 December 1984

... Ethiopia's ambassador to Switzerland, denied reports Wednesday from relief organizations that government aircraft bombed a column of starving refugees trekking in the Tigray Province toward the Sudanese border. The alleged attack Dec. 3 was confirmed by a number of independent observers who had treated survivors.

The Christian Science Monitor, 20 December 1984

Mr. Harris said there was a confirmed report that Ethiopian Air Force planes attacked a refugee trail on Dec. 7, killing 7 and wounding 18.

The New York Times, 28 December 1984

The Government's official position is that it has no internal enemies other than "bandits" and "terrorists." Western diplomats dispute that and say there are some 25 active rebel organizations, representing virtually all of Ethiopia's main ethnic groups....

The New York Times, 9 January 1985

Some Western diplomats in Addis Ababa are predicting that the Government may began [sic] a new military offensive against the insurgents within the coming months.

"What the Government has to consider is can they afford another major military operation and can they count on the donors to continue supporting the relief effort while they are fighting," a Western diplomat said.

The New York Times, 9 January 1985

Although ... few people involved will talk about it, it is an open secret among relief workers that more than half the famine victims in Ethiopia are not being reached by the government's programs.

The Nation, 19 January 1985

The problem in our country's northern region, which is deep-rooted, has become worse and the suffering of the people prolonged because they [insurgents] were hindering all efforts made by the government and the people to solve the problem before it reached this stage. They rob people of the aid given them during this difficult situation.... Today when men and animals are dying in the thousands, they slaughter their farming oxen and drive people at gunpoint to Sudan.

Radio Addis Ababa, 13 February 1985

Those insurgents are clearly the largest hurdle to the success of the relief effort.

The New York Times, 17 May 1985

... offers by Mr. Jansson [UN Asst. Secretary-General] to lead unarmed convoys carrying food into rural areas of Tigre and Eritrea have been rebuffed by the Ethiopian Government of Lieut. Col. Mengistu Haile Mariam.

The New York Times, 26 May 1985

Western diplomats in Addis Ababa, the Ethiopian capital, say at least 14 trucks have been attacked in recent weeks by anti-Government insurgents operating near Ibnet.

The New York Times, 9 June 1985

Ethiopia's Marxist government seeks to combat the rebels in part by using hunger as a weapon and keeping gift food out of rebel-held areas. Other nations, eager to improve relations with Ethiopia, are unwilling to circumvent the Ethiopian blockade in a significant way....

The Christian Science Monitor, 14 June 1985

The senior Red Cross official in Ethiopia said today that the famine had grown "much worse" in parts of the country where Government troops and rebel forces remain in conflict....

The New York Times, 16 June 1985

Tigre and Eritrea contain a total of about 7 million people. About half live under guerrilla control, in arid, mountainous, thirsty, hungry areas among the hardest hit in all of Africa....

Mengistu denies any political motives associated with food relief, and claims there is "no area" of Ethiopia he does not control. Western aid officials concur that this is not so.

The Christian Science Monitor, 18 July 1985

One look at the records suggests that Western aid has helped the Ethiopian regime to finance its civil wars; and perhaps finance the absurd and extravagantly pretentious maintenance of the OAU [Organization of African Unity].... Certainly Western aid has enabled the regime in Addis Ababa to pursue policies which, without such help, would have brought it down much more quickly and saved Ethiopians from so much misery.

We have seen only too vividly that a billion dollars has not been used to pursue agricultural, social or economic policies which could have equipped the rural population far more effectively to cope with the drought. A billion dollars has provided the regime with foreign exchange, perhaps to help pay for Soviet tanks to use on its citizens and certainly to sustain conscription. It has helped the Dergue to suppress policies of private trade in favour of public monopoly; to expropriate assets, particularly American ones; to expel unpopular groups to cause major refugee problems in the Sudan.

... If Western aid agencies persist in giving money to rulers on the basis of the poverty of their subjects, that means that policies which persistently cause the impoverishment of local populations will in effect be rewarded though the rewards may only be visible in the amount of weapons bought or in the life style of officials in the capital.

The Times, November 1984

The war in the north has generally been a low key affair since the government reasserted control over most towns in Eritrea in 1981-82.

The campaign, however, is costing Addis Ababa about £400,000 a day and has tied up half the 300,000-man army in Eritrea and the neighboring Tigre province where guerrillas are also fighting for secession.

All the rebels two weeks ago announced their willingness to suspend military operations to assist the famine relief program but the government never responded.

Daily Telegraph, 15 November 1984

Agencies' Dilemma

Agencies, mandated to work only with governments, neither act independently to channel aid to the starving in the contested areas nor do they make any public statements to contradict Ethiopian government descriptions of the crisis. Many private aid agencies are also silent about this, claiming they wish to avoid jeopardizing operations on the government side.

The Boston Globe, 26 November 1984

International relief agencies ... maintain that secrecy is necessary because if the central government became aware of their involvement in rebel-controlled areas it would hamper their efforts elsewhere in Ethiopia or even expel them from the country altogether.

The Boston Globe, 2 December 1984

"The attitude that we can't do anything about it so we had better accept it tends to be rather habit-forming," the aid worker said. "Personally, I would rather stand up and get punched than lie down and be walked on."

The New York Times, 21 January 1985

Among the donors the thought regularly stirs of whether it is worth providing help that saves lives but also props up a squalid and hostile regime, one that has countenanced massive suffering — especially in rebel-held areas — to stay in power.

The Washington Post, 8 May 1985

As a relief official who wishes to remain anonymous put it, Eritrea's is a "politically sticky" famine....

... Indeed, officials at the American Council for Voluntary Agencies, an umbrella organization of US relief groups, put the total value of private American famine-relief funds going to the government side in Ethiopia at more than $8 million annually vs. less than $900,000 for Eritrea and Tigre, another province where antigovernment insurgency rages.

This almost 9-to-1 ratio exists although as many or more people are starving in Eritrea and Tigre as are starving in government-held areas of Ethiopia. In Eritrea, 85 percent of the population is estimated to live in antigovernment areas....

Several agencies — including the UN-sponsored World Food Program — refuse to work with nongovernmental bodies such as guerrilla movements, even if these groups offer the only organized access to stricken populations.

The most commonly offered explanation for eschewing work in Eritrea is the fear of antagonizing the Ethiopian government and jeopardizing existing projects in government-held areas.

Catholic Relief Services (CRS) concedes that its large-scale relief efforts in Ethiopia and Eritrea cannot hope to reach most of the starving population because CRS works only through government channels.

"We're concerned that the government [of Ethiopia] would be very upset if we worked directly with the Eritreans," says Jim DeHarport of CRS's Africa Programs section. "That could jeopardize our ongoing work in the rest of Ethiopia." . . .

"People are dying out there in Eritrea, but we just don't know how to get around these political roadblocks. I wish I knew what the answer was."

Another organization that has avoided work in Eritrea, but that is now reconsidering, is California-based World Vision. . . .

"Privately, World Vision told us they couldn't help because they didn't want to make the Ethiopian government angry," Mr. Tesfa [director of the New York office of the Eritrean Relief Committee] recalls. "But publicly they said it was because there were already many other organizations helping us . . ., which isn't true because very few humanitarian groups are belonging to us."

Dr. John McMillin, World Vision's director of relief and rehabilitation, confirms that the key issue in his organization's denial of the Eritrean Relief Committee's request was the fear of invoking the displeasure of the Addis Ababa authorities.

"We have a long history in Ethiopia, with a large investment in staff and resources," Dr. McMillin explains. "We had to make a choice and we tried to serve the most people in the best way."

"But looking back on it now," he adds, "knowing what we know now about how serious the situation in Eritrea is, I'm not sure that I wouldn't make a different choice today. In fact, we're now reevaluating whether to start up some work in Eritrea."

One organization that has opted for a strong Eritrean involvement is the Mennonite Central Committee. Recognizing, as associate executive secretary Edgar Stoesz puts it, "that the neediest people are not reachable through government channels," the organization last year funneled $25,000 in aid to rebel-held Eritrea.

The Christian Science Monitor, 20 July 1984

Throughout that period, relief workers complained privately that local authorities were hampering their efforts to provide food, clothing and shelter, presumably because of suspicion that the assistance would benefit rebel forces and their supporters in the area.

The New York Times, 17 December 1984

The UN's Position

A senior World Food Program official in Rome commented: "Until the government concentrates all its efforts on the drought, it will need more and more support."

The WFP [World Food Program] and some private agencies are reluctant to criticize the Addis government openly, for fear of jeopardizing existing relief shipments and programs.

The Christian Science Monitor, 3 April 1985

. . . the evacuation of Ibnet, which witnesses described as forced, poorly planned and brutal, could blind international donors to the need for—and the need to pay for—the eventual closing of all the feeding camps in Ethiopia.

"People cannot live in these places forever. They are a drain on the resources of the Ethiopian government and of international donors," said Alan Court, a senior official here with the United Nations Children's Fund (UNICEF).

The Washington Post, 14 April 1985

Returning here tonight from Ibnet, Kurt Jansson, the United Nations assistant secretary general for emergency operations in Ethiopia, said the evacuation was "done with too much haste and with inadequate preparation. It is also clear that there has been and will be suffering as a result of the hastiness."

In his remarks at the airport in this Ethiopian capital, Jansson said that the evacuation of Ibnet made sense in principle because it is time for peasants to return to their homes to resume farming. He added, however, that the government had not gone about the evacuation in the proper way and said that in the future Ethiopia will handle this more efficiently.

Dawit Wolde Giorgis, commissioner of the Ethiopian government's Relief and Rehabilitation Commission, which is responsible for famine relief here, told the Reuter news agency that the story was a "fabrication" by a "cub reporter" trying to please his employers.

... Ethiopian party officials provided reporters with three versions of how Ibnet was burned. All versions denied involvement of soldiers. One version described the burning as an accident, a second called it a sanitation measure and a third said it was the act of one misguided person who is now in jail.

The Washington Post, 3 May 1985

UN Assistant Secretary-General Kurt Jansson, chief coordinator of famine relief in Ethiopia, denied Wednesday that there have been large diversions of food aid, saying 97 percent of donations in the past six months have been accounted for. The statement was issued in response to a May 23 article in the French newspaper *Le Monde*, which alleged that 30,000 metric tons of food aid disappear every month.

The Christian Science Monitor, 30 May 1985

Alleged Facts vs. the Need for Information

... the Western Ethiopia Planning Zone Office is engaging in the necessary studies in Illubabor and Kefa regions to ensure the proper utilization of natural resources and to develop the productivity of the people.

Radio Addis Ababa, 26 October 1984

The Ethiopian government is systematically covering up the fact that it lacks access to the starving, and most of the international humanitarian aid community is complicit in this coverup by remaining silent about it. One result is that food aid is becoming a powerful political weapon in the battle for control of the region, and thousands of innocent civilians are dying unnecessarily....

The Boston Globe, 26 November 1984

What is needed now is immediate and full disclosure of the political dimensions of this crisis by aid agencies, governments, UN organizations and media alike.

The Boston Globe, 26 November 1984

American news coverage should not merely be a recitation of the horrors of death by starvation. It should reflect the complex phenomenon that creates African famine: climate, geography, history, culture, local and international politics all play a role.

Until the American people understand why Africans are starving, U.S. aid will only serve as a band-aid for a problem which will certainly surface again in five to ten years.

The Boston Globe, 4 December 1984

... Some say they [celebrities and assorted world officials] come to assess the efficiency of relief programs. But the brevity of their visits—as enforced by the Ethiopian government—makes such assessments cursory, at best.

The Washington Post, 10 December 1984

Members of a Canadian fact-finding mission said today that they had found no evidence to substantiate reports that famine relief aid was being sold commercially or was being misused.

The leader of the mission added, however, that he favored further investigation into the reports....

"I feel some more work has got to be done in the area of monitoring," said David S. MacDonald, Canadian Emergency Coordinator for Relief in Africa ... [he] had spent five days in Ethiopia....

According to a Canadian Embassy official, the members of the fact-finding mission asked 16 nongovernmental relief organizations here if they were aware of any misappropriations and all said they were not.

The New York Times, 17 December 1984

... It occurred to me that in the entire trip from Addis Ababa, crossing half the country by air and land, I had not seen a single square foot of topsoil.

Christopher Matthews, an administrative assistant to the Speaker of the House, *The New Republic,* 21 January 1985

"Mister Blaine, a woman, her baby died. You want to interview her?" The questioner was my "minder," an employee of the Ethiopian Ministry of Information and National Guidance....

... I followed my minder (and my translator)....

Blaine Harden, *The Washington Post,* 17 March 1985

Appendix G

Addis Zemen (The National Ethiopian Newspaper)
Taisas 6, 1977 (Ethiopian Calendar)

The Ministry of Construction Visited the Sites Created for Settlements

Asosa. Comrade Kassa Gebre, member of the Alternate Central Committee and the Minister of the Committee for Water Resource Development, visited an area created to deal with the drought reconstruction in other parts of the country. This happened to be in Wollega Region, the Province of Asosa. The local peasants happily built a new center for fellow Ethiopian comrades [settlers] around Bombasi village, beyond the Yabuus River. The man in charge of construction, Kassa Gebre, in cooperation with the Committee for Water Resource Development team, agreed to get the materials needed as fast as possible to get the work done faster. Additionally Gebre is giving seed for fast-growing vegetables to be planted in gardens around the houses that are to be built for the settlers by the local people. Gebre also encouraged the settlers to work hard and do their best to become self-sufficient in the new area. Negussie Fanta, Central Committee member and the regional administrator of Wollega region, was also there.

A Good Start in a New Settlement
[accompanied by pictures]

Because of the lack of rain, and the problems that have been created for our people, it is very important that our people be moved and be accepted as fellow citizens in the new fertile land. What has been so sad — creating so many tears and weak bodies — has been reversed within a month's time thanks to our new settlement program.

This new beginning and new settlement has taken place in the west. It rebuilds the settlers and makes them able to stand on their own. This gives us great happiness and is due to our unity and our revolutionary spirit and thought.

Due to man-made and natural disaster, many times our unity was threatened and questioned, but today, due to the formation of the Ethiopian Workers' Party, there is a correct political line and there is a forum for finding a large range of solutions to the problem of drought for famine victims. Part of this political program is that many people who have been suffering from drought and famine must understand that their problem cannot be solved by only feeding them where they are, they must be moved to fertile land and guaranteed that this will not happen again. Our economy makes our ability to carry out this big settlement impossible; such a program requires the cooperation of a world effort in finding a long-term solution to this humanitarian problem. Today, because of world cooperation in the relief effort, we have been able to save many of our beloved people from disaster. Many of our people have been moved from this disastrous area to the most fertile area in our empire — at this time a good example is in Wollega, Illubabor and Kefa regions.

We have been able to resettle many of these victims; this should be considered as the revolutionary duty of all Ethiopian residents. All these guidelines are given by the Workers' Party of Ethiopia, which is a Marxist-Leninist party, which gives at last a victorious outcome. Because of this, today in western Ethiopia (Wollega, Illubabor, Kefa) all party members and participants in the party are carrying out the policy of this party. The local people in these three regions are building them houses, feeding them and increasingly showing them friendship. A short time ago Comrade Legase Asfaw, the Member and Secretary of the Politburo, went to the three regions to see the most efficient way of finding settlement areas in these three regions. On his visits he has seen the groundwork laid for 372 villages (28,550 family households) in the Wollega region. He also visited in the three different areas where he saw temporary shelters in clusters of 350 units that could accommodate 22,500 people at one time. In the same administrative region in four different districts and 13 subdistricts and at different *kebeles* (local party organizations), 824 sheltering houses were built. In Wollega and in Kefa the shelters are already built. Our brothers [those who have been hurt by the drought] who aren't in Kefa are in the process of building their own small houses to have their own quarters. For this purpose planning and clearing work has been going on and shall continue.

In the Illubabor administrative region, the job that has been done or the work that is going on in the resettlement program differs in form, although in essence a similar type of job has been executed and is also in process. This means that instead of building a temporary shelter the main and permanent living quarters have been built for the settlers. This is like when a child is moving out, all parents try to settle their children with the essential household items. Thus the residents of this area today — because of the drought, and for those people who have lost everything and have been uprooted from all that they had, and who are consequently planning new lives — are preparing what is necessary for the new settlers to live. Even the plow and the yoke have been remembered, the people have provided everything for them. Even in some of the areas in this region everything has been provided for our brothers so that they can be self-sufficient as quickly as possible. Their brothers [local residents] have begun farming for them. This example should be the cornerstone, the main centerpiece or model, for others to follow in settling famine victims.

Appendix H

The Anuak

Anuak have fled to Sudan in three distinct waves. In 1980, as a result of forced conscription and government takeovers of their land, about 1,000 left Ethiopia for Sudan; some of these Anuak later returned to their homes or to nearby forested areas. In 1982 an undetermined number of Anuak fled to Sudan and settled in the area of Jucco, Marakei. Most of these two groups were later resettled by Sudanese authorities in Gallaheil, Marakei. About 600 Anuak remain in this camp today. To avoid resettlement inside Sudan many Anuak fled to Sudanese cities or back across the border.

In 1984 additional Anuak arrived, but Sudan did not recognize this group as refugees. They were suspected, it seems, of being, or at least collaborating with, Anyanya II or SPLA (Sudan Peoples' Liberation Army) guerrillas — mostly Nuer and Dinka fighters — who resumed their fight for autonomy from northern Sudan in the late 1970s.

Anuak refugees from Ethiopia claim that Sudanese officials could not have been more wrong. They claim, for instance, that beginning in 1983, Anyanya II began to operate from its base camp of Makal near the Amabal airport in Ethiopia and to attack Anuak villages.

Anuak interviewed in Sudan in 1985 claimed that since the Dergue came to power the Anuak's culture and social organization have been systematically destroyed. To substantiate this claim they pointed out that prior to the Dergue's era, Anuak "chiefs" ruled according to specific collective agreements. Even after the Dergue came to power, Anuak village representatives were elected by villagers in free elections. With the promulgation of the land reform, however, Anuak leaders were arrested for being "landlords" because traditionally they had the power to decide how land would be allocated each year. Anuak leaders are now appointed by outsiders — by Dergue officials. The Anuak we interviewed pointed out that many of the Anuak who are appointed are uneducated; therefore they are unable to keep the required records, which would allow others to hold them responsible for the actions they take on fiscal and policy matters.

Another Dergue policy cited as destroying indigenous culture was the forced change in an important economic practice followed at marriage. Traditionally, when Anuak men got married they gave a bead, valued at E$150, and two cows to the bride's family. The government began to forbid this practice and to collect the beads by force. Those who refused to hand over the beads were beaten; some were even killed. According to those interviewed, the "Ethiopians" took the beads and put them in a museum.

Even clothing styles have changed as a result of the Dergue's government. Women used to wear skirts with long slits up the side. Those were taken by the army. Before, women were bare breasted, but now they are told to cover themselves.

Anuak villages in Ethiopia have been organized into peasant associations. As one man said, "Now we must attend meetings even if we need to be in our fields." Food produced communally in the peasant association goes directly to the government; the producers do not receive payment for it. All the food is stored in central granaries. Some of the food is periodically taken away for the army and the militia in trucks that are driven by persons unknown to the Anuak.

According to one of those interviewed about the operations of peasant associations in Anuak country, people cannot be elected to positions of power in the peasant associations until they have been "trained." One of the persons interviewed had been elected chairman of his local peasant association, but he did not want to be put in the position of being between the people and the government. When he refused to accept the chairmanship, he insisted that it was "a strike against him," i.e., he was looked upon with disfavor by the officials.

Anuak live in 50 to 100 villages along the rivers. Up until the Dergue took power, they subsisted through raising crops (maize and sorghum), rearing livestock, hunting and fishing. Today each member of the peasant association is given about one hectare to cultivate, but birds and other predators get much of the crop. Few Anuak have extensive herds now because their grazing lands have been taken by the state, and they are no longer allowed access to them. The state has also curbed hunting. One of those interviewed fled to Sudan in order to avoid being arrested for suspicion of hunting. Another problem is that water buffalo are moving into the area and bringing tsetse flies with them; it is now against the law to kill the buffalos.

Some of the Anuak harvest twice a year in their areas. For the most part, they try to live on their own and be self-sufficient. Many times, however, government taxes and contributions force them to come up with additional money that they can get only by selling part of their produce. The land tax is E$27 per year, and the peasant association fee is E$5 per year.

If Anuak need to sell produce to pay taxes or contributions they can usually find a merchant from Gambella interested in buying it. Anuak reported receiving about E$10 per tin of grain. The merchants, in turn, either sell the grain as is or make beer from it.

The peasant association chairman is seen as an assigned "flunkie" who has "to do everything for the government." He can make no independent decision in the interest of the people or in response to their wishes. One year, for example, the chairman tried not to call the meeting during periods of agricultural labor, but district officials showed up unexpectedly and forced him to hold meetings. Most of the officials that are at the district level speak to the Anuak in Amharic or Oromo. According to the Anuak interviewed, many of them know Oromo, the lingua franca of the region.

After the Anuak were organized into peasant associations, the villages lost most of their traditional lands. Ever since that time the government has brought "so-called farmers to the area." One Anuak we interviewed insisted that the European Economic Commission recently gave US$28 million for development in the Anuak area, but only one road was built with this money. Those interviewed did not see how all that money could have been spent as it was intended. In 1980, about 31 Anuak were taken away for agricultural training but they never came back.

The Anuak were disarmed by the Dergue government. Only the local Anuak selected to be in the militia and guard the villages are armed by the government after completing a required training course. Anuak have been taken away by force to fight in the Ethiopian army. One man interviewed said that four friends from his peasant association were taken to fight in Eritrea.

Anuak areas have also been targeted for resettlement, a policy about which the indigenous people had no say. Anuak do attempt to accommodate newcomers whom the government imposes upon them. As a result, the Anuak explained, people indigenous to these areas of resettlement have less to eat. For example, the Nuer, with government support, have begun to take more of the land.

In the past the Anuak and the Nuer had a symbiotic relationship. The Anuak would produce crops on the areas along the rivers and the Nuer would graze their herds on the higher lands. During the dry season, after the harvest, the Nuer would bring their herds in to eat the stubble on the Anuak's fields. Drought, population pressure and land reform make this difficult. Also, it is more difficult than before for the Nuer to move across the border. The Nuer have also started to compete directly with the Anuak for certain foods such as fish. In the past only the Anuak ate fish. Neither the Nuer nor the Oromo thought it was suitable food. Through a United Nations program the Nuer obtained fish nets, however, and they now fish so much that many of the rivers have been depleted of fish altogether.

For further information on the Anuak, see: Anuak Decimated by Ethiopian Government, *Cultural Survival Newsletter* 5(3) 1981:19; and The Anuak — A Threatened Culture, *Cultural Survival Quarterly* 8(2) 1984:75-76.

CULTURAL SURVIVAL PUBLICATIONS

CULTURAL SURVIVAL REPORTS

Southeast Asian Tribal Groups and Ethnic Minorities in the 1980s. Proceedings of a Cultural Survival-sponsored conference. (No. 22, 1987.) $8.

Coca and Cocaine: Effects on People and Policy in Latin America. Edited by Deborah Pacini and Christine Franquemont. Proceedings of the conference "The Coca Leaf and Its Derivatives — Biology, Society and Policy." Published with the Latin American Studies Program, Cornell University. (No. 23, June 1986.) 169 pages. $8.

Anthropology and Human Rights. Edited by Theodore E. Downing and Gilbert Kushner, with Human Rights Internet. (No. 24, 1987.) 250 pages. $10.

The Spoils of Famine: Ethiopian Famine Policy and Peasant Agriculture. By Jason W. Clay, Bonnie Holcomb, Peter Niggli, and Sandra Steingraber. (No. 25, 1987.) 200 pages. $10.

A Sea of Small Boats. Edited by John Cordell. (No. 26, 1987.) 300 pages. $12.95.

Indigenous Peoples and Tropical Forests: Models of Land Use and Management from Latin America. By Jason W. Clay. (No. 27, 1987.) 150 pages. $7.

(Cultural Survival Reports continue the Occasional Paper series.)

OCCASIONAL PAPERS

The Chinese Exodus from Vietnam: Implications for the Southeast Asian Chinese. By Judith Strauch. (No. 1, December 1980.) 15 pages. $1.50.

East Timor: Five Years After the Indonesian Invasion. Statements by M. Al-katiri, R. Clark, J. Dunn, J. Jolliffe, Amnesty International, E. Traube and B. R. O'G. Anderson to the Fourth Committee of the U.N. General Assembly; articles by D. Southerland (*The Christian Science Monitor*) and T. Harkin (*The Progressive*). (No. 2, January 1981.) 42 pages. $2.25.

The Cerro Colorado Copper Project and the Guaymí Indians of Panama. By Chris N. Gjording, S.J. (No. 3, March 1981.) 50 pages. $2.50.

The Akawaio, the Upper Mazaruni Hydroelectric Project, and National Development in Guyana. By William Henningsgaard. (No. 4, June 1981.) 37 pages. $2.

Brazilian Indians and the Law. Proceedings of a Cultural Survival-sponsored conference of lawyers and anthropologists in Santa Catarina, Brazil, in October 1980. (No. 5, September 1981.) 14 pages. $1.25.

In the Path of Polonoroeste: Endangered Peoples of Western Brazil. Articles by D. Maybury-Lewis, D. Price, D. Moore, C. Junqueira, B. M. Lafer and J. Clay. (No. 6, September 1981.) 66 pages. $2.75.

The Plight of Peripheral People in Papua New Guinea, Volume I: The Inland Situation. Edited by Robert Gordon. Contributions by J. Flanagan, P. Huber, D. Jorgenson, J.-C. Martin and F.-R. Ouellette, N. L. Maclean, and E. L. Schieffelin. (No. 7, October 1981.) 95 pages. $5.

The Dialectics of Domination in Peru: Native Communities and the Myth of the Vast Amazonian Emptiness. By Richard Chase Smith. (No. 8, October 1982.) 131 pages. $6.

The San in Transition. Volume I: A Guide to "N!ai, the Story of a !Kung Woman." By Toby Alice Volkman. Published with Documentary Educational Resources. (No. 9, November 1982.) 56 pages. $2.50.

Voices of the Survivors: The Massacre at Finca San Francisco, Guatemala. Published with the Anthropology Resource Center. (No. 10, September 1983.) 105 pages. $5.

The Impact of Contact: Two Yanomama Case Studies. By John Saffirio & Raymond Hames, and Napoleon Chagnon & Thomas F. Melancon. Published with Working Papers on South America. (No. 11, November 1983.) 66 pages. $4.

Micronesia as Strategic Colony: The Impact of U.S. Policy on Micronesian Health and Culture. Edited by Catherine Lutz. (No. 12, June 1984.) 109 pages. $6.

The San in Transition. Volume II: What Future for the Ju/Wasi of Nyae-Nyae? By Robert Gordon. (No. 13, July 1984.) 44 pages. $2.50.

The Eviction of Banyaruanda: The Story Behind the Refugee Crisis in Southwest Uganda. By Jason W. Clay. (No. 14, August 1984.) 77 pages. $4.

Resource Development and Indigenous People: The El Cerrejón Coal Project and the Guajiro of Colombia. By Deborah Pacini Hernandez. (No. 15, November 1984.) 54 pages. $3.50.

Native Peoples and Economic Development: Six Case Studies from Latin America. Edited by Theodore Macdonald, Jr. (No. 16, December 1984.) 103 pages. $6.50.

Art, Knowledge and Health: Development and Assessment of a Collaborative Auto-Financed Organization in Eastern Ecuador. By Dorothea S. Whitten and Norman Whitten, Jr. Published with the Sacha Runa Research Foundation. (No. 17, January 1985.) 126 pages. $7.

The Future of Former Foragers in Australia and Southern Africa. Edited by Carmel Schrire and Robert Gordon. (No. 18, October 1985.) 125 pages. $8.

Ethnic Diversity on a Corporate Plantation: Guaymí Labor on a United Brands Subsidiary in Costa Rica and Panama. By Philippe Bourgois. (No. 19, December 1985.) 52 pages. $4.

Strategies and Conditions of Political and Cultural Survival in American Indian Societies. By Duane Champagne. (No. 21, December 1985.) 56 pages. $5.

SPECIAL REPORTS

Brazil. Articles translated from "A Questão de Emancipação" (Comissão Pro-Indio, São Paulo, 1979) and "Nimuendaju" (Comissão Pro-Indio, Rio de Janeiro, 1979). (No. 1, December 1979.) 68 pages. $1.

The Indian Peoples of Paraguay: Their Plight and Their Prospects. By David Maybury-Lewis and James Howe. (No. 2, October 1980.) 122 pages. $4.

Amazonía Ecuatoriana: La Otra Cara del Progreso. Edited by Norman E. Whitten, Jr. Contributions by N. E. Whitten, Jr., E. Salazar, P. Descola, A. C. Taylor, W. Belzner, T. Macdonald, Jr., and D. Whitten. Published with Mundo Shuar. (No. 3, 1981.) 227 pages. $2.50.

Fishers of Men or Founders of Empire? The Wycliffe Bible Translators in Latin America. A U.S. Evangelical Mission in the Third World. By David Stoll. Published with Zed Press. (No. 4, December 1982.) 344 pages. $12.99.

Please send check or money order for the amount of order plus $1 postage and handling to Cultural Survival Publications, 11 Divinity Avenue, Cambridge, MA 02138. Bookstores and those needing publications for classroom use should write for special rates.